So You Want to ᴜe a

GAME DEVELOPER?

Let's make it happen in just 30 days

Start making your dream game today!

Aaron Craig

So You Want To Be A Game Developer by Aaron Craig

Published by Lulu

lulu.com

© 2021 Aaron Craig

Cover by Tiana Praise.

Book ISBN: 978-1-7367824-0-8

This book is dedicated to all the teachers out there who helped me in my journey. I can recall a dozen specific teachers and their names, from middle school to college, who were kind, dedicated, and challenging. The calling of teachers is undervalued in today's society, and yet they are one of the most important jobs you can do. Teachers change lives every day by going to work, listening to their students, pushing them to be their best, and not giving up when others might.

So, to all the teachers out there who feel their work is underappreciated, know that you are valued, cherished, and loved. Keep up the amazing work because you are changing the world, one day at a time.

I also want to give a huge thanks to my wife. Not only has she sacrificed so much to allow me to write this book and follow my dreams, but she's remained encouraging and loving along the journey. She is my love, my light, and my courage to keep moving forward. This book, my channel, and my game development journey wouldn't even exist without her constantly pushing me forward, encouraging me when I'm down, and giving me the time to work on my projects.

Contents

Acknowledgments

This book was kickstarted by this list of awesome people! I am eternally grateful for their belief, support, and financial backing to get this book made!

Martin Goodson

J.P.

"Awesome Big Bro" Jason Craig

Elijah Purvey

Keaton Richards

Johannes

Rose Craig

amysarah

Scott Ager

Osama Imran

Michael Vincent Capone

Michael Fullarton

Ronald Payne

Joseph "TheGoldSwabbie" Greentree

Michael Pasquariello

Charles Hewitt

James Donnelly

Anthony Colon

Taylor Scrivner

Eliot Hochberg

Oliver Roberts

The Pittman Family

Anihbal Rivera

NHB

Warren Long

Meghan Cassidy

Josef Vaccaro

Joy Alynne Miller

Danny Ramirez

bbsamurai

Marko Zakrajsek

Michael White

Will

Leilabelle

Sunbeam Sovan

Steven and Victoria Pack

Michael Keith

Kevin

David Wehle

Keith Migliaccio

David Krause

Raymond Bryne

Frank Kergil

D57X

pompom

ALEJANDRO MORALESHILARIO

Patrick "PAVERICK" Meyer

Adam Jacomb

Jared Carvalho

Vinz

———

Feldenthorne

Andy Wright

Donovan "Darcovian" Saunders

flashjaysan

Max Clark

Ronald Alexander Cadena

Benjamin Truman

Fenne

Stuart Benoit

Keith Duckett

Ivan Rodrigues

Aldie

andifroen

SaucyJack

Steven Lim

Jess Taylor

Sarah Sugas

Nick Dufault (Vimlark)

The Creative Fund by BackerKit

Danae

Introduction

Are you Ready to Become a Game Developer?

Well, are you? Because that's what's going to happen by reading this book. By picking this book up and reading it every day you'll gain all the skills to make your dream game come true. You won't just learn how to code, there's thousands of books that can help you with that. No, this book will transform the way you think, learn, and approach life. Once you begin to think like a game developer, nothing will be off limits. You'll be able to solve complex problems and learn new skills with ease.

A game developer isn't someone who just sits at their desk typing away, coding all day. Instead, they are the people who solve the problems others can't. They think in terms of efficiency, new possibilities, and create unique experiences for the world. You won't just learn to code in this book, you'll learn how to approach problems in a new way, a different style of thinking. And that new way of thinking will transform how you look at everything. Which is great!

Day 1

Taking the First Step

Getting the Software

Are you ready to start your game dev journey? Although, to be honest you've already taken the first step in getting this book and reading this paragraph. You've got the desire, now let me guide you in how to use that passion to create games of all shapes and sizes. Because after you've completed this book and done the work, you'll be ready to make the game of your dreams. So, let's go ahead and get started.

First thing you'll need is GameMaker Studio 2. Head on over to YoYoGames.com, and look for the Get Started button in the top right corner **(Figure 1.0)**. Then you'll be taken to a page where you choose which version of GameMaker you want **(Figure 1.1)**. For this book, the free trial version will suffice, granting you full access to GameMaker without needing to pay anything up front. The creator option is for a 12-month license, and the developer is for permanent ownership of GameMaker Studio.

Go ahead and register, you must have an account with YoYo to use their software, and then download and install it. Once you've got all that done, it should pop up on your screen looking like **(Figure 1.2)**. I have previous games I've opened in GMS, but your recent projects side should be empty, although not for long!

Figure 1.0 Downloading GMS

Figure 1.1 Choosing the Right Version

Figure 1.2 New Project Screen

Figure 1.4 Gamemaker Studio

Figure 1.3 New Project

Exploring GameMaker

So, let's go ahead and create a new project **(Figure 1.3)**, and be sure to choose Game-Maker Language. The other option, Drag and Drop is a visual scripting language, which can be great for beginners on their own, but you've got me; in the long run GameMaker language will allow you to create games faster, and more complex.

Name your project anything you'd like, such as First Game, or I Love Making Games, it's all you. This project will be your first game, albeit a simple one, it will still teach you a lot of important things to take into the big project of this book. After you click save, Game-eMaker will open **(Figure 1.4)** and you're now ready to start creating games. Do note I have a custom background, and later I'll show you how to change yours. But before we dive too far in, let me give you a brief rundown of how the most important window works, the Asset Browser.

Asset Browser

The Asset Browser is where every resource for your game is stored. Every sprite, object, and piece of code is there, and can be organized any way you see fit. By default, it has groups with a label for each different resource, but you can delete and rename any of them. You can stuff fonts in scripts, or create a new folder called Room 1 and put everything related to room 1 in there. You have total freedom in how you organize the Asset Browser.

By default, it has groups for every kind of Asset/Resource you can have in the game. At the top is the search bar where you can find anything in your game by simply typing it in there. To the right is the add asset button, then filter, and finally extras, which include the room manager, and other important options. Below all of those is the Quick Access section which you can remove in the preferences if you prefer. And then below that are the assets themselves, with default groups for organization. Near the bottom is the zoom control, and below that is the recent windows. We'll touch on all of these as we progress, but for now just take away that you can organize this section however you prefer, and you do not have to copy what I do; do whatever works for you.

With GameMaker open, press F5 or the small triangle button below Tools, near the top left of the screen **(Figure 1.6)** to run your game. A few seconds of compiling will occur and a new window will pop up. That is your first game **(Figure 1.7)** congratulations! Now

Asset/Resource

Many times, used interchangeably, an asset or resource refers to the different kinds of things you can have in your game. Sprites, objects, timelines, tile sets, etc... are all assets and resources in your project.

Quick Access

Quick Access contains the recent, favourites, room order, saved searches, tags, and game options sections. Most of these are easy to understand by their name alone, but I will explain the ones that aren't. Room order actually controls which level your game begins in, indicated by the little house next to the room name. Tags can be custom added to any assets, to easily see all assets with like tags. And finally, game options control many important features, such a frame rate and publishing graphics.

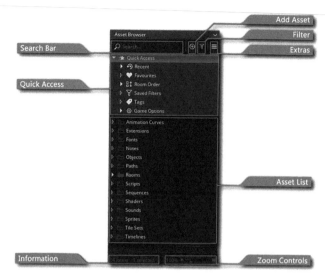

Figure 1.5 Asset Browser

Compiling

Every program written on a computer must compile, or ready itself, so it can run on that computer. Compile-Time errors, such as missing brackets or spelling errors, will be caught at the time of compiling.

Figure 1.6 Running a Game

I'll admit, that by most standards what we just created isn't actually a game. There's nothing you can do in it, no images, no objects, no interactivity. But it's a good first step, because now it's time to add some of those things into our game.

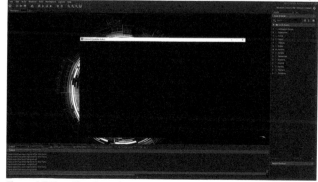

Figure 1.7 Your First Game!

Creating Sprites

Right click on the folder called Sprites and hover over create, then find Sprite and click **(Figure 1.9)**. If you happen to click directly on the folder itself, you'll instead get a color selector to pop up **(Figure 1.8)**, which isn't what

Figure 1.8 Changing Folder Color

Figure 1.9 Creating a Sprite

Sprite Editor

The Sprite Editor controls all meta data, and visual data, for a given sprite. You can change how fast it plays in game, where the origin is, its collision mask, and more. By clicking on Edit Image, or double clicking on the current frame, you can open up the Image Editor to change the image itself.

you want. Move over a little, and right click again. A new window will pop up, called the Sprite Editor **(Figure 1.10)**, and this is where we're going to create our first image for our game. Rename it to sprFlower, either in the Asset Browser itself, or in the Sprite Editor near the top left. This sprite is called flower, and I give it the prefix of spr which stands for sprite. Many developers prefer to use an underline between words like this: spr_flower. If you prefer that, I'll take no offense. I have used what's called Camel Case my entire programming life, which is where you capitalize each word after the first, and don't add spaces or dashes. No one way of coding is inherently better than another, simply choose the one you can read and remember to use and stick with it.

Figure 1.10 Sprite Editor

Now click on Edit Image to open the Image Editor **(Figure 1.11)**. To minimize the side and bottom bars, click F12 and you'll have a full screen, ready to draw in. If there's one thing you should know about me, it's that I'm not an artist. Anything I hand draw in this book will look terrible, so don't feel like you need to copy exactly what I do. Express yourself in your art and do take the time to familiarize yourself with the tools and powers of GMS.

Figure 1.11 Image Editor

Although most game developers won't use the Image Editor to create their sprites from scratch, they'll use third party software, you absolutely can do so, and make some incredible things to boot!

Go ahead and create a flower, like mine **(Figure 1.12)**, or spend some time and create something even more awesome. The image editor has drawing tools, fill, select, text, and more. Near the top you can adjust the size of the brush. New sprites are created at 64x64 pixels, which means you've got 4096 pixels you can use to create this flower. Anything not colored will be left transparent, meaning you can see through that part of the sprite to the background, or another sprite in the game. Many pixel art games use sprites at 32x32 or even lower, while some use much higher to create a very modern and detailed look. The size of your sprite doesn't determine the kind of game you'll make, but 32x32 is what you'll find many free assets in, so getting used to working in this size range is immensely useful.

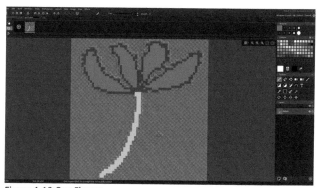

Figure 1.12 Our Flower

What you've just created is a Sprite, the backbone of everything you'll see in your game. Most games will have hundreds, or thousands of sprites. The background will be a sprite, the tiles will be a sprite, and every different animation you want your character to play will be a sprite. We'll touch on animation soon, but for now just know that a sprite can have multiple frames, although this one just has 1. Close out of our image editor window, near the top left, and return to Workspace 1 **(Figure 1.13)**.

Levels and Layers

Let's now open the first level in our game **(Figure 1.14)** and put that sprite in it. Find Rooms in the Asset Browser, press F12 again to bring it back or click on the little arrow on the right of your screen and open the folder. Double click on Room1 and a new window

Camel Case

One of many different styles of naming assets and variables. Camel Case begins with a lower cased letter, and each word after is capitalized with no spaces or dashes between words.

Image Editor

The tool to edit images. It has everything necessary to make awesome, fully animated sprites inside of GameMaker Studio.

Sprite

An asset made up of one or more frames. Sprites are what you see inside of your game, and can range in size from 1x1 to nearly anything (although very large sprites, like above 2000x2000 may get shrunk down by GameMaker to save memory).

Figure 1.13 Closing Windows

Figure 1.15 Layers

Figure 1.16 Layer Properties

Room Editor

The Room Editor contains all options for rooms. The layers control depth and what can be placed in the room. The layer properties changes based on the selected layer, and the Properties itself contains options for views, cameras, physics, creation order, and creation code.

Figure 1.14 The First Level

will appear, showing you the room. We've also got another side panel that popped open, so let's break that one down. The left panel is called the Room Editor and contains all the options for the levels, such as their layers, properties, views, and more. For now, let's just look at the Layers.

(Figure 1.15) The first type of layer you can create is a background, which this room has one already. Click on the Background layer near the top left, and you'll see the layer properties **(Figure 1.16)** change. You can select a sprite, change the color, and do a dozen other things. For now, let's just change the sprite. Click on No Sprite and select your flower. Your room may not be centered and so the flower may be partially invisible, to fix this click on the center icon **(Figure 1.17)** and you'll see it fill the screen perfectly.

Figure 1.17 Room Viewing Options

Go ahead and experiment with the options for the background layer. You can tile the sprite, stretch it, change where it starts, and more. Try changing the horizontal or vertical speed and then run your game by pressing F5 or that little triangle. Your sprite will now melt together and look super weird! This occurs because GameMaker needs a background to draw upon, or strange things start happening. Add another background layer in your game, move it beneath the background with your sprite, and run the game again. You'll see it now works as expected if you still have the speed set.

Layers

In the Room Editor, a layer controls what can be put into the room, such as instances, backgrounds, tiles, and paths. The layer also controls the depth, the order in which everything in the room gets drawn. Higher up layers get drawn on top of lower layers, so never place a background layer as the first, otherwise it will cover everything.

Figure 1.18 Confirm Making New Layer

And that's everything you need to know about the background layer for now. Reset it back to normal, take off the sprite, and delete the added background layer. You'll need to set the color back to black, although you can choose any color you want.

Let's now click on the instances layer. You'll see the specific property layer is empty. Drag the sprite from the Asset Browser into the room. A confirmation dialogue will appear **(Figure 1.18)**, warning you that a sprite can't be put on an instances layer. If you click create, it will make an Asset Layer for you, where you can place sprites and sequences. But our flower will just be a static image in the room, which is still quite boring, no real difference from the background. What we want to do now is make an object and add a little code.

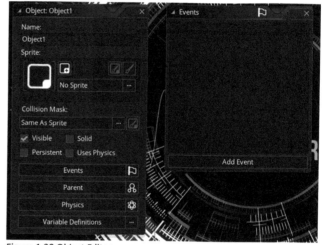
Figure 1.20 Object Editor

Creating an Object

Delete the asset layer, if you created one, and click on the Objects folder in asset browser. Now click on the plus icon at the top of the asset browser which will pop up the create asset window **(Figure 1.19)**. Select object, keep the amount at 1, and click create.

We now have an object in the Objects folder, or wherever you had selected in the asset browser at the time you clicked create, and the Object Editor **(Figure 1.20)** open. An object is another kind of asset/resource, and it's the one that will run all the code we write for our games. But, like the sprite, we need to name our object

Figure 1.21 Invalid Name Error

because as projects get larger, you'll find you have dozens to hundreds of objects. I'm going to name mine objFlower, with the prefix obj to easily identify it's an object. In GameMaker, and coding in general, you can't name two things the same. So, if I didn't add the spr and obj prefix,

Figure 1.19 New Assets

Asset Layer

A layer where you can place sprites and sequences that will appear in your room. These won't be associated with any objects, so no code will be run. They will animate, or play, so it can be great for making a menu

Figure 1.22 Object with Image

Object Editor

The Object Editor controls all the meta data for objects, such as visibility, inheritance, physics, and more. It's also where we assign a name, sprite, and add events to specific objects.

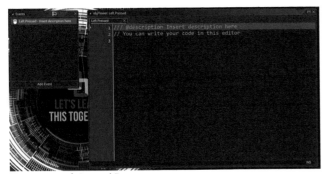

Figure 1.24 Left Pressed Event

and tried to name both my sprite and object just flower, I would get an error **(Figure 1.21)**.

Our object editor allows us to change many properties, but all we'll focus in on now is the sprite and adding events. Click on No Sprite and assign our flower to that object. Now when we see this object in our game, we'll see the flower, as the two are connected. Let's go back to our room, and on the instances layer, drag in our objFlower (you'll notice the flower is now also the image for our object in the asset browser) **(Figure 1.22)**. In our room, if you had the instances layer selected, you'll now see the flower in the room. We could run the game again, but so far, it's no different than if it was a background or asset layer. Time to change that!

Events and Coding

Before we write our first line of code, I want to explain how GameMaker works. All code in our objects run in Events, and you can think of events as things like that in the real world. An event could be you open a door, taking a drink, picking up your phone, or turning the page in this book. Each of these events sends out a little message asking if it should run any code, and if we've added code to that event, it will execute that code, otherwise it continues doing nothing. If I told you to jump on one foot every time the doorbell rang, then the code would be to make you jump, and the event would be the doorbell.

And so now let's look at some of the events we have access to for our object. Return to our workspace by double clicking on our object or choosing Workspace 1. Click on Add Event and peruse the different options we have available **(Figure 1.23)**. Many of them you can sort out for yourself, like create, destroy, and key pressed. But many of them will sound obscure and confusing and that's totally ok right now. Mouse down to the Mouse event, it will present many new options, and select Left Pressed. That event will appear in the Events section, and a new window will appear **(Figure 1.24)** with some green writing in it. This is where we can write our code.

During this book we will use many of the events available, and I'll explain the ones we don't use. For now, let's start simple with the Left Pressed event. This event triggers each time we left click on the object. We must click on the object, not somewhere else in the game, for the code to execute. Right now, we're going to type in this:

x = x + 50; (Figure 1.25)

GameMaker levels are on a Grid-based system, using x and y as coordinates. This line of code says to move 50 pixels to the right each time this code is run. So, let's try it! Press F5 to run your game and click on the flower object. When you do, it will move to the right 50 pixels. You can continue to click on this until it's off the screen. But you can also see that clicking somewhere besides the flower has no effect, which is exactly what we wanted. As you can imagine, there are events for clicking anywhere, but we don't want to use that just yet.

Figure 1.23 Adding an Event

Events

GameMaker is event oriented, meaning nothing happens without an event being triggered. The Step event bypasses this by triggering every frame/step of your game, which means for most games it will execute code 60 times a second. There are dozens of different events, and there is no limit to how many an object can have.

Error Help

- If your flower isn't moving, be sure that you have your object in the room, in the instances layer. Delete any other layers besides the Instances and Background layers. If you have an asset layer and try to click on the flower in that layer, it will do nothing. The asset layer is for sprites, and sprites cannot run code, only objects can.

- If you get the error variable only referenced once **(Figure 1.26)**, double check that your x's are lower cased. They should turn green, not blue.

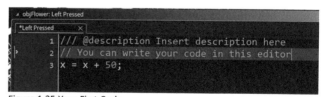

Figure 1.25 Your First Code

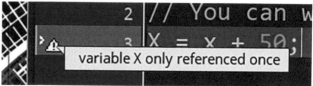

Figure 1.26 Variable Refrenced Once

19

Grid

GameMaker uses a grid, with x and y coordinates, to control where everything is positioned in each level. The grid begins in the top left corner of each room, at 0, 0, and increases as you go right and down.

Conclusion + Challenge

And now you've written your first line of code and created your first game. Again, it may not look too impressive yet, but you should understand that you are now a programmer who understands how to create sprites, objects, and events in a game development software capable of producing incredible games. Everyone starts somewhere, and this is your beginning.

Tomorrow, we'll go deeper into objects. If you're still interested in doing more today, play around with the events and see if you can figure out what they do.

Day 2

Functions Aren't for Fools

Introduction to Functions

Yesterday we covered a lot of material! When learning something new, especially software, there's a lot to see and experiment with. The good news is you've already got most of it down and have seen 70% of what goes into making a game. Over this next month you'll grow more and more familiar with the software and programming, until it feels like second nature. Give it time and have patience with yourself, you will get there!

Today we're going to turn our little project into more of a game. As it currently stands, it isn't much fun to play, but we can fix that! The first thing we're going to learn about are Functions. A function is a way to reuse code in an efficient manner all over your game. GameMaker already has many, many functions built-in to make your life as a game developer easier. We can also create our own functions, which we'll do on later days.

Back in our project, open our objFlower and go to the Left Pressed event. The only code we should have in here is what we wrote yesterday, the x = x + 50;. If you have anything else in there, go ahead and remove it. What we're going to do now is change where the flower is at randomly when we click on it. This will involve several new aspects of coding which I'll break down as we do them.

First off, remove the right side of the equation so you only have x = remaining. Now we're going to use a function that GameMaker has built-in called random. Type the word random, lower cased, and you should see a box appear with lots of different function names; this is Auto Complete which can be helpful. Once you've finished typing, you'll notice that random has changed color **(Figure 2.0)**, indicating it's a different from the x or the number we used before. GameMaker uses a color system to differentiate things like constants, Built-In Properties, functions, and more. You can change all the colors in preferences if you desire.

Functions

An isolated chunk of code that can perform a series of actions quickly by calling its name. A function is given any appropriate name (one that isn't already reserved by GameMaker) and then the code will run, sometimes returning a value for you to work with.

Figure 2.1 Function Arguments

Auto Complete

Auto Complete looks at what you're typing and suggests functions, variables, or other properties it thinks you might be trying to type out. You can scroll through this list and choose one and it will place it on the line where you were just typing. Auto complete isn't perfect, especially when it comes to instance variables, but on the whole it's extremely useful.

Built-in Properties

GameMaker does a lot of heavy lifting by storing properties like room size, sprite width, the starting x and y coordinates of every object in your game, and more! These are color coded green, and you should use them everywhere you can. The exception is speed, health, score, and direction, which we often times take over control for ourselves.

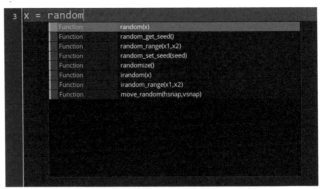

Figure 2.0 Functions

Now type a left bracket, which looks like this: ((shift 9), and at the bottom of the event window the function name appears with brackets and something inside it **(Figure 2.1)**. Many functions accept Arguments, or data, and then use what you passed into them to run their code. In this instance the function wants to know the limit on the number it should return to us. To see an explanation on the arguments, or even what the function does, you can click inside of the function and press F1, or middle click the function, and it will open the Manual **(Figure 2.2)**.

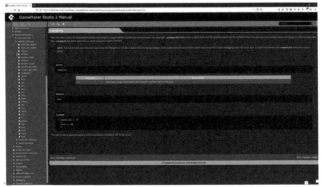

Figure 2.2 The Manual

GameMaker's manuál, unlike many other manual's you've probably tried to read, is concise and helpful. I'll be referring to it very often throughout this book, and I encourage you to browse through it for functions, or just in your spare time to familiarize yourself with GameMaker. In this case, it's opened the page explaining what the function random does, what we should pass in, and what it will return, including an example at the bottom. Syntax simply means what we type to use it, and Real (in the returns area), which is a Data Type.

We can read that this function will return a number from 0 to whatever we pass in. So if we pass in 10, it random will give us a number between 0 and 10, including decimals to the 6th place. Knowing this, let's return to our object and pass in the number 1366, then close it with a right bracket and end the line with a semi-colon **(Figure 2.3)**. The semi-colon is like a period in programming, it tells the computer to stop looking for something more. Try and get used to using it, because there are times if you forget it, GameMaker will not function correctly. Many other languages also require the semi-colon, though not all.

Run your game and click on the flower. You'll see it move randomly along the x axis in your room. That's cool, but we can do even better! Exit the game and below where we assign our x, let's do something similar for our y. Type this:

```
y = random(768);
```

And then run your game once again. Now your flower can move all around the game room, nowhere is off limits. You may be wondering why those numbers specifically, and I can tell you they aren't random. Open your Room1 up and check out the properties near the bottom left, you may have to expand it by clicking on the grey title and find the Width and Height properties. This is the default size GameMaker assigns to new rooms, which is why I chose those numbers, so our flower could go anywhere.

Sprite's and Their Origins

If your flower completely vanished at one point, it's because the random number happened to return the absolute maximum height or width of the room. There are several ways to prevent that happening again, so let's explore them.

The first is changing the origin of our flower. Open your sprFlower by double clicking on it in the Asset Browser or

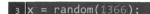
Figure 2.3 The Random Function

Figure 2.5 Origin

Arguments

Functions often accept arguments, or data that can be passed in to alter the outcome of the function. A function can accept 0 to nearly unlimited arguments with arrays. Arguments are traditionally named in a helpful manner to indicate what piece of data should be passed in.

Figure 2.6 Instance Details

Figure 2.4 Opening a Sprite

Figure 2.7 Flower in Room

Manual

GameMaker's manual is an extremely helpful tool to learn the software, functions, and the other features available to you. I highly encourage you to browse through it often, and refer it whenever you get confused.

Data Type

Every piece of data in GameMaker has a type, such as a whole number (-3, 0, 5, 6), real number (-1.53, 2.2222), and more. Data Types are essential to understand when adding variables together, as trying to combine certain types will result in errors, such as a string and a number.

Origin

The origin controls where that sprite is placed in the room. For most sprites you'll want middle center, especially for characters with movement, but the origin can be anything.

clicking on the little paint icon with a white rectangle in the object **(Figure 2.4)**. With the Sprite Editor open, look at the top right of the window where it says Top Left and click on it **(Figure 2.5)**. You can now set the origin of this sprite to any of those options. A sprite's Origin controls where the flower is at in the room. Those x and y's we've been setting have been the origin for the object based on this sprite's origin.

Return to your room and move your flower to the top left corner and double click on it, opening an instance details window **(Figure 2.6)**. Notice the X and Y are both at 0, because the flower's origin is in the top left. Now return to the sprite and change its origin to Middle Center. Go back to the room and notice it's now moved **(Figure 2.7)** because we changed its origin. Our object is still at 0, 0 in our room, but it's moved. All of this is to show you that the origin of your sprite is particularly important and will cause issues later if you have some sprites set to Middle Centre and others set to something else. We will be using Middle Center for almost all our sprites, and I want to show you how to change that in preferences now to save time and frustration.

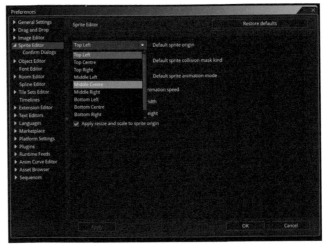

Figure 2.8 Changing Preferences

Click on File (near the top left) and go down to Preferences. It will open a new window. Find Sprite Editor (fourth from the top) and click on it. The first option now available on the right is 'Default sprite origin'. Click on the drop down and select Middle Centre **(Figure 2.8)**. Click OK to exit. There are a lot of settings in there, and I encourage you to look through them, just be careful what all you change.

Using A New Function

If we run our game now the flower will never disappear completely, although it may sometimes be halfway out of the room. This is better, but still a slight problem. Now let's look at the second thing we can change to keep the flower visible and inside our room on every click, which would be limiting the number we get from our function.

There are two ways to go about this, both involving new functions. We're going to do the easiest one, because as developers our primary job is to be lazy. And I'm not joking here. The more you code, the more you'll come to see that being lazy is a benefit. The less code you can write to get the same job done, the better!

Let's now change our function from being random to random_range (the underscore is necessary, as the function is named with that in it). Immediately you'll see several things happen **(Figure 2.9)**:

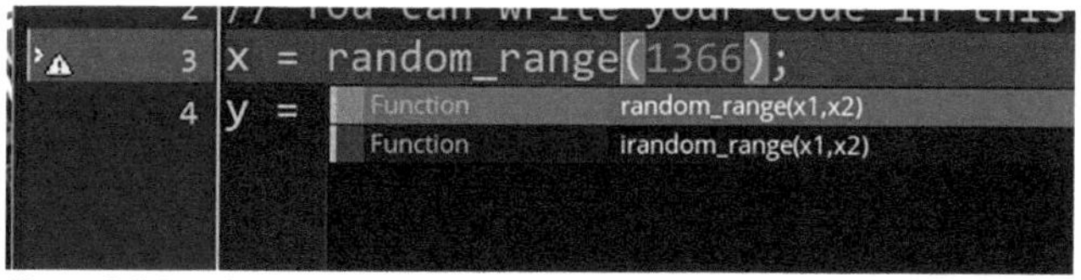

Figure 2.9 Random Range

1) Auto complete will present two options, we want the one without an i in front.

2) A yellow warning symbol will appear on the line you changed. This warning says it expected 2 arguments but only received 1, which is a fair warning since we haven't changed our arguments yet.

I mentioned before that functions can take many arguments, and this one we want to use takes 2, a minimum and a maximum. Whereas before the random function had a set minimum of 0, we can now set to whatever we want, which is awesome. To ensure our flower stays in

the bounds of our x, we need to set the minimum to 32 and the maximum to 1334, go ahead and do that now **(Figure 2.10)**. The reason for 32 and 1334 is our origin is now center, so there's 32 pixels on the left and right of our sprite we must account for. Try moving your object to the left and right in your room and look at its X position, and you'll see that on the edge it's at 32 and 1334 respectively (you may have to turn off grid snapping in the room, which can be done by pressing the little grid icon near the top right **(Figure 2.11)**).

Figure 2.10 Fixing Random Range

Figure 2.11 Grid Icon

Now let's fix the setting of the y coordinate as well by changing the line to this:

```
y = random_range(32, 736);
```

Built-In Properties

Run your game again and you'll now see it will always stay inside the room. But what if we changed the room size, or the sprite? Then our numbers wouldn't work anymore. Fortunately, there are ways around that problem! What we've done so far is called Hard Coding, not because it's difficult, but because those values are fixed and won't work if we change anything about our game. In general, you don't want to hard code values unless you're working on a small prototype, or know for certain you'll never change those values.

A way to get around hard coding values in your game is to use built-in properties. We've already used some of them, such as the x and y coordinates of our object. Built-in

Hard Coding

When you put in the data exactly as it is, without accounting for changes in the future. Hard coding values is a bad practice in general, as future changes can destroy your code. Whenever possible, use built-in properties and variables.

properties are color coded to green and are essential for getting and setting properties of our sprites and objects. For example, let's take the first argument in our functions, the 32, and replace it with this line:

sprite_width / 2

Sprite Width gets the width of the current sprite the object is using, which in this case is our flower at 64 pixels. When we divide it by 2 we get 32, which is the same number we had in there before. The difference now is that number isn't hard coded, so if we changed the size of our flower, this number would remain correct. Let's now subtract that same value (sprite_width / 2) from the second argument in our function **(Figure 2.12)**. But what about those numbers we have in there? They're still hard coded, and we don't want that.

```
/// @description Insert description here
// You can write your code in this editor
x = random_range(sprite_width / 2, 1334 - sprite_width / 2);
y = random_range(sprite_width / 2, 736 - sprite_width / 2);
```

Figure 2.12 Subtracting Sprite Width

Built-in properties to the rescue again! Take the 1334 number and replace it with room_width. It turns green, because room_width is a built-in property that holds the width of the room you're currently in. Now replace 736 with room_height **(Figure 2.13)**. Our 2 lines of code are now much longer but will work if we change our sprite or our room size. Go ahead and try it! Alter the room size to something like 400 x 400 and play your game (be sure your flower starts in the new room size though).

```
x = random_range(sprite_width / 2, room_width - sprite_width / 2);
y = random_range(sprite_width / 2, room_height - sprite_width / 2);
```

Figure 2.13 Final Code

It's a little more work to type all that out compared to the numbers we had in there, which may seem like it goes against my whole laziness speech from earlier, but, it doesn't. What takes more work, using built-in properties to make our object always work correctly, or needing to change the numbers every time we change room size or sprite size? Sure, sure, if we never changed room or sprite size, then the second one is faster, but that's unlikely. Room size changes all the time! The first option will be faster, and work better in the long run, than the quick and dirty option of using hard coded values.

Sprite Width

The width of the sprite currently assigned to an object. You can get the width of sprites not assigned to objects, but that requires using a function, not this built-in property.

Conclusion + Challenge

Your challenge for today is to play around with auto complete and see what functions are available in GameMaker. There are hundreds, and many of them can be intuited by their names alone, while others require the manual and a lot of research. We don't quite have a playable game yet; we'll do that tomorrow. But for now, continue to play around with the functions you have available, and see what awesome ones you can discover.

Day 3

Your First Real Game

Variables

It's time to turn our little project into a game, one that has all the properties of an actual game. There are still more things to learn, and so today we're going to focus on Variables and a few more events in our objects. We'll focus on variables first, as they're a basic building block for all programming projects.

Figure 3.0 First Variable

To start it off, let's just create a variable and then examine how they work. Open your objFlower and add a new event, this time add the first one on the list, the Create event. We get to name our variables almost anything we want, but there are a few rules. It can't be the name of a built-in property like room_width or x, and it can't start with a number like 2. For our first variable, let's use the name clickScore, using camel case once again. Try this:

clickScore = 0; (Figure 3.0)

You'll notice a little warning symbol again, but we can ignore it for now. What we've just done is created a container called clickScore and assigned 0 to it. We've used the = sign several times already, but I think we should break it down a little more right now. In math, = means equals, but in programming it tells the computer to set whatever's on the left side to equal whatever's on the right. It's not checking for equality, instead we are telling it what its value is, like we did yesterday with the functions.

Our variable is going to hold the score for our game, and we can change it during the running of our game. Let's return to the Left Pressed event by double clicking on it in the Events section or pressing the little window in our code window **(Figure 3.1)**. Add a new line below our functions, and let's increase the value of our variable whenever we click

Variables

A variable is a container for data that you're allowed to name almost anything (it can't be the name of a function or a built-in property). Variables can hold any kind of data, and in GameMaker they can change what they're holding at any time.

on this object. There are several ways to do this, so let's quickly explore those now.

```
clickScore = clickScore + 1;
```

Figure 3.1 Changing Events

Code runs from right to left, always retrieving values before assigning them. So, this line of code reads like this: get the value of clickScore, which is 0, and add 1 to it. Now assign whatever the result of that math is to clickScore and save. The first time we click on our flower it will become 1, then 2, and so on.

```
clickScore += 1;
```

This line of code does the same thing but allows us to type less. The += is code for grab the variable on the left, add the number on the right to it, and then assign that result to the variable. You can of course add any number you want; it doesn't need to just be 1.

```
++clickScore;
```

And finally, we have my favorite way of increasing a variable by 1. The ++ in front of a variable adds 1 to it and saves the result in that variable. It is only good for adding 1, unlike the others where we could change the number to anything. This method also has the reverse where you can subtract 1 at a time by using --. This specific method is the most succinct and quickest to write, but also probably the most confusing.

Go ahead and choose one of those three and put it below the functions in the Left Pressed event. I'll use the first method for now, as I think it's the easiest to understand when starting out **(Figure 3.2)**. Now whenever we click on our flower, our variable goes up by 1.

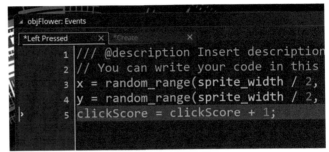

Figure 3.2 Increacing ClickScore

Showing the Score

We now have a goal in our game, to reach the highest score possible. But we need to display this information to the player somewhere, because if they can't see their score, they have no way of knowing they even have one. It's time to add another event to our object, this time it's the Draw event. Select the event that simply says Draw, even though there are many options to choose from **(Figure 3.3)**.

The draw event is a special event that triggers every frame of our game, which is 60 frames a second by default. This means whatever we put in here will run many times, so we must use this event with caution. The other thing to note is by adding this event, we've now told GameMaker we will oversee all drawing related to this object, even controlling when this object shows up in the game. Press F5 to run your game now and you'll see the flower is invisible. Let's fix that!

Close your game, and add in this event on line 3: draw_self(); It doesn't accept any arguments, and it doesn't return anything we need to save or store in a variable. This function will now render our object in the game so we can see it. You must add this function anytime you use the draw event, or you won't be able to see your object.

But if we run into some problems when using the draw event, then why even use it? Because the draw events are the only place we can use the draw functions! And these functions allow us to manually draw whatever we want on the screen, including text. There are dozens of different draw functions, and we'll learn many of them in this book, but for now we're going to start with the simplest text drawing one available: draw_text. Press enter and type our draw_text on the new line (Figure 3.4). You'll see auto complete once again trying to assist you, but we don't need the other functions right now, we just want the first one. The red error appears if we don't add the brackets at the end of calling a function, so go ahead and add (); now.

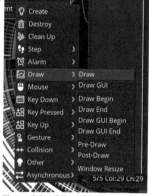

Figure 3.3 Adding the Draw Event

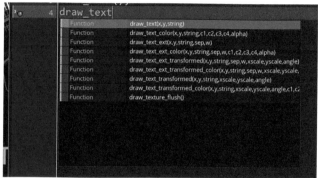

Figure 3.4 Draw Text

Click inside of the brackets and look at the bottom of the code window to see which arguments it's expecting. The x and y are where we'll draw the text in the game, and string is a data type; a String is just any words and/or characters between 2 quotes "". This function will automatically convert variables of a number data type, like our clickScore, to a string and display it properly if it's the only thing we're trying to draw. Let's give it a try.

In the draw_text function add 32 for x, 32 for y, and clickScore for the string to draw. At this point if you make a typo in our variable name, you'll get another yellow sign with the warning you've only referenced it once **(Figure 3.5)**. This time we need to pay attention to this warning, as it would cause our game to crash if we ran our game with it. And actually, let's go ahead and crash our game, then I'll explain what's happening. Press F5 to run your game.

Create

The create event will run code only once when that object is first added into the game. This makes it the best place to initialize variables and run any code that needs to only run 1 time.

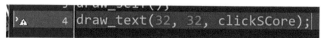

Figure 3.5 Warning with Variables

(Figure 3.6) This box will become your worst enemy as you begin making larger games if you let it. But it doesn't have to be! If we look closely, we can read why the game

Draw

The draw event is a special event that runs every frame of our game. By default, GameMaker is drawing our object in the level, but once we add this event it becomes our responsibility to handle that. We can only use the draw_ functions inside of a draw event. If you want to see your object in the game, then add draw_self() to your draw event.

crashed, which line of code caused the crash, and exactly how to fix it. In my case I used a capital C in clickScore (variables must be spelled exactly the same every time we use them), and so GameMaker thought I was referencing a variable with that specific name and spelling. We never created that variable or gave it any data, and so when our function tried to draw the contents of clickSCore onto the screen it couldn't find the variable and crashed.

Error Help

- A variable not being set before reading it is the most common error you'll run into. It almost always means there was a spelling error when it occurs outside of the create event. Double check spelling and look for those little yellow signs indicating a variable is referenced only once. If you create a variable in the create event and then use it somewhere else, GameMaker sees it's been referenced more than once, and that sign disappears.

Let's correct this error and spell our variable correctly **(Figure 3.7)**. Now let's run and see how that looks **(Figure 3.8)**. Fantastic! We now have a score in our game that increases as we play. Click on your flower to see the score go up. The only problem is that number has no context. Most players will figure out it's their score, but if we started drawing any other numbers on the screen, like a timer, it will get confusing without a label. Fortunately, we can draw more than 1 thing at a time!

Figure 3.6 Code Error

```
4  draw_text(32, 32, clickScore);
```
Figure 3.7 Correct

Inside of our draw_text function, we can add more information to draw, such as the word Score. We could add another draw_text function before the score, but doing so becomes trickier than you might think, as the number grows, it might grow to the left or right and overlap our word (you can direct how font is drawn exactly, but that's beyond the scope of what we're doing right now). So instead let's add the word Score as a string to our variable, like this:

```
draw_text(32, 32, "Score " + clickScore);
```

This is what we want, to draw the word Score before our number. But running this produce an error. Go ahead and try it **(Figure 3.9)**. This time the error is a little more confusing. What is DoAdd :: Execution Error? The name isn't very helpful, which is partially why I wanted to bring it up now because you'll probably run into it many times in the future.

Figure 3.8 Our Game with a Score

```
DoAdd :: Execution Error
at gml_Object_objFlower_Draw_0 (line 4) - draw_text(32, 32, "Score" + clickScore);
############################################################################
gml_Object_objFlower_Draw_0 (line 4)
```

Figure 3.9 Another Error

- DoAdd :: Execution Error happens when we try to add data types that aren't compatible. The word "Score" and clickScore are a string and a number, respectively. We've told GameMaker to add them together, but it doesn't know how to do that. Do you know how to add a word and a number together? There are many ways you could approach it, and computers cannot deal with ambiguity. If it's not clear, they will throw an error. To fix this, we need to make them compatible data types. We know we can add numbers together, but we can't very easily convert the word Score to a number. Instead we go the other direction and convert our variable to a string.

And again, there's a function for exactly what we want to do. The function string() will convert whatever's inside of it to a string (it won't change anything about the contents or make it so we can't add more to it later). That way we can add, or concatenate, the two words together. For a computer, they can add words/strings together by just combining them into one long string. Let's give it a try! Use the function string() on our clickScore variable and run the game **(Figure 3.10)**.

Figure 3.12 Matching Brackets

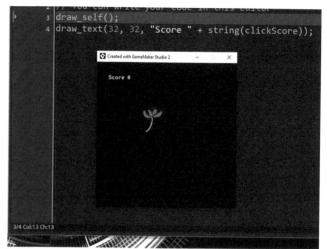

Figure 3.10 The Game with Score

Figure 3.11 Another Error

- **(Figure 3.11)** If you get a red error that says Got ';' (;) expected ',' don't worry, it's just your line is missing a bracket. When you add another function inside of a function, the brackets really start adding up. This unintuitive error is telling you that the semicolon was found before it was expected, and you need to line up your brackets. An easy way to find the missing bracket is to click to the right of the last bracket and see where it lines up **(Figure 3.12)**. In this image it only goes back to the string() function, but it needs to go all the way back to our draw_text() function. Add one more right bracket and it'll be right as rain!

Figure 3.13 Alarm 0

> • If you got a red error saying Got 'string' (id) expected, it's because you forgot the + symbol. Without that, GameMaker expected something else instead of our string() function. Add the + between the string "Score" and string(clickScore) and you're good to go.

String

Another data type, the string is used for holding words and characters. They must be between two quotes like this: "Hello!". A string can be as simple as one letter, or as lengthy as a book. Strings in variables can manipulated through many of the built-in functions.

Debugging is a big part of being a programmer and making games. Try not to be frustrated by problems but look at them as a logic puzzle. Something's gone wrong but you can figure it out! Take it step by step, use Ctrl Z to undo and Ctrl Y to redo to find when things were working, and then make one small change at a time. This is a skill, and nobody starts out being an expert debugger. Give it time and you'll be able to fix bugs and glitches and errors in no time at all.

Completing our Game

All these problems solved, let's now turn our little project into a full-fledged game. The way we'll do this is add a timer that ticks down, turning the clicking into a game of speed and reaction. At the end of the timer, we'll show the final score and ask if they want to replay.

Let's return to our create event of objFlower and set an Alarm. Alarm's are like timers for our objects and can have up to 12 running at any time. They tick down once per frame, and are great for delayed events, timers, or in specific situations when you need to run code just 1 frame later (like changing rooms). What we're going to do is use the alarm as both a timer and message for the player, to show them their final score.

Beneath where we set our clickScore variable, let's set the first alarm to 300 like this:

alarm[0] = 300; **(Figure 3.13)**

The alarm events are an Array, which is another data type we'll discuss later. For now, just know to use the alarm events, you need the square brackets ([]) which are found to the right of the letter p on your keyboard. Set the number you want to use and give it a number. That alarm is now set to that number, 300 in our case, and will count down until it reaches 0 and then execute its code. The big caveat to alarm's is that you must have the alarm event in the object you call it, or nothing will happen. So right now, our alarm 0 will never go down, it will just stay at 300 forever.

To ensure our alarm works, let's add the alarm 0 event to our object. Now it will count down and trigger the code in here after 300 frames, or 5 seconds. Let's add a debug message in here to check that it's working. The function we'll use is show_message() and it's meant only for debugging purposes, not for use in game, but we can definitely use it for this project. Add a string inside the function letting the player know their final score and the game will restart when they click ok. I'll challenge you to do this on your own, before looking at my solution. Go ahead and give it a try!

Here's the code I'm going to use:

```
show_message("Game Over! You got
a score of " + string(clickScore) + ". If
you click ok, you can play again.");
```

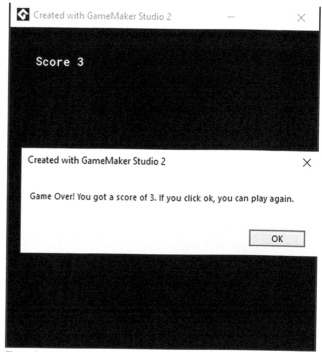

After 5 seconds, the message appears **(Figure 3.14)**. There're just 2 things left to do. The first is to show the timer on screen, so the player sees how much time they have left. And the second is to restart the game. The first one you can probably do on your own, so I'll challenge you to try that out. The second is a bit more difficult since you're not familiar with the specific function you'll need. Let's tackle them in reverse order to give you the chance of solving it without me.

Figure 3.14 Message

To restart a game from scratch, we use the function game_restart(). No arguments needed, just call that and your game resets to almost how it was when it first ran (there are some differences, but none we need to be worried about for this game). Let's add it right after our show_message() function. While that message is on screen, the game is paused, but once the player clicks ok the game resumes, and our game_restart() function will trigger **(Figure 3.15)**.

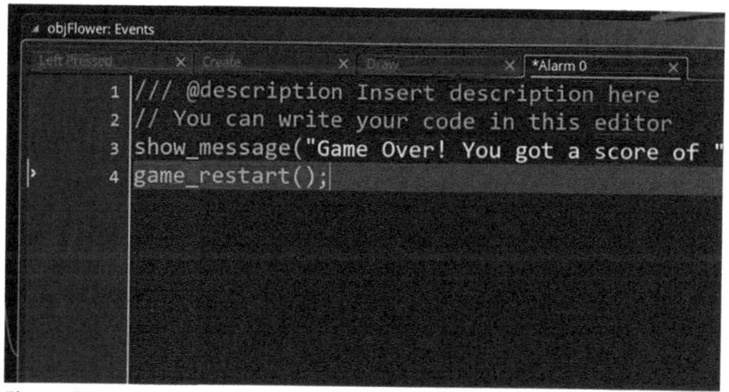

As to showing the timer, we could create another variable and display that as the timer. But the cool thing is that the alarm itself can function as the timer we show, too. We just need to do a little math, but don't worry, I do mean just a little.

Figure 3.15 Restarting

Figure 3.16 The Game with Timer

Figure 3.17 Randomize

Seed

A seed, in GameMaker, is a specific number value that will always produce the same results. By default, the seed is the same each time you play your game. You can change this by using the function random_set_seed() and passing in a value, or by using randomize() which truly randomizes your game every time.

Return to our Draw event and add another draw_text() function, with the x at 32, and y at 48. Then we'll say something like "Time Left" and add the alarm[0], but divide it by 60. The alarm[0] / 60 must be in a string, since we're adding it to our other text. It should all look like this:

```
draw_text(32, 48, "Time Left " + string(alarm[0] / 60));
```

With that done, we can now see how much time is left in our game, and we'll show a message to the player with their score **(Figure 3.16)**. And we have a game! It's not flashy, but there's a clear goal, a little bit of fun, and endless replay ability. But if you've played it very much, I'm sure you've noticed your flower is always in the same spot. What's up with that? We're using a random function, and yet it doesn't seem random.

The reason is GameMaker always sets the same random Seed in your game, which makes testing it easier. To get around this, call the function randomize() in the create event of our flower **(Figure 3.17)**. It only needs to be called once in your game, and then it will set the seed to be something totally random each time, giving your game a unique experience each time. If you want to control the randomness, there are functions to manually set the seed, like in Minecraft, or other games with procedurally generated worlds.

Conclusion + Challenge

Our game is now playable, unique, and fun. Take a moment and be proud of what you've done! Share this with your friends and family. You're 3 days into your game making journey and you've already got a game, and a ton of new knowledge under your belt. There's a long road ahead of you, and even though the journey never really ends, it's good to take a look back and see how far you've come.

Today's challenge is to add a cool background to your flower game and keep the flower from appearing behind the text we're drawing. Good luck!

PRO TIP

Is There a Best Game Engine?

Aaron Craig
Let's Learn This Together

LetsLearnThisTogether.com

A question I hear a lot is, 'what game engine is the best?' And there's a huge problem with that question that most people don't realize. Not only is 'best' subjective, which means everyone is going to have their own opinion on it, it's also assuming that there is one that's the best. Imagine asking a musician which instrument is the best to learn when your goal is just to play music. Or ask an athlete which sport is the best to take up when you just want to play a game.

In the end, a game engine is a tool you use to create your vision. If it isn't working for you, then find another one that will. There are dozens of engines to choose from and they all have their appeals and drawbacks. Some are better for 2D while others excel at high fidelity 3D games. There are engines specifically made for online games, integrating Twitch and YouTube into their core tools, while others focus on creating single player experiences with no regard to networking.

One engine isn't worse for not having certain features, and one isn't better for having said features. It all comes down to what you are creating. If you're working on a small indie team who wants to craft a heart filled narrative game, you'll gravitate towards the engine that allows for easy dialogue, and that's what you want to happen.

So, the next time you begin to ask, or hear someone else ask, 'what's the best game engine', steer the conversation towards what really matters: what engine is best suited to help me create my game?

Day 4

Diving into Fluffy Heroes

Getting the Assets

Today we're going to begin building the big project in this book. It's a platformer, puzzle, rpg-like game called Fluffy Heroes, where you get to play as 3 adorable characters, solve puzzles, collect power ups, and jump your way to victory! You can download the entire project on my github if you want to check out the source code, play the game, or just mess around with it. It's an awesome game, and while we build it together, you're going to learn everything you need to make your dream game, even if it doesn't fall into those game genre categories.

So, go ahead and open GameMaker Studio and create a new project with GML (game maker language). We're going to be using third party assets for this project, and I've credited the authors in the back of this book where necessary, so you'll need to get those assets to follow along. I've also included other similar assets, such as other terrain sets, objects, enemies, etc. so you can experiment and create a game that's totally unique to you! Download the assets and open the folder **(Figure 4.0)**. You'll see two folders, the one we're going to spend our time in is Fluffy Heroes, where all the assets are labeled and organized. The other folder contains the original download where I got the assets from, along with attributions and license notes. There's a lot to explore in that folder, including the art source files, so give it a good look over, as you might find some art in there you prefer over what I chose.

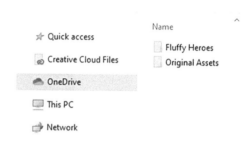

Figure 4.0 Assets

Taking Pinky for a Walk

But when you're ready, open the Fluffy Heroes folder, go into Sprites, then Pinky, and find Pink_Monster_Walk_6. This is our first Sprite Sheet and contains the animation for our first character to walk. We're going to organize our project differently than the default, which means we need to create a folder for our player. In GameMaker, right click in the gray area of the asset browser and select Create Group **(Figure 4.1)**, and name it Player. If you clicked on a folder and did this, it will now be nested inside that folder, but don't fret! You can drag that folder out by left clicking and pulling it to the bottom or the far left.

We now have a folder for all our player sprites, sounds, and objects. This method of organization is purely subjective, and you are free to organize it however you see fit.

Figure 4.1 New Group

Sprite Sheet

Sprite sheets contain related images that when played together result in an animation. Sprite sheets can be large, containing every animation for a character, or small, containing a single animation. Good sprite sheets will be spaced evenly and consistently, making it a pleasure to use, while others will be just cobbled together and require more work on your part to pull out what you want.

Just know I'll be referring to specific folders I've created in the future when talking about where assets are, and where to import new assets.

In the Player folder, add yet another group, and this time we want it to be nested in there. Name it Pinky, as this is where we'll place all the sprites related to this specific character. Then drag and drop the walking sprite sheet into the Pinky folder and the sprite will appear **(Figure 4.2)**! The sprite sheet comes in as just one image though, and we need to fix that. Double click on the frame at the bottom of the image editor or click Edit Image. A new window opens, and we now have access to more options for working with this sprite. You may have noticed already, but GameMaker has context sensitive menus, which means the toolbar at the top changes depending on what window you're in **(Figure 4.3)**. So, if you're looking for a room specific option, be sure to open a room and it will appear.

Figure 4.2 Pinky Walking

Figure 4.3 Contextual Menu

The option we're looking for is in the dropdown menu for Image, then Convert to Frames **(Figure 4.4)**. This allows us to split up a sprite sheet based on how many images we want out of it, where they're positioned, and how far apart they are from one another. A good sprite sheet makes this easy, while a bad one can take a long time to discover the correct numbers. Fortunately, this is an excellent sprite sheet! The file name of the sprite even tells us how many frames are in this sprite sheet: 6. Set the Number of Frames box to 6. You'll notice that nothing happens, and that's because the second box is saying there's only 1 frame per row, by default. But for our sprite sheet, there's only 1 row, and all six of our images are in that 1 row. So, let's change the Frames per Row to 6. Now there's white boxes around all the frames we want. The width and height are set to 32 by default, and that's the size of this sprite. The offset options are to set where the first sprite begins on the sheet, remember they can be very large sheets, and you can left click and move the first box's starting position around (which I've found to be the easiest way). Set them back to 0 if you did click in there. Finally, the separation options are for when the frames aren't so close together, as sometimes they have space between them.

The final values to be in the boxes should look like **Figure 4.5**. If they do, then click on Convert. We now have a sprite with 6 frames that show our player walking. Try

p	Image	View	Effects	
	Cut Selection			CTRL+X
	Copy Selection			CTRL+C
	Paste Clipboard			CTRL+V
	Select All			CTRL+A
	Cancel Selection			ESCAPE
	Invert Selection			CTRL+SHIFT+I
	Add Frame			SHIFT+A
	Insert Frame			Insert
	Delete Selected Frames			Delete
	Import Image(s)			CTRL+SHIFT+A

Figure 4.4 Convert to Frames

Figure 4.6 Play

Number of Frames	6	
Frames per Row	6	
Frame Width	32	
Frame Height	32	
Horizontal Cell Offset	0	
Vertical Cell Offset	0	
Horizontal Pixel Offset	0	
Vertical Pixel Offset	0	
Horizonal Separation	0	
Vertical Separation	0	

Figure 4.5 Correct Options

clicking on the play button to see them in action **(Figure 4.6)**! Woah hold up there! Pinky is going crazy, click the pause button to stop. Pinky was going so fast it looked awful, what happened? The problem is our speed is set too high; we need to lower it. Close the window we're in and return to Workspace 1. Here we can see some more properties of our sprite that we haven't talked about yet **(Figure 4.7)**.

Figure 4.8 Center Button

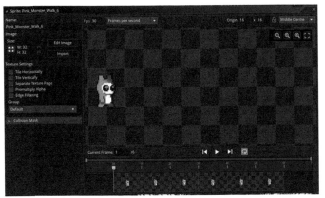

Figure 4.7 Pinky

The first thing we'll change is the speed of sprite, which controls how fast the images are played. FPS here stands for Frames Per Second and controls how many frames are played per second. Change it from 30 to 10 and then press play to see the result. It's much smoother and looks rather good to me. Whatever you set it to here will be the default in game as well. There are ways to speed up and slow down a sprite without altering its fps, but we'll get to that later in this book. Pinky is currently walking forever, and that's being controlled by the playback mode, two buttons to the right of play. There are three options for playback, which also applies elsewhere in GameMaker, and they are loop-ing, ping pong, and not looping. The first and last are easy to understand just from their terminology, looping will play forever, not looping will only play once, but ping pong is a little more abstract. Try changing it to the ping pong setting, the one without a circle, and play the animation. The sprite plays from left to right, then right to left, and back again forever. Like the game of ping pong, it goes back and forth. In all my time I've never used this for an animation, but it's still good to know you have the option.

Click on the center button to bring Pinky into full view **(Figure 4.8)**. If you didn't change the preference of the origin when I did, be sure to set the origin to Middle Centre, not Top Left. If you forget this, it will cause some issues down the road. Lastly, let's rename our sprite to sprPinkyWalk. That's everything we need to do for this sprite, of course we'll need many more sprites later, but for now let's take Pinky out for a walk!

Cameras and Views

Create an object in the Player folder and call it objPlayer. I'm specifically putting this object in Player, not in Pinky, as we will have multiple characters to play as down the road. Assign the Pinky sprite to the new object. Open the Rooms folder and double click on Room1. My Room Editor tab opens a bit large sometimes, but it's easy to resize all the

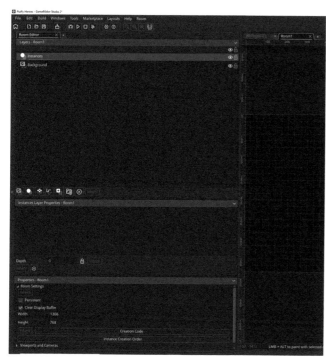

Figure 4.9 Large Room Editor Tab

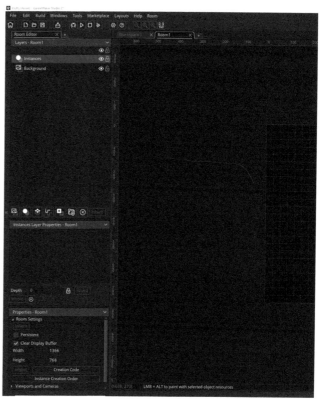

Figure 4.10 Resizing

Figure 4.11 Layer Properties

Frames Per Second

The number of frames played every second. This is the default speed type in games, and probably what you'll always use. 30 is the default and can look good for sprites with dozens of frames. For smaller animations, you want a smaller playback number. This setting here will be the default playback speed in the game for this sprite, so if it looks good in this preview, it will look good in your game.

Figure 4.12 Cameras

Figure 4.13 Camera Properties

Viewpoints

The viewport is the window the game runs in. Most games these days run full screen at the monitors max resolution, and this controls the resolution. It can also be used for allowing multiple cameras in your game, such as for multiplayer, or minimaps.

Cameras

The camera is the view into your game. It controls what can be seen, and the dimensions of the width and height are directly related to the viewport width and height. If these two are not scaled to each other properly, then your sprites will appear deformed. You can have up to 8 cameras in your game.

tabs in GameMaker **(Figure 4.9)**. Move your mouse to the edge of the tab and drag it left or right until it fits nicely **(Figure 4.10)**. Now center the room but clicking on the centre button, same look as the sprite centre button. Add our objPlayer into the room.

You'll notice the object is quite small. Run the game, and you'll see that doesn't change. Remember the sprites we are using are only 32x32 pixels, so pretty small compared to modern standards. Fortunately, there are many tricks to making small sprites appear big and still look great! GameMaker uses a camera system, which controls how much of the room we see, the size of the game screen, and the scale of it all. We're going to create a custom camera later, but for now let's use a simple one to enlarge our player on the screen.

Minimize the Layers and Instance Layer Properties by clicking on the small down arrow on the right **(Figure 4.11)**. That maximizes the Properties section, which contains all the options for Viewports and Cameras, which we're going to now adjust. Expand Viewports and Cameras by clicking on the little arrow to the left of the text. Now checkmark Enable Viewports, and then expand Viewport 0. There are a lot of options here, but let's just focus on what's necessary to make our player look big.

Check the box that says Visible and you'll notice a white border appear around the room **(Figure 4.12)**. We have enabled everything necessary for cameras, and that white border is our first camera, and it's showing us what it can see. But seeing the whole room doesn't help us, and probably isn't what you want in your game. Think about most games you've played, maybe even all games, and you'll realize the room changes as you move your character, you don't see the entire room all at once. We want to do the same thing here, showing only a portion of the room and having the camera follow our player around.

To get that effect, we must change the width and height of our Camera, which you can find under Camera Properties **(Figure 4.13)**. Change the width to 256 and the height to 144. Immediately you'll notice the white rectangle shrinks down, indicating the camera can now only see that much of the room. It may not look like much, but when using small sprites, that can be a large section of your game. Before we run the game again, we must set the Object Following property, or the camera will not be focused on the player. Click on No Object and find objPlayer. The camera doesn't move, but when the game starts up it will look for the player and show them. Give it a try **(Figure 4.14)**.

Our player is in the corner, which isn't exactly what we want. The reason for this is the border properties. Beneath where we selected our player are the Horizontal and Vertical border options. By default, they're both at 32. The border option tells the camera how close the object it's following can get to the camera. We can't move our player in game yet, but if we could and moved to the right, the camera would move with us. If we moved to the left, it wouldn't move until we got 32 pixels away from the edge. To center our player, change the border options to 320 and play the game again. Perfect! Our player is now in the center. The border options are larger than necessary, as we could have also set them to 256 and 144, but I wanted to show you that anything over those numbers will also work.

Figure 4.14 Camera on Player

Then there's the viewport, which controls the window size of our game. Depending on what kind of computer and monitor you're using, your resolution may be different than mine. The most common resolution these days is 1920x1080, but if you know yours, you should use that here when adjusting the viewport. Under Viewport Properties, adjust the width and height to 1920 and 1080 respectively. Run the game and it will fill up your screen completely. If it doesn't, then you have a larger resolution. If you cannot find the bar at the top to close the game, then your monitor may have a smaller resolution and you'll need to force close the game window (on Windows, use Alt+F4. On Mac Cmd+Q). We can control the border at the top, and even make our game full screen through code, but we won't do that until we can also quit our game from in the game. Change the Viewport Properties until you find a size you like and keep it there; I will keep mine at 1920x1080.

Comments

Let's focus on our player object now, so go ahead and close the room window. In our first game we used several events and you learned about functions. Now I want to expand your knowledge and introduce you to the event you'll probably spend the most time in, the Step event. The Step event, like draw, is a special event that triggers every frame of your game. You can use it to check for input, health, states, collisions, and more. There are special events, like key press, mouse press, and collision, but if you want full control over your object, you'll want to put those checks in the step event. As we build it up, you'll see why, so let's get started!

Add a new event to objPlayer, the Step event. There are three options, select the first, just Step, and add it. It's also time to talk about the green code that appears at the top of every new event, as it will help you write better code and maintain large projects. Anything following two slashes (//) in GameMaker, and several other languages, is a Comment. GameMaker ignores comments, they are only used to leave messages/descriptions for yourself or other humans. They don't impact speed or performance, so you

Step

The step event runs every frame of your game is where most of your objects logic will reside. The reason for this is it gives you more control, whereas the collision event triggers when we collide and gives us access to that one object, we can use the step event to check for all collisions occurring, filter them through a list, and pick out a specific object. The same goes for all other circumstances: coding it in the step event gives more control, which is essential for crafting better games.

can add in as many comments as you like. The primary reason for comments is to help yourself, or others, understand what's being done in a specific section of code. As your game grows, it will also get more complicated, and some sections will be difficult to simply look at and understand what's happening. This is where comments come in handy! I highly suggest you leave comments all over, not

Figure 4.15 Description

just frivolous ones, but really describe what a section of code is doing, especially if you struggled creating it. Odds are when you return to it in a couple of days, without any comments, you'll have no idea what it's doing, or how to fix it if there's something wrong.

You can leave multi-line comments, too. A single slash followed by an asterisk begins the multi-line comment (/*) and the reverse ends it (*/). Useful for longer comments, or if you want to comment out a section of code for debugging or testing a new section of code.

Comment

A comment is for human use only and ignored by GameMaker when running a game. Leave comments on tricky code to help you remember what it's doing when you return to it down the road.

And the last thing about comments for now is the special comment in events, the @description on line 1. This controls the text in the event section, and I recommend you replace it with something useful. Try changing it now and see how the events pane changes, too **(Figure 4.15)**. I always set a description myself. They're more helpful on smaller events, such as draw or destroy, when I can concisely say what's happening in just a few words, but I still give descriptions to all my events because I think they look better that way.

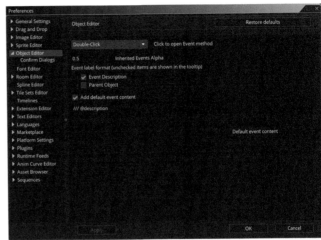

Figure 4.16 Changing Comment Settings

One thing to note here is the comments that appear when creating an event can be changed from the preferences. I'm going to change mine now by going to File, Preferences, and expanding Object Editor. I'm going to erase the Default event content and leave only /// @ description, which will save me the time of deleting that portion every time I make a new event **(Figure 4.16)**.

Conclusion + Challenge

And this is where we're going to end for today. It may not seem as though we did much, but the introduction of cameras, sprite sheets, and comments are all important game dev topics. The cameras especially are essential, and I encourage you to play around with them and their settings.

Today's challenge is to get our player moving in the game. Use the other events, such as key down, to get them moving. Do note that on a black background, it is impossible to see that player moving. So, add in some other sprites that you can walk by, to see if you're moving or not.

Day 5

What if We Animated Pinky?

What If?

If you took me up on the challenge from yesterday, you probably have some events in objPlayer like Key Down Left and Right, to get your player moving. Awesome work! If you didn't, that's alright, too. We're going to tackle moving and animating our fluffy hero today, and introduce the concept of conditional statements, also known as if else statements. Before we dive into that, remove any other events or code you have in your player, as we're going to do it all in the step event.

The first thing we're going to learn is Conditional Statements as we need them to control how our player is going to move. Up until now, all the code we've written has executed no matter what, but there are many times we only want code to run when a certain condition is met. That condition can be literally anything, although it's usually based on the value of a variable or function. The example I like to use goes like this:

You look out your window. If it's raining, you'll grab an umbrella or raincoat, if the weather is fine, you won't. The data being checked here is the weather, and based on if it's raining or not, you will react differently. The code we're going to write will be the exact same, using some of the same words as well! Let's dive into the code, and I'll continue to explain how it works and why it's so important.

On line 2 in our step event, write this code **(Figure 5.0)**:

```
if (keyboard_check(vk_left) == true) {

    x -= 2;

}
```

This code is going to move our player to the left while we're pressing the left arrow key. I'll explain how it all

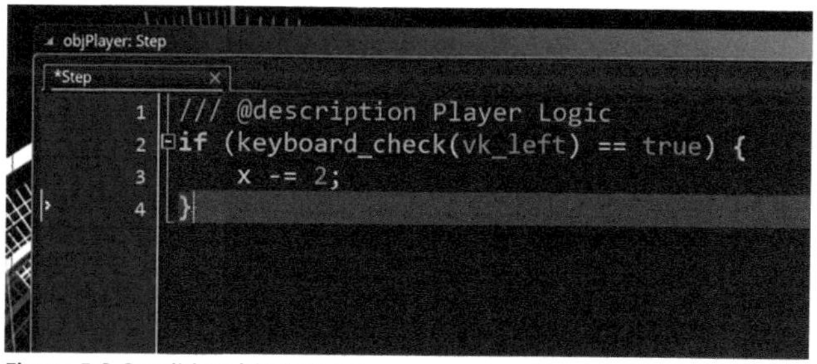

> ### Conditional Statements
>
> *Conditional statements alter the flow of code, allowing it to react to variables and other data. This usually takes the form of an if statement, or a switch. You can think of these as asking a question about a piece of data, and then, based on the answer, running a specific chunk of code.*

Figure 5.0 Conditional Statement

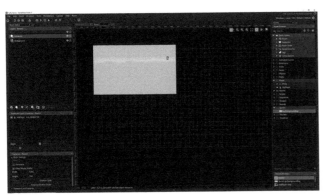

Figure 5.1 Setting Background

works in just a moment, but first let's add a background in our game so we can see the player moving. In the Fluffy Heroes assets folder, open Backgrounds, and drag Background Day into the Sprites folder. Rename it to spr-BackgroundDay. Now open Room1 and assign that sprite to our background layer. If you have any trouble accessing it, because we moved some tabs around, you can click on Room (up at the top) and select 'Reset Windows On Current Desktop' to reset it all back to the way it was in the beginning.

Now assign the background and move the player so they're in the top portion of the background **(Figure 5.1)**. With that all in place, we can run our game and move Pinky to the left, give it a try! You'll notice Pinky only moves when we hold down the left key, even though we have code in our step event that tells it to move.

Constant

A constant is data that cannot be changed once a game is running. It will always return the same when accessed and is useful for many things such as setting the fixed size of an inventory, or possible options in the menu.

Error Help

- If pinky begins moving left without your input, check where your parenthesis's are located. It's possible to not close the function keyboard_check immediately after vk_left like you should, and instead add the == true inside of it. If you did this, then Pinky will move forever left and you cannot stop it. Check **figure 5.0** again, and double check your brackets line up perfectly.

The conditional statement is checking to see if we're pressing the key, and only when that is true, does the code in the curly brackets run. The function keyboard_check accepts one argument, which is the key to check for, and if that key is being held down, it returns true otherwise it returns false.

Moving More and More

Let's explore the vk_left and keyboard input a little more before adding more code. Middle click on vk_left or left click on it and press F1 to open the manual. It opens the section on Keyboard Input and has a long list of every key you can check for. The special keys, like every non-letter, non-number keys have a special Constant associated with them that begin with vk, which stands for virtual key. To access the letters and numbers you use a special function called ord and pass in the letter you want in quotes **(Figure 5.2)**. There's no need to memorize all the constants, but rather memorize that the list is here in the manual and how to get to it quickly for future reference. Being a programmer isn't about memorizing everything a language can do, or all the functions you can use in your game engine; it's about knowing where to find the knowledge you'll need in the future.

```
1   /// @description Player Logic
2   if (keyboard_check(ord("A")) == true) {
3       x -= 2;
4   }
```

Figure 5.2 Ord

So, we can move left, which is a great start, but now we need to move right. We can accomplish this in two ways, which may look similar, but have significant differences. The first, and most obvious way, is to add another conditional statement (if statement) to check for the right arrow. This will work but does lead to a small problem, but I believe that experimentation is the best form of learning, so let's go ahead and do it and discover the problem naturally.

Add another if check for the right key, this time increasing x by 2 instead of subtracting **(Figure 5.3)**. Run the game and you'll see it works great! But now try pressing both keys at once and you'll notice you don't move at all. Our if statements are cancelling each other out. This is an opportunity for you to begin stretching your game design legs. Nothing says this method is wrong, and it's up to you to decide if it's best for the game you're making. Does it feel right? When it's play tested do people get confused by it? Those are all things you'll discover as you build games, and nobody can just give you the right answer.

```
5   if (keyboard_check(vk_right) == true) {
6       x += 2;
7   }
```

Figure 5.3 Right Movement

But let's move on to the second way of handling moving right, which is to add an else on line 5, before the word if. Be sure there's a space between the two words, it should read: else if (....) **(Figure 5.4)**. The else if statement works like a line, where if the first statement returns false, then it will go onto the next one and check there. If it's true, then it stops, otherwise it continues down the line until it either finds a statement that is true, just an else state-

```
objPlayer: Step
Step
1   /// @description Player Logic
2   if (keyboard_check(vk_left) == true) {
3       x -= 2;
4   }
5   else if (keyboard_check(vk_right) == true) {
6       x += 2;
7   }
```

Figure 5.4 If Else If

ment (which we'll get to soon), or the end of the conditional checks. With this one tiny change, run your game again and check it out.

Pinky will now always move to the left when both keys are held down. The order of our if checks is vital here, as the first one to return true has its code run, and the others get ignored. Again, you need to ask yourself if this feels right or wrong. How do you want it to play out? How will you handle this if it's on a console? A controller doesn't have the ability to move the stick both left and right simultaneously, so you may not have this specific issue at all if that's where your game ends up. These are all things you'll discover on your journey of game dev, but just remember that in the end, it's up to you!

And now it's time to mention the third way of moving right, the secret way that you probably don't want unless your game is a sidescroller where the play can't stop moving. This time let's remove everything on line 5 except the word else and the curly bracket **(Figure 5.5)**. Run the game. You'll notice, aside from the background getting all screwy, Pinky moves right unless we're holding down the left key. That's the power of else, it gets triggered in the line of conditional statements if everything else is false. The else statement is extremely useful, just not so much in this situation.

Personally, I prefer having Pinky stop moving when both keys are held, so that's what I'm going to revert my code back to with Ctrl+Z. You're free to use whichever method

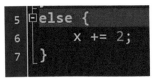

```
5  else {
6        x += 2;
7    }
```

Figure 5.5 Else Statement

Image Speed

Image speed is a built-in property of objects that references the sprites FPS that was set in the Sprite Editor. A speed of 1 will play the sprite at the speed set in the Sprite editor. A setting of 2 will double the playback speed, and 0.5 will half it. It's easiest to get an animation looking good in the Sprite Editor, than to change the image speed of the object, as that will effect every other animation that object might play.

you like. But with that settled, it's time to get Pinky to start animating properly, because it looks a little silly right now.

Controlling Sprite Animation

Recall back to Pinky's sprite, and how we set it to run at 10 FPS (frames per second), which is what it's doing right now. That looks good when Pinky's moving, but not standing still. What we want is Pinky to animate only when we're holding a key down, which is something we already have set up! So, inside our first if statement, above where we subtract 2 from x, add another line. Then type this:

```
image_speed = 1;
```

Image Speed controls the speed of Pinky's animation. 1 means it will play at the speed we set, which is perfect. Add this line to the right movement check as well. Now when we go left or right, we'll animate at the correct speed. But now we need a way to not animate when we're standing still. Fortunately, there's a special check for when no key is being pressed called vk_nokey. Let's add another if check with this special virtual key, and when it's true, set the image speed to 0 **(Figure 5.6)**.

```
objPlayer: Step

*Step                          ×
 1  /// @description Player Logic
 2  if (keyboard_check(vk_left) == true) {
 3      image_speed = 1;
 4      x -= 2;
 5  }
 6  if (keyboard_check(vk_right) == true) {
 7      image_speed = 1;
 8      x += 2;
 9  }
10  if (keyboard_check(vk_nokey) == true) {
11      image_speed = 0;
12  }
```

Figure 5.6 Animation

Give your game a go and see how it looks. You'll notice right away that it looks a little funky unless Pinky is moving to the right. We're animating correctly, but not looking the right direction. To change that, we're going to change the built-in property of image_xscale. Image Xscale controls scaling. Any value other than 1 or -1 will result in the sprite looking misshapen, but when used at these specific values, it allows for left and right movement with only one sprite.

Beneath where we're setting image_speed in our if checks, let's set image_xscale. For moving left, set it to -1, and for moving right, set it to 1 **(Figure 5.7)**. Run the game and see how it looks. Pinky should now turn left and right accordingly! It's starting to look a lot better, yeah?

Figure 5.7 Image Xscale

Image Xscale

Another built-in property, Image Xscale controls the horizontal scaling of the sprite. A cool trick when animating 2D sprites is to reverse the xscale when moving right or left, so only one sprite is needed for animating in 2 directions.

This system we have in place is simple but can be used to great effect in some games. We've built it up to show off several built-in properties that GameMaker has, but for our final movement system it's going to be quite a bit different. And that's how much of game development, and programming in general, goes. It's referred to as Agile Development, a form of software creation that can accept changes quickly and not get bogged down in plans that may no longer be the best. My goal isn't to teach agile development in its entirety, but I mention because that's how we'll be developing Fluffy Heroes; piece by piece, changing older systems as we add newer ones. Don't let this annoy you, build on it, and see that it allows for fast prototyping, and easy changes to your game.

Being Idle

Pinky, and our other heroes, have more sprites that we're going to use. One of those sprites is an idle sprite, for when we're not moving. Pinky will look much better once we bring that in and set it when we're not moving, so let's do that now. Open the assets, go to Sprites, Pinky, and find Pink_monster_Idle_4. Import that into Pinky's folder and rename it to sprPinkyIdle. Then open the sprite and convert it to frames, like we did for the walk sprite. Click on Image, Convert To Frames, and set the first two boxes to 4. Click Convert, and we now have an idle animation.

Close the Image Editor window and set this animation to 9 FPS. Make sure the origin is middle centre, and we should be all set. Now back in our object, we're going to delete all the changes to image_speed, as I find it best to get the animation looking great in preview, and just leave image_speed always set to 1. So, for the first two if checks, replace the changes of image_speed to this:

```
sprite_index = sprPinkyWalk;
```

And the last image_speed change to:

```
sprite_index = sprPinkyIdle;
```

Sprite index controls which sprite is currently associated with that object, and it can be changed anytime. While we're walking, we want the walk sprite, and when we're not, we want the idle sprite **(Figure 5.8)**. Run the game and see the results. It's starting to look much better. The animation is smooth, Pinky's looking the right way, and we have an idle animation when we're not moving. A great days work!

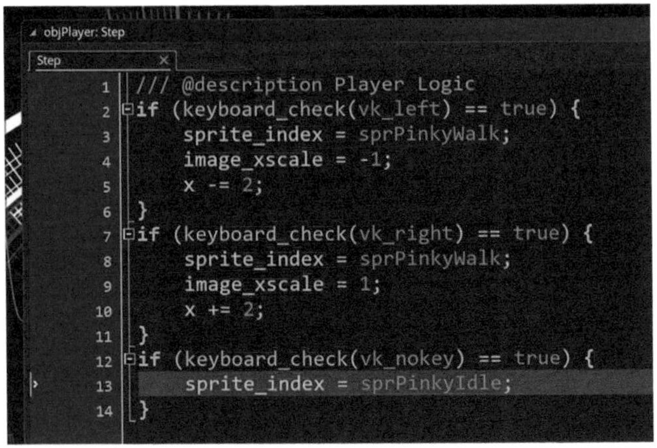

```
/// @description Player Logic
if (keyboard_check(vk_left) == true) {
    sprite_index = sprPinkyWalk;
    image_xscale = -1;
    x -= 2;
}
if (keyboard_check(vk_right) == true) {
    sprite_index = sprPinkyWalk;
    image_xscale = 1;
    x += 2;
}
if (keyboard_check(vk_nokey) == true) {
    sprite_index = sprPinkyIdle;
}
```

Figure 5.8 Idle Sprite

Conclusion + Challenge

Tomorrow we're going to tackle collisions, so that we can eventually add in our own gravity to the game. It's all connected, but I'm going to do my best to build it up one piece at a time.

Today's challenge is to get Pinky running. There isn't a separate sprite, instead change the image_speed and how fast Pinky's moving across the screen while holding down the left shift key. Good luck!

Day 6

Homework Review

How did the challenge to get Pinky running go for you? I hope you're trying these challenges, because the best way to solidify what you're learning is put it into practice on your own.

My solution is **figure 6.0**. The only new thing I used was another keyboard function to check when the shift key was released to set the image speed back to 1. There are keyboard functions for single presses, held down, and released. Each one is useful in different areas, and you can combine them like this to great effect.

Now let's jump into today's exercise where we'll tackle Booleans, collision masks, and more!

Boolean

A data type indicating a value is true or false. In most programming languages they are represented with the constants true and false, equaling 0 and 1, respectively. GameMaker also honors these values, but they go one step further and allow anything 0 and below to be false, and anything 1 and greater to be true.

```
12    //Sprinting
13    if (keyboard_check(vk_shift)) {
14        image_speed = 1.5;
15        if (keyboard_check(vk_left)) {
16            x -= 2;
17        }
18        if (keyboard_check(vk_right)) {
19            x += 2;
20        }
21    }
```
Figure 6.0 Sprinting

Booleans

I've mentioned data types before, and now it's time to learn another important one: the Boolean. A Boolean is either true or false, and get used in conditional statements like we've been using for the movement code. The double equals true in the if statement

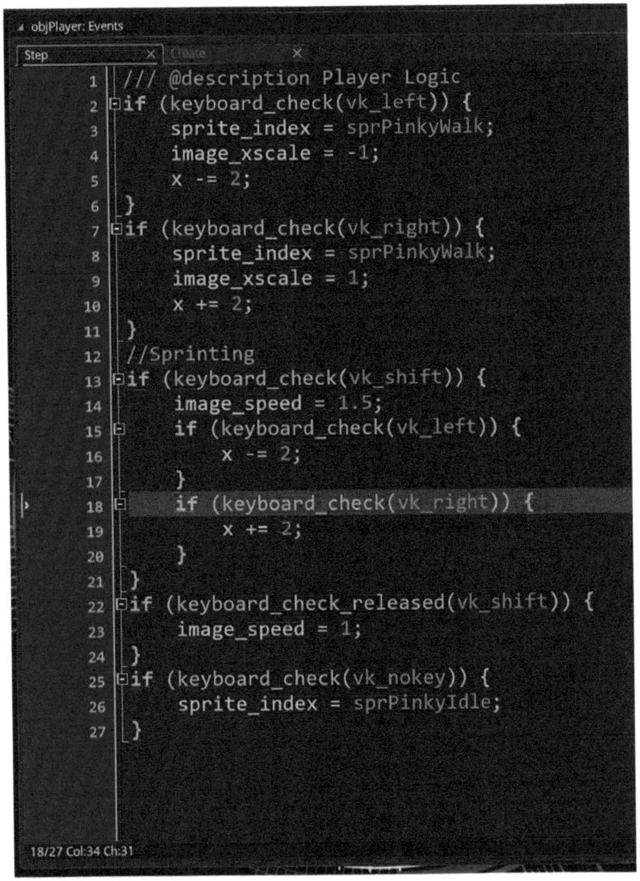

```
▲ objPlayer: Events
  Step                    ✕  Create              ✕
  1  /// @description Player Logic
  2  if (keyboard_check(vk_left)) {
  3      sprite_index = sprPinkyWalk;
  4      image_xscale = -1;
  5      x -= 2;
  6  }
  7  if (keyboard_check(vk_right)) {
  8      sprite_index = sprPinkyWalk;
  9      image_xscale = 1;
 10      x += 2;
 11  }
 12  //Sprinting
 13  if (keyboard_check(vk_shift)) {
 14      image_speed = 1.5;
 15      if (keyboard_check(vk_left)) {
 16          x -= 2;
 17      }
 18      if (keyboard_check(vk_right)) {
 19          x += 2;
 20      }
 21  }
 22  if (keyboard_check_released(vk_shift)) {
 23      image_speed = 1;
 24  }
 25  if (keyboard_check(vk_nokey)) {
 26      sprite_index = sprPinkyIdle;
 27  }
```
18/27 Col:34 Ch:31

Figure 6.1 Simpler Checks

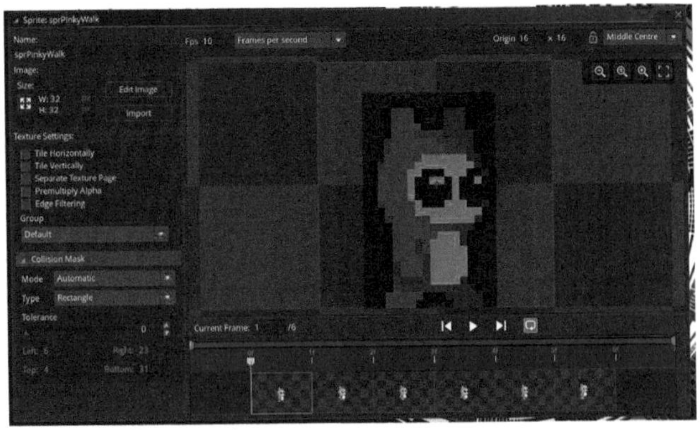

Figure 6.2 Collision Mask

is an equality check, looking to see if what the function keyboard_check returns is the same as true.

Let's take a look and see why this code even works. Add a Create event to Pinky and use the function show_message to display the value of keyboard_check and true with this code:

```
show_message(false);
```

Run the game and see how it prints a 0. Now replace the constant false with true and run the game again. This time it's a 1. So far, so good. True and false are constants with an integer of 1 and 0, but what about our function? We can use show message to display what we get back from a function, too. Try this:

```
show_message(keyboard_check(vk_
nokey));
```

Run the game and you'll get a 1 because you're not holding down a game when this function is being checked (don't try to hold a key down either, you'll just end up typing it instead of your game registering it). So, our keyboard functions just return a 0 or 1 depending on what it's checking. Then when we use the double equals, that's comparing the values to see if they are the same. If they are, then our conditional code executes, and if not, it won't.

What this means is we can shorten our conditional statements considerably by removing the == true at the end **(Figure 6.1)**. In this case it's still easy enough to read when we take that out. There will be times it's a little more confusing, and then I suggest you keep the == true or false so you can understand what the code is really checking when you look at it a week later. Clarity is always better than brevity (shortness), but sometimes the two can be the same.

In the end though, the choice is yours and your code will run the same as mine, so feel free to leave in the double equals if it helps you understand what's going on. We'll continue to use Booleans throughout this project and see even more ways of comparing data types, such as less than or greater than.

Collision Masks

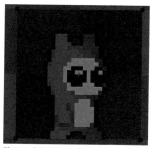

Figure 6.3 Manual Mask

GameMaker has events specific for Collisions with other objects, and these events can be useful in the right circumstances. But the downside of these events are they'll only trigger after a collision has been detected, and there's no way to see if something is going to collide. The ability to see if a collision will occur is powerful and something we need in this game. It could be used to display if a projectile would hit an enemy, changing colors of the cursor if a spot is open and free to be built upon, and so forth.

Before we get into checking for collisions, we need to understand how GameMaker handles collisions and what it sees as a collision. Open Pinky's walking sprite. On the left is a drop down labelled 'Collision Mask', expand that. You should now see a dark silhouette around Pinky **(Figure 6.2),** this is her Collision Mask. This is what GameMaker checks against to see if there is a collision. Notice that the silhouette is slightly larger than Pinky on any given frame. The reason for this is the collision mode is set to automatic, so GameMaker gets the maximum height and width of all the frames and set the mask to those values. This is extremely important to remember on larger sprites, like explosions, where there might be small 1- or 2-pixel strokes on the edge of the sprite, causing the collision mask to be a lot larger than we would want.

Fortunately, we can take over control of the collision mask for our sprites, which we often want to do. This collision mask is really well done, and we won't need to change anything, but it would be good for you to see all the different options now, so we can easily change them later on. The Mode types are Automatic, Full Image, and Manual. We've seen automatic already, so change it to Full Image. Now the collision mask expands to cover all of Pinky, even the transparent portions, definitely not what we're looking for.

How about Manual? Now there are four dots in the corner **(Figure 6.3)**. We can grab these handles and move them around ourselves. Manual mode is great for setting the mask just the way we want it to be. However, you'll notice it's still always as a rectangle, what if we had a circle or some other shape? Click on Type to view all the options and select Ellipse. Each type provides a different type of collision mask, and can be combined with each of the Modes. The last thing to play with is the Tolerance, which can only be set when the Mode is on automatic. It determines if partially transparent pixels are accounted for in the mask, with a higher tolerance removing them, and a lower tolerance including them. Beneath tolerance are the manual numbers for the collision mask, but I've never used those, instead preferring to use the handles on the sprite to move the

Collision Mask

Every sprite has a collision mask, the thing that GameMaker uses to determine if it's colliding with another sprite. The mask can be automatically set by GameMaker, or manually adjusted to fit your sprite exactly. The more precise the collision mode, the more power it takes to compute it. On any modern computer, a few precise collision checks won't be noticed, but be careful if you use it on many objects at once, as it could impact performance and slow down your game.

Collisions

Collisions occur in GameMaker when two objects overlap the same space. There are many kinds of collisions, such as precise and solid. The collision mask is what's checked on the objects, and that can be controlled manually or automatically.

Figure 6.4 Solid

Figure 6.6 Tool Box

mask around.

Go ahead and reset Pinky to Automatic Rectangle, with a tolerance of 0. This is the mask we'll be using in the game to check against other objects and see if we are, or would, collide with them based on our movement. The collision mask your object has assigned to it is directly connected to the sprite it's displaying. This means if we had a drastically different mask for idle compared to walking, then switching to idle would change the mask and possibly cause issues. The workaround for this is to manually set the collision mask on our object, which works great when the sprites are close to the same size, such as for our characters.

Sprite Sizes and Alpha

Now onto running into things! But before we can run into something, we need another object to collide with, as we currently only have Pinky. Rename the Paths folder to System by right clicking or selecting it and pressing F2. This folder will contain sprites and objects that are invisible to the player but help our game run smoothly. Add two folders in System, one called Sprites, and the other called Objects. Being organized helps immensely as projects grow, and it's never too early to start!

In the Sprites folder in System, create a new sprite and name it sprSolid **(Figure 6.4)**. We are going to be using 32x32 sprites for this entire project but notice that our new sprite comes in at a size of 64x64. This is GameMaker's default and can be changed in the preferences. However, we won't be creating too many sprites ourselves, so I don't find it necessary to change that setting. We do need to change the size of this sprite though, otherwise when we use it in the game it won't fit correctly. Click on the arrow button to the left of the size.

A Resize Properties window appears which allows us to scale the image or resize the canvas **(Figure 6.5)**. Scaling an image will change what's inside and skew it to the new dimensions, sometimes altering it beyond recognition. Moving from smaller to larger, GameMaker does an impressive job at keeping it looking good, but shrinking an image is another story entirely. Resizing the canvas will cut out parts of the sprite and leave everything else looking the same. Since our sprite is empty, we can choose either one, they'll both do the job. On the scale image size, change the width from 64 to 32 and the height will also change, because the Maintain Aspect Ratio box is ticked. Click Apply.

Nothing much changed, except the small gray outline in the Sprite Editor shrunk. Now let's fill up the sprite. Click on Edit Image and this time we'll use the fill tool from the

Toolbox. Choose one of the red colors (or any color really, I prefer red for my solids as it indicates the player cannot go there), and double click on it. That brings up the Colour selection window **(Figure 6.6)** which allows you to select from thousands of colors. What we want to do is change the Alpha from 255 to 100. Now click OK and click anywhere in the sprite with the fill tool to fill up the sprite with our color **(Figure 6.7)**.

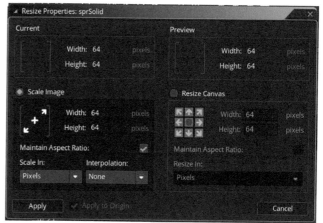

Figure 6.5 Resize Image

Collisions

Now let's close this window and create a new object in the Objects folder of System and call it objSolid. Assign our sprite to our new object. The goal with this object is to place it anywhere we want our player to collide with the environment. We'll be using tile sets to design the level, and this object to simulate walls and ground. There is a more advanced technique of using the tilesets themselves as collisions, which you can find on my YouTube channel LetsLearnThisTogether, but for starting out, we'll use a simpler system. But don't think that this one is only the one to start with, you can make entire games with this system, there's nothing wrong with it.

Later on we'll make this object invisible in the game, but for now let's use it to get our collision system up and running. Open Room1 and select the instances layer. Drag our objSolid to form a half rectangle **(Figure 6.8)**. Then go into objPlayer's create event and remove the show_message function. Leave the event, we'll use it momentarily. Now run the game and try to move into the solid.

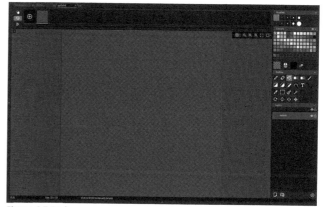

Figure 6.7 Red

You should notice two things. Firstly you can move right into it, there's nothing stopping Pinky. Just because we've named it a solid, doesn't mean it knows to act like one. Secondly, Pinky is behind the object, altering the color of our player. Once we get the collision system in place we won't be able to go behind the object, so we don't need to worry about this color alteration. Close the game.

Figure 6.8 Collision Shape

Figure 6.9 Solid

Figure 6.10 Far From the Wall

Alpha

Alpha controls the transparency of a color. 255 is full visible, and 0 is invisible.

Before we implement the final collision system, I want to show you why we're doing it. Let's try using GameMaker's built in collision functions and see what limitations they have. Return to objPinky and add a Collision event with our objSolid. We don't need to add any code in here, just having the event is enough. The only other thing we need to do is check the Solid box on the object properties **(Figure 6.9)**. Now run the game and try to move into the solid and you'll see that you can't. It works for going both directions and seems to work perfectly fine.

And sure, it works great when the movement speed is low. But what would happen if we were flying fast, or falling from the sky and we wanted to collide with this solid? Change the speed of the player when moving left from 2 to 20. Now run the game and move left. Pinky zooms across the screen and is several pixels away from the wall **(Figure 6.10)**. Move to the right a smidge and then move left again. You'll notice, depending on how many times you do it, that Pinky won't move close to the wall if she's closer than 20 pixels. GameMaker moves Pinky, sees there's a collision, and then puts her back where she started. This isn't ideal at all! We need a system that can move us close to the wall, stop us right next to it, and then set our speed to zero.

A Better Movement System

Close the game and delete the Collision event from Pinky. Uncheck solid. Revert the speed back to 2. To use this more advanced collision system, we need to check how fast we're moving right before we might collide with a solid. Currently we've got a value of

Figure 6.11 Pinky Data

2 in for our movement speed, except when we're sprinting. This hard-coded value isn't great, and we should replace it with a variable that holds our current speed.

Open the create event and create a variable called xSpeed and set it to zero. This variable will always hold our current speed along the x axis. Beneath it create another variable called walkSpeed and set it to 2 **(Figure 6.11)**. This variable will control how fast we walk when we press an arrow key. Ignore the yellow warnings for now, in the create event those warnings don't mean very much since we haven't used them anywhere else yet. I'm also going to add the description of Pinky's Data at the top.

Now let's use those variables we created in our step event. Replace every 2 with the walkSpeed variable. A quick way of doing this is using the Ctrl+F feature of search and replace. You put in what you're looking for, which is 2. Then click the little icon to the left of where you just typed to bring up the replace portion. There,

Figure 6.12 Find And Replace

type walkSpeed. You can replace 1 at a time with the single checkmark, or all at once with the multi check box **(Figure 6.12)**. This Find and Replace is only for Pinky's Step event, if you press Ctrl+Shift+F it will bring it up project wide. Doing a replace in project wide will trigger a warning that it can't be undone, so use that with caution.

After we've replaced the 2's, we need to change the code from moving the player immediately while we're holding down a code, to assigning our walkSpeed to xSpeed. So what we want is this:

```
xSpeed = walkSpeed;
```

Instead of:

```
x -= walkSpeed;
```

On the left key, for both walking and sprinting, put a negative sign (-) in front of walkSpeed **(Figure 6.13)**. This will make the value negative, which allows us to move left. Without it, xSpeed will always be positive and you'll move right even when holding the left key. And on the sprinting,

```
objPlayer: Events
*Step          Create
 1   /// @description Player Logic
 2   if (keyboard_check(vk_left)) {
 3       sprite_index = sprPinkyWalk;
 4       image_xscale = -1;
 5       xSpeed = -walkSpeed;
 6   }
 7   if (keyboard_check(vk_right)) {
 8       sprite_index = sprPinkyWalk;
 9       image_xscale = 1;
10       xSpeed = walkSpeed;
11   }
12   //Sprinting
13   if (keyboard_check(vk_shift)) {
14       image_speed = 1.5;
15       if (keyboard_check(vk_left)) {
16           xSpeed = -walkSpeed;
17       }
18       if (keyboard_check(vk_right)) {
19           xSpeed = walkSpeed;
20       }
21   }
22   if (keyboard_check_released(vk_shift)) {
23       image_speed = 1;
24   }
25   if (keyboard_check(vk_nokey)) {
26       sprite_index = sprPinkyIdle;
27   }
```

Figure 6.13 Movement Speed with Variables

```
12   //Sprinting
13   if (keyboard_check(vk_shift)) {
14       image_speed = 1.5;
15       if (keyboard_check(vk_left)) {
16           xSpeed = -walkSpeed * 2;
17       }
18       if (keyboard_check(vk_right)) {
19           xSpeed = walkSpeed * 2;
20       }
21   }
```

Figure 6.14 Sprinting with Variables

```
25  if (keyboard_check(vk_nokey)) {
26      sprite_index = sprPinkyIdle;
27      xSpeed = 0;
28  }
```

Figure 6.15 xSpeed to 0

multiply the walkSpeed variable by 2 so Pinky will actually run **(Figure 6.14)**.

The reason we're doing this is we need to check for a collision before we try to move Pinky, and if we immediately move when pressing a key that check will need to be repeated everywhere we press a key, which is awful. Whenever possible, we don't want to repeat code. So, instead we're going to assign where we want to walk and then check if that area is clear to move.

At the very bottom of our Step event, add this code:

```
x+= xSpeed;
```

Now we've isolated our movement to the end of the code in just one spot. So, we can check for collisions on where we might move and stop us from colliding somewhere, we shouldn't. But if you test your game now, you'll notice that Pinky continues moving when we release left or right, and that's because her xSpeed variable never gets set back to 0. So, on the if check where we're setting Pinky to idle, also set xSpeed to 0.

Conclusion + Challenge

But that's going to be tomorrow's work! There will be a lot that goes into manual collision checking, including introducing loops. They're exciting but can also lead to big problems when used incorrectly!

Today's challenge comes in two parts. The first is a little bit of reading. Open GameMaker's manual and look up loops. Getting a primer on them before we tackle them will help you understand how they work. They're a little difficult, but a versatile and powerful tool we'll utilize in Fluffy Heroes!

And the second is to find the bug we've introduced in Fluffy Heroes today and try to fix it. I'll give you a hint: it has to do with the keys and what we're checking specifically. Good luck!

PRO TIP

Following the fun!

David Wehle
Game Dev Unlocked

GameDevUnlocked.com

I was testing the first level of my fox adventure game The First Tree when my wife looked over my shoulder and said "it feels kinda lifeless and empty... you should add some other animals running around." So that led me to HerdSim, a Unity asset that would spawn NPC animals around the environment, like bunnies. I decided to test it out, so I bought it, added the bunny template, put in the variables, and hit play—then immediately noticed a bunny the size of a house towering over my scared little fox. I had forgotten a decimal point for the "max size" variable, so inevitably some of the bunnies got really, really big.

I thought it was funny enough to share on Twitter, so I made a quick GIF and posted it without thinking much of it. It quickly became the most viral post I ever made, being retweeted by prominent game developers and celebrities alike. Even David Bowie's son found it amusing. I posted it later on Reddit and Tumblr where it gathered even more views and comments. The #1 comment I kept seeing: YOU NEED TO ADD THIS TO THE GAME! So sure enough, I added a giant, hidden Easter Bunny (like an easter egg... get it?) in the first level to honor the thousands of big bunny lovers out there.

When people find the giant bunny, they also unlock the test level where I initially tested out the HerdSim asset. It's now an achievement I added for all platforms including Xbox and PS4, and it always make me smile seeing the achievement completion rate go up, knowing thousands of players are being surprised by the giant bunny like I was.

Day 7

Upgrading our Collision System

Day 6 Challenge Solution

So, were you able to discover the bug? If not, don't worry, we're going to cover it now. To see it in action, run your game and begin moving. Hold down another key, besides left or right arrow, and release the arrow key you were holding. Pinky still moves! Until we're not pressing down any keys, Pinky continues to move in the last direction she was moving. The reason for that is our if check is looking for the constant vk_nokey, which will only return true when no key on the keyboard is pressed down.

Instead of looking for no key being held down, let's change it to when the left or right key is released! That will fix the problem. Let's copy the if check and paste a duplicate beneath it. Then change the first if check to look for keyboard_check_released on vk_left, leaving the code inside unchanged. Then do the same on the duplicated if check, except look for vk_right (**Figure 7.0**). Now Pinky's moving when she should.

There is one strange thing now though, and that's Pinky is playing her walking animation while standing still. Before we changed to idle when no key was being held down, but now we only do so when we release the left or right key. An easy fix for this is to change which sprite Pinky starts on to idle, instead of walk. Let's do that now and it will look much better!

```
25 if (keyboard_check_released(vk_left)) {
26     sprite_index = sprPinkyIdle;
27     xSpeed = 0;
28 }
29
30 if (keyboard_check_released(vk_right)) {
31     sprite_index = sprPinkyIdle;
32     xSpeed = 0;
33 }
```

Figure 7.0 Day 6 Challenge

You might be wondering if there's a better way to do that then copying our code and having essentially two chunks of code doing the same thing, only slightly different. And the answer is a definite yes there is! The answer is conditional operators.

Conditional Operators

Conditional Operators

There are many conditional operators, and they expand the power of expressions, like if checks and loops. There are many different kinds, and it's worth reading up on them in the GMS manual, but the primary ones you'll use almost daily are the assigning (=), combining (&&, ||), and comparing (<=, ==, !=) operators.

Conditional Operators are used all the time, and we've already used several in our game. When we create a variable, we use the assigning operator to set that variable's value. In our if checks, when we use the double equals, that's a comparing operator. But the one we're interested in right now is the combining operator. It allows us to check more than one statement in an if check, saving us code and time.

There are three Combining Operators, the and operator (&&), the or operator (||), and the xor operator (^^). Of the three, xor is the black sheep and is rarely used, so I won't cover it here. But the other two are staples, and you need to remember them, as you'll probably use them every time you work on a game.

The first combining operator is and, which checks to see if both expressions evaluate to true. In GML you can type the word and or use two ampersands, &&, and it will work the same way. I encourage you to use the && over the keyword and, as nearly every language follows the same syntax for combining operators. GMS allows you to use the word and, but very few other languages will.

Let's open objPlayer and go into the Create event. Add a few lines at the bottom, and let's play around with the and operator. Type this code in:

```
if (xSpeed == 0 && walkSpeed == 2) {

    show_message("It's true.");

}
```

Run the game and see if the message appears.

Combining Operators

Combining operators are a specific kind of operator that allows you to check for more than one condition in an expression, like an if check or loop.

> **Error Help**
>
> - If you typed it in correctly, it does. If it doesn't appear, you may have assigned a different value to walkSpeed, so just update your if check to the same number you used before.

The two ampersands, &&, allow the if check to only run if both Expressions are true. Try changing one of the numbers so one of the expressions evaluates to false and run the game. No message this time. Both sides of the and operator must be true, or it won't work.

Now change the && to two pipes, ||, which are found above the enter key. Hold shift to get the straight lines, instead of the slash. Don't change any of the code, leave one expression true and one false, and run the game again. The message appears! The or operator just needs one of the two to be true, and it doesn't care which side is true.

The operators can also be combined to form long checks, and you can use both in one if check or loop. There are a few things to note, however. The first is there's no shortcut when it comes to using these operators, even though it would be so much more convenient! By shortcut, I mean you can't have this code:

```
if (xSpeed == 1 || 0)
```

Even though I want it check if xSpeed is equal to 1 or 0, the computer can't read my mind. It will read the code exactly as I've written it, and not as I want it. When using combining operators, you must write out each expression fully.

Second, you can have as many combining operators as you want, but when you have more than two, it's a good idea to add parenthesis to understand the order you want them resolved in. In **Figure 7.1** notice the parenthesis after the && symbols. Read this expression as xSpeed must be 0 and walkSpeed can be either 2 or 4. This can get as complex as you want, but a good rule of thumb is if it exceeds 2 combining operators, it's probably too complex and should be simplified with a variable. We'll get at how to do that later.

```
5  if (xSpeed == 0 && (walkSpeed == 2 || walkSpeed == 4)) {
6      show_message("It's true.");
7  }
```

Figure 7.1 Combining Operators

With all this knowledge, let's go and fix our duplicated if check in the step event. Be sure and delete all the code in the create event we just added, first. In the step event, let's add an or check for the other key being released **(Figure 7.2)**. The length of the line increased quite a bit, but we did save 4 lines of code, and this is easier to read all at once, since we now have just one place we're setting Pinky to idle instead of 2.

```
25  if (keyboard_check_released(vk_left) || keyboard_check_released(vk_right)) {
26      sprite_index = sprPinkyIdle;
27      xSpeed = 0;
28  }
```

Figure 7.2 Solution with Operators

Combining operators are an essential programming skill to have, as you'll end up using them everywhere. The cool thing is these are the same across nearly all languages, so if you most onto C# or Swift, you'll already know how to use them!

Expressions

An expression is a mathematical phrase that can include numbers and operators and evaluates to true or false. If checks take an expression, as do loops. While that expression evaluates to true, the code will run inside.

For Loop

For loops will iterate (execute) a block of code a certain number of times, decided by you. The syntax for it is confusing at first, but this loop is probably the most powerful and useful loop of them all. For loops can be used to display many items on the screen at once, checking an area of the game for a condition, or anything else you need.

While Loop

While loops take just one expression and while that expression is true, the code inside of it will continue to run forever. It's amazingly easy to create an infinite loop using while loops, and when that happens the game must be force closed. But even though they can cause issues, while loops provide immense power to check over great deals of data and have many uses in game development.

The last thing I'll add is an explanation to the xor operator (pronounced x-or, not zor). It is when neither expression evaluates to true. So, if you wanted to check if two things were false, you could use xor. I've personally never used this operator in GMS, as it's just as easy to use an or operator to check if two things are false, but there may be times you want this operator, so keep it in the back of your mind.

Loops

If you took up yesterdays' challenge to read about loops, the rest of today should go well, if not, then just have a little more patience than usual. Loops are powerful, and with great power comes great frustration and the ability to crash your game in 0 seconds flat.

Open up objPlayer and scroll down to the bottom of the Step event and find the line where we're moving our object. Our goal for today is to add in horizontal collisions here and understand the different kind of loops available in GML. There are several kinds of loops all together, but two of them are used more often than the others: the for loop and the while loop.

The For Loop has the most confusing syntax of them all, and yet is the one that's used the most. Nearly all programming languages have some form of a for loop, so understanding how to use it will be essential, and we'll spend a good deal of time on it later in this game. The While loop is simpler use but will be the cause of many of your game crashing bugs. Think of a while loop like an if statement, the way we'll write it is similar, but the code inside of the loop pauses your game while it runs. When the loop works correctly, the pause is so brief that the player will never notice it. But when the loop doesn't stop correctly, it will pause the game forever, causing it to eventually crash or force the user to manually shut it down.

There are a few other kinds of loops in GML, such as repeat and do until, but they're rarely used and once you know how to use the while and for loops, you'll be able to understand how the others work and use them if necessary. The loop we're working with today is the while loop, as it's the one to use when we don't know exactly how many times we want to iterate over a block of code. Iterate means to perform an action, and is a common programming term you should memorize, as you'll hear it all over in tutorials and lectures.

So, let's get down to the code now! On the line before we change our objects x position, press enter a few times to add some space. Now let's add in a simple while loop to familiarize ourselves with the syntax (syntax means how it's written).

```
while (1 == 1) {
```

```
show_debug_message("hi");

}
```

We use the Statement while, add parenthesis like an if check, and put in an expression. Then we use the curly brackets and put some code inside of them. And that's all there is to it. This while loops will run forever because the expression, we used will always be true. Before you run this code, though, you should know it may freeze your computer. There is a stop button in GMS, to the right of the player button near the top **(Figure 7.3)**. Try running your game and see what happens for a second, then press stop (if you can't stop it, you'll need to force close it). Nothing showed up, right?

Statement

A typical line of code is a statement and ends with the semicolon. GameMaker interprets the statements and then runs them. But there are also special statements like the while loop and break keyword, which don't require a semicolon after use and have a bolder font than other code.

Figure 7.3 Stop Botton

The game window never appears, because the while loop is still running, keeping all other code in the game from running. But the function we called in the while loop is executing, and it's showing the message hi in our output window **(Figure 7.4)**. The debug message function writes it there, whereas the show message function creates a pop up, both can be useful in the own way for debugging.

Figure 7.4 While Loop

There are two ways to exit a while loop. The first, and the one you should use most of the time, is to get the expression to become false. This is done by calling a function in the while loop, or checking if a variable is a certain value, while also changing that variable in the loop itself, so it eventually does become that specific value. A great example of that is stretching a sprite to a certain factor, like resizing a dialogue box to fit on the screen, even after the player changes the size of the screen in the settings.

The second method is using the statement Break. This causes the while loop to exit or be broken. I don't suggest relying on break, however, as it's usually better for a loop to complete itself naturally. To use break, place it anywhere in a loop, and then when it

Break

The break keyword ends a loop or with call immediately, moving on to the next section of code after the loop. Break is also used in switch statements. It should be used cautiously in loops, as the preferred method for exiting a loop is for it to complete its job, not be broken by using this keyword.

runs the loop will be broken, and code will continue to run. Try using it in our while loop **(Figure 7.5)**. Now run your game and you'll notice that the message still appears, but the game works normally. That's how break works.

```
29  while (1 == 1) {
30      show_debug_message("hi");
31      break;
32  }
```

Figure 7.5 Break

Horizontal Collisions

Alright, let's get down to colliding with our solid object. Remove the code inside the while loop and the expression in the while loop. Ignore the red warning that appears, we'll add an expression in just a moment. The question is though, how do we check if our player would collide with a solid? Well, there's a function for it, of course!

The function place_meeting accepts three arguments, an x position, y position, and object. It will essentially move our character to those coordinates and if it detects a collision with the object, will return true, otherwise it will be false. We don't just want to check our current x and y position though, as we know we're not currently colliding with a solid (and we know this because we've placed our object free from the solid object). Instead, we want to check our x position plus our xSpeed to see if we will collide with a solid.

Figure 7.6 If and While

The first thing to do though, is wrap our while loop inside an if check. The reason is we need to check if we will collide, and then use the power of while to get right next to the wall. If we just had the while loop checking to see if we'd collide, we will get stuck in an endless loop. And this is also where indentation really becomes important **(Figure 7.6)**, because without it the code becomes much harder to read. Use the built-in indentation that GameMaker does, especially when nesting if checks and while loops, it will save you a lot of time and frustration in the long run.

Now, the if we want to check for is the place_meeting function I just told you about. Add in this code:

```
if (place_meeting(x + xSpeed, y, objSolid) == true)
```

The double equals true isn't necessary but does make it obvious what we're doing. So, if we are going to collide with a solid object on our next move, we want to instead get as close as we can to it and stop. This is how we do pixel perfect collisions, and it can be used in any kind of game you make, not just platformers.

In the while loop, we want to move just one pixel closer to the solid until we are only one pixel away. To do that, we'll use the place_meeting function again, but this time only looking one pixel ahead, instead of our xSpeed:

```
30  if (place_meeting(x + xSpeed, y, objSolid) == true) {
31      while (place_meeting(x + 1, y, objSolid) == false) {
32          x += 1;
33      }
34      xSpeed = 0;
35  }
```

Figure 7.7 Collision

```
while (place_meeting(x + 1, y, objSolid) == false)
```

And then inside of the while loop, move Pinky's x position by 1. The loop will continue to run while we are not going to collide with a solid in 1 pixel. And finally, outside of the while loop, but inside of the if statement, set our xSpeed to 0 **(Figure 7.7)**. Once the while loop completes, Pinky will be just one pixel away from the object, and we don't want to move anymore.

Let's try it out! Run the game and move to the right and collide with the solid. Pinky gets right up to the wall and stops perfectly, awesome! Now move to the left and try it there. Woah! What just happened? Pinky warped from the left side to the right side instantly. That's certainly not what we wanted to have happen. Let's go back to the while loop.

Remember that our xSpeed variable can be negative or positive, so when we check in the if portion of the code, it's working properly. It triggers the while statement whether we're colliding left or right. However, the while loop is specifically checking for a collision on Pinky's right and moving Pinky to the right when we collide. So when we collide with a solid on our left, the if check triggers, then the while loop begins to look for a collision on the right of Pinky, and there's empty space there, so it moves Pinky over until it finally finds a solid, then stops. If we didn't have a solid on the right, we would end up in an infinite loop because it could never find a solid on the right but would keep trying forever.

We can fix this small problem with the sign function. Sign is a function that you pass in an integer, and it will return -1 if that number is a negative, 0 if the number is 0, and 1 if the number is positive. This is exactly what we need, since we don't want to duplicate our code to check if the collision is on the right or left, we want to just have one block of code that can handle both situations. So, replace the + 1 in the while loop with + sign(xSpeed). Replace both instances, in the while loop, and when moving Pinky **(Figure 7.8)**.

Now let's try our game and see if the collisions are correct. Viola! They work going right and left. Now we have horizontal collisions in our game, and I'm going to comment this section of code. If you don't totally understand what we just did, that's ok! I've created several courses and tutorials about this code, and I still struggle with it sometimes. Try to break it down, delete it and try to recreate it from scratch. You'll make mistakes, but each mistake will help you understand what not to do, and how it works overall.

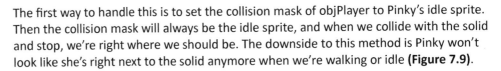

```
30   if (place_meeting(x + xSpeed, y, objSolid) == true) {
31       while (place_meeting(x + sign(xSpeed), y, objSolid) == false) {
32           x += sign(xSpeed);
33       }
34       xSpeed = 0;
35   }
```

Figure 7.8 Fixed Collision

Tomorrow we're going to handle vertical collisions, which uses the same system as this, just going up and down, so you'll get some more experience then.

One thing you may have noticed, is that when we get right next to a solid and stop moving, Pinky's idle sprite goes into the solid just a little bit on a few frames. The reason for that is when we're moving, or collision mask is set to the moving sprite and that's what we're checking against collisions. But when we stop moving, we're not checking against collisions at all, so Pinky's idle sprite can move into the solid.

The first way to handle this is to set the collision mask of objPlayer to Pinky's idle sprite. Then the collision mask will always be the idle sprite, and when we collide with the solid and stop, we're right where we should be. The downside to this method is Pinky won't look like she's right next to the solid anymore when we're walking or idle **(Figure 7.9)**.

The second way to handle it would be to create system that checks for any collision whenever we change sprites. You can use a lot of the same code we used for the horizontal collisions, but it will cause Pinky to be pushed back when becoming idle and look a little strange.

The third option is to have your sprites all be the same size and range for their animations. But that would mean hiring an artist and paying money, which I wouldn't recommend for your first dozen games.

Personally, I don't mind Pinky's idle hand moving on top of the solid, but you can set it however you desire.

Figure 7.9 Idle Collision Mask

Conclusion + Challenge

And that's all for today! There's no coding challenge, instead I want you to find and play a 2D game and think about it from a developers perspective. How did they create certain effects, are their collisions pixel perfect? Once you become a game dev, you'll look at all games in a totally new light. Give it a try.

Day 8

Jumping & Falling with Grace

Were you able to find a game and play it? What did you discover? I'd love to hear your thoughts, and you can reach me on YouTube or Twitter anytime.

Making Our Own Physics

Figure 8.0

Today we're going to tackle creating an artificial physics system in our game and tackle vertical collisions. It's a lot, but it's all stuff we've done before, just slightly different. And you'll find, as you code more and more, that's what most development is. Sure, there can be totally new things and methods from time to time, but usually it's a variant on a skillset you already have, and you just need to look at it a different way.

The first thing to discuss before we code anything is why we're going to create a physics system ourselves when GameMaker already has a physics engine built in. If you open any object and look near the bottom of the first floating window, you'll see a Physics button **(Figure 8.0)**. Click on it and it expands to show all the options for this object in the game world. I'm not going to cover them because we won't be using this option for this game.

The reason we're not using GameMaker's system is it's too much for what we want. If you want to use their system at all, you've got to totally commit to it. Each object needs to be physics based, the world needs to have physics enabled, and you need to use entirely new physics specific functions to move objects around. That's great and all if your game is purely physics based, like Goat Simulator or Angry Birds, but all we want is to be able to jump and fall. There's no need for full world physics, it's overkill, and really does take some time to understand how to use properly. But I thought it worth noting in case you want to make a physics game down the road. Close the physics window.

Open the Create event in objPlayer and let's create a few more variables. To simulate gravity, we'll need a gravity variable; it will control how fast Pinky falls to the ground when she's

Figure 8.1 Jumping Variables

Figure 8.2 Maximize

in the air. All of the numbers we'll be using in this chapter are what I've found looks and feel good for a standard platformer, but I highly encourage you to tweak every number to see exactly how it effects Pinky and game movement. No number I use is the best number by any means, so find what you like best.

We can't use the variable name gravity because it's a built-in property, so let's name it gameGravity instead and set it to 0.25. The 0 isn't necessary, but for the sake of clarity let's leave it in for now. We'll apply our gameGravity in the step event, so it continually pushes down on us, accumulating on itself every frame, which is why we need it to be such a small number.

Next let's add a jumpSpeed variable and give it a value of -4. This will control how high we can jump and will be applied all at once. It must be a negative value, because we want to go up and the y axis begins at 0 at the top of the room. And just like our horizontal movement for xSpeed, we also need a ySpeed to control vertical movement. Create a variable called ySpeed and set it equal to 0. We now have 3 variables ready to be used to create a jumping system **(Figure 8.1)**.

Up until this point we've been coding in the small windows that appear when we click on an event. These are fine when we have just a little bit of code, but when an event grows large it's helpful to have more screen real-estate to use. In the top right corner of the event window is a little maximize button **(Figure 8.2)**. Click on that button to expand your code into its own workspace. Our events now take up the entire screen, the workspace has been

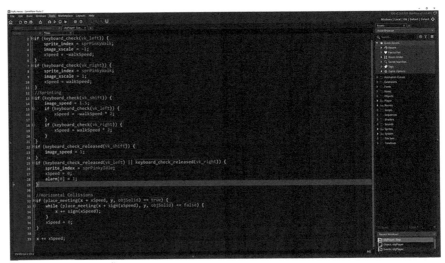

Figure 8.3 Maximize Coding

renamed to our object name, and we have tabs for each event **(Figure 8.3)**. This is how I prefer to work most of the time, but it's purely a preference thing so do what works best for you. I will note here, that if you create another event in the object you have full screened, it will appear as a regular little window in the other workspace. But you can grab the event tab and drag it into the other workspace. Or you could close all the code for the object, then open each one again and press maximize.

Adding Gravity

Navigate to where we coded the horizontal collisions yesterday. Right above that is where the jumping and gravity code will go. It's not necessary for it to go here, it could potentially go anywhere in the step event, but it logically makes sense to me to place the jumping code after the moving left and right code. There are times the order of code is essential but not currently. Add a few lines before the horizontal collisions to begin working in.

The first thing we need to establish is how to differentiate when Pinky is on the ground and in the air. We'll only apply gravity when she's not on the ground. Often the simplest solution is the best one and in this case that's true. We know how to check for collisions with a solid to the left and right, let's do the same for right below, like this:

```
if (place_meeting(x, y + 1, objSolid) == true) {

    ySpeed = 0;

}
```

The y + 1 checks directly beneath our player to see if we're standing on a solid. If we are, then we don't want to apply any gravity, instead we want to set our ySpeed to 0. Next, add an else statement after this if check, and in there we'll apply our gravity to the player.

Inside the else brackets, add our gameGravity to ySpeed like so:

```
ySpeed += gameGravity;
```

Remember the += is a shortcut to adding the two variables together and assigning that combined value to the variable on the left. You could also write it as ySpeed = ySpeed + gameGravity if it helps.

Now scroll down to where we're moving Pinky with the code x += xSpeed. Beneath that, or above it, add the same for the y coordinate and our ySpeed. That's all we need to implement a basic gravity system. Now we can test it out.

Figure 8.5 Stuck Pinky

Figure 8.4 Floating Pinky

Open Room1 and place Pinky a little above a solid object **(Figure 8.4)**. Run the game and check out our gravity system in action! Boom, Pinky falls and stops at the solid. Well, she stops in the solid, not exactly what we wanted **(Figure 8.5)**. The reason for getting stuck in the solid is we're only checking for one pixel beneath the player, but our gameGravity accelerates our ySpeed to a much higher speed than one, so Pinky's inside the solid by the time that if check becomes true.

Do you want to see exactly how fast? Because you can! Let me introduce you to your new best friend, the debugger.

The Debugger (Your New Best Friend)

The Debugger is an incredible tool you should be using anytime your game starts acting funny. It's the best tool to find out what's going wrong and how to fix it. To use the debugger, you simply press F6, or the little bug icon next to the play button **(Figure 8.6)**. You may have already clicked on it by accident and gotten confused. It does take a while to become familiar with the debugger, and even I barely scratch the surface on what it can do.

Figure 8.6 Debugger

To fully utilize the debugger, you'll want to set a breakpoint. Breakpoints are the primary way to interact with the debugger, as it allows you to pause your game at a specific line of code. Let's give it a try. On the line where we set ySpeed to 0, click to the left of the line number, or highlight the line and press F9. A big red circle will appear indicating a breakpoint **(Figure 8.7)**. Now run the game in debug mode by pressing F6 and watch what happens.

```
31   if (place_meeting(x, y + 1, objSolid) == true) {
32       ySpeed = 0;
33   }
```

Figure 8.7 Breakpoints

Depending on your setup, a new GameMaker Workspace will appear labelled Debugger with a whole new look to it **(Figure 8.8)**. I have a dual monitor setup and the debugger appears on one, while the game continues to run on the other, which I find very helpful. Inside the debugger, try hovering over any variable and you'll see a value appear above it. If you look at ySpeed, you'll notice it's got a larger value than one, in my game it's 5.75.

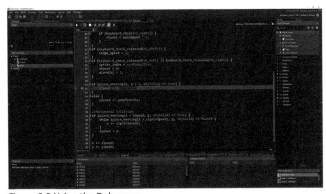

Figure 8.8 Using the Debugger

Our game has paused on the breakpoint, waiting for us to continue in some way. The debugger has the power to go line by line in our code, which is immeasurably helpful in finding extremely specific issues that plague your games. Let me break down how to use the primary features of the debugger.

First are the debugger controls, which is a new set if buttons near the top **(Figure 8.9)**. Starting on the left, there's Continue (which resumes your game), Break (which will pause your game while it's running), Restart (which restarts the entire game), and Close (which shuts down the game). Those ones are all intuitive from their iconography, but the rest are a little more confusing.

Figure 8.9 Debugger Buttons

Next up is the Step Into button, which is the arrow going into the curly brackets. This button will go line by line as you press it, the game executing the line of code you're currently on. Press it now. The line jumped from ySpeed = 0 to the next if check. If you hover over ySpeed now you'll see it's set to 0, because that line just got executed. It skipped the else since the else block only runs when none of the if blocks do.

After the Step Into button comes the Step Over button. This won't go inside of any curly brackets, instead jumping right to the next function or main line of code. Try pressing it a few times. The way it works is a little confusing, as it can seem to do the same thing as the Step Into button. Unfortunately, we don't have any code to show off this button very well, so just know it will not go into curly bracket code. I don't find myself using this button often, as I usually want to see my code run line by line.

And the last code moving button is the Step Out button, which will completely skip entire events. The only code we have running in our game right now is in objPlayer's step event, so clicking this button will just return you to the step event, just as the top of it. This button is especially useful, because when there's many objects in your game, the debugger shows you every one of them. Being able to skip events where you know there's no bugs is genuinely nice.

The second to last button is one you should tick on. It enables real-time debugging, allowing you to see changes to variables and other data as it happens in game. I use this feature frequently, to see if the values I expect to appear are there. And the last is to close both the game and debugger. Use this when you're done with the debugger.

There's a whole lot more we could cover, but I'll save it for another time. Right now, we need to fix our game gravity collision problem. Remove the breakpoint you placed in the code.

Breakpoints

A breakpoint tells the compiler to pause everything on that line of code. It will only work if you run your game in debugging mode though. When debugging, if the compiler sees a breakpoint, it will bring up the debugger to the breakpoint and pause the game, allowing you to inspect every object, variable, and piece of data.

Vertical Collisions

Above the horizontal collision code, write another check for meeting a solid, but this time check against the ySpeed. It should look like this:

```
if (place_meeting(x, y + ySpeed, ob-
jSolid) == true) {

}
```

Just like our xSpeed, our ySpeed can be both negative and positive so this one if check will catch above our heads and beneath our feet. Then write a while loop, almost the same as the horizontal collision check, but for y and ySpeed. Here's how it should come out:

```
while (place_meeting(x, y + sign(y-
Speed), objSolid) == false) {

y += sign(ySpeed);

}

ySpeed = 0;
```

This code moves Pinky as close as possible to the nearest solid in the direction they're moving and sets their ySpeed to 0. Add a comment about what it does, I'll label mine vertical collisions **(Figure 8.10)**. Now run the game and Pinky should land gracefully on the solids.

Error Help

- If you forget the == false on the while loop, or make another mistake, you may find your game freezing up and unresponsive. Your game is in an endless loop and must be force stopped. A good tip when writing while loops that could cause this issue is to run your game in debug mode. If you run into an infinite loop you can pause the game and exit it from the debugger. It's an easier way to quit, but it will also show you exactly what's going wrong if you inspect the loop and variables in it.

Fantastic stuff! We can now fall and collide correctly. The last thing to get working is the jump. What's the point of falling if we can't jump back up? We've already created the variables necessary, so let's just put them into play.

Above where the gravity is getting applied, add a check for the spacebar being pressed once. The function is keyboard_check_pressed and the spacebar constant is vk_space. Inside the if check set the ySpeed equal to jumpSpeed. That should launch Pinky upward. Run the game and try it out.

Well, that doesn't quite work does it? What's happening? Let's use the debugger to find out. Add a breakpoint to

```
38    //Vertical Collisions
39    if (place_meeting(x, y + ySpeed, objSolid) == true) {
40        while (place_meeting(x, y + sign(ySpeed), objSolid) == false) {
41            y += sign(ySpeed);
42        }
43        ySpeed = 0;
44    }
```

Figure 8.10 Vertical Collisions

where we set ySpeed equal to jumpSpeed and run the debugger. Try to jump in the game and the debugger will pause at the breakpoint. Now let's walk through it line by line to see the problem **(Figure 8.11)**.

```
31  if (keyboard_check_pressed(vk_space)) {
32      ySpeed = jumpSpeed;
33  }
34
35  if (place_meeting(x, y + 1, objSolid) == true) {
36      ySpeed = 0;
37  }
38  else {
39      ySpeed += gameGravity;
40  }
41
```

Figure 8.11 Jumping Problem

Did you find the problem? It's the order of our code! When we press jump our ySpeed does get set to launch us upward, but then the if check to see if we're on the ground triggers and sets our ySpeed back to 0. We'll never take off like this!

Do you remember me saying how the order of code can be vitally important? This is one of those times. Cut out the keyboard jumping code and place it beneath the gravity applying code. Now try to run your game and see if you can jump.

Excellent, it works! And maybe it works a little too well. Keep jumping and you'll notice you can do it forever. That's great if we want to make a Flappy Bird clone, but not so much for this platformer. We've got our code in the right order, checking for a jump press after seeing if we're on the ground, we just have it in the wrong place. When do we want to allow the player to jump? Only when they're on the ground. So, let's cut out jump code once more and place it in the ground check, immediately after setting ySpeed to 0 **(Figure 8.12)**.

```
31  if (place_meeting(x, y + 1, objSolid) == true) {
32      ySpeed = 0;
33      if (keyboard_check_pressed(vk_space)) {
34          ySpeed = jumpSpeed;
35      }
36  }
37  else {
38      ySpeed += gameGravity;
39  }
```

Figure 8.12 Jumping Solution

When cutting/copying and pasting code, the indentation can get all whacky. Be sure to line it all back up properly. Alright, one more time now with feeling, run the game. Viola! It works as expected this time, only allowing a jump while on the ground. Now play around with it, add some more blocks above and around Pinky to see how it feels.

As you play around you may not several things not working perfectly. (Depending on if you set Pinky's collision mask directly, you'll find some of these issues don't apply) If you stand directly against a wall and jump, it won't work. You can glitch into the edges of solids. Sometimes Pinky will be slightly inside of a solid or above it. This is all fine. We're going to fix it... tomorrow!

Conclusion + Challenge

Your challenge for today is to use the debugger and see if you can find out why some of these glitches are occurring. Don't spend too much time on it though, it took me quite a while to figure out exactly why all of this was happening when I was making the game, so I don't expect you to find and fix all these. But do spend time in the debugger, play around with it, perhaps check out my YouTube channel and watch the debugger tutorial on there. Give it your best.

Tomorrow we'll fix these small bugs and add a few specific platformer tricks.

Day 9

Perfecting our Jump

Removing Those Pesky Bugs

So, what were you able to discover through the debugger yesterday? Did you find out why we had these small problems? Let's go over what's happening and how to fix it now.

The first issue we'll tackle is the inability to jump while next to a wall. To show you this, I'm going to introduce some new functions. I want you to follow along here, as this will be helpful to you in future games of all genres.

Open objPlayer and add a new event, this one being a Draw Event. Choose the first event on the drop-down list, the one that simply says Draw. We've talked about the draw event in the first game we made together, so recall that it's an event that runs every frame of our game and is where we can manually draw things to the game screen. Once we add this event, the object will no longer draw itself in the game, so if we want to see Pinky, we must call draw_self. Currently, you don't need to add that in.

Next, we're going to draw the collision mask we have on our sprite. The way to do this is by drawing a rectangle around the bounding box. The Bounding Box is a set of built-in variables that hold the data about where the collision mask is on the sprite, relative to the room. We can use this to draw an outline, or full rectangle, of our player object. The function we'll use to do that is draw_rectangle, which takes 5 arguments, 2 x coordinates, 2 y coordinates, and if the rectangle should just be an outline. The code for it looks like this:

```
draw_rectangle(bbox_left, bbox_top, bbox_right, bbox_bottom,
false);
```

So, we're drawing the first x as the left bounding box, the first y as the top bounding box, then continuing so it's a rectangle. And lastly, we tell it to not draw as an outline, this method will make it much easier to see where the problem is. If you manually set the ob-

Bounding Box

The bounding box are the coordinates of the collision mask for a specific sprite, relative to the room it's in. There are four bounding boxes and their values change as the object moves around. These are read-only variables, which means they can't be set in code. If an object has no collision mask, these built-in variables will instead return the x or y position of the object.

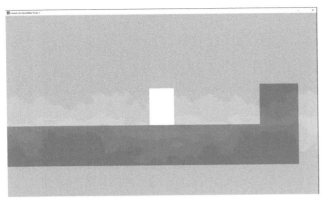

Figure9.0 Rectangle

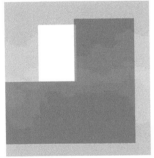

Figure 9.1 Inside Wall

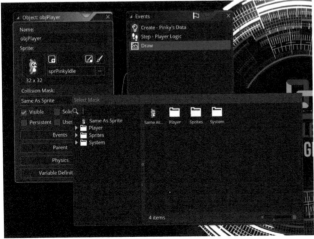

Figure 9.2 Manual Collision

jPlayer collision mask to be one of Pinky's sprites, change it back to being the same as sprite for now. Run the game now and you'll find Pinky replaced by a white rectangle **(Figure 9.0)**.

That's what we wanted. That rectangle represents the collision mask on Pinky. Try moving next to one of the walls. Notice how the size of the collision mask changes when we move. This is because the collision mask is set to copy the current sprites collision mask, and the collision masks are different sizes. When we run next to a wall, the collision mask never enters the wall, but once we stop moving, the mask expands to be slightly inside the solid **(Figure 9.1)**. That's why we can't jump! Our code checks for a collision with the wall, and if we have run all our speeds get set to 0. So even though we press jump, before we move our ySpeed gets set back to 0.

To fix this issue, we could manually check every time we change collision masks if we're inside a wall and then move out of it. Or we can manually set the collision mask to always be the same, that way we never clip inside of it. That's the approach I'm going to take now, but if you're up for an extra coding challenge, try to work out how to fix it the first way.

Return to objPlayer and click on their collision mask **(Figure 9.2)** and choose either Pinky's walk or idle. Then run the game again and see how the collision mask doesn't grow or shrink when we move. The clipping problem is solved, and we can now jump when we're next to a wall. Excellent!

Onto the next problem we have, that of getting stuck inside the corners of the solid object **(Figure 9.3)**. Leave the draw event for now, it will still be of great help in solving this problem. I will admit this problem stumped me for a while. Most tutorials on platformer collisions only cover what we've already done and call it good. But that's never felt perfect to me, always leaving a few errors here and there. So, out of frustration I worked and worked at it until I came up with a solution.

78

The reason for this clipping into the corners is we're not checking for all the collision possibilities right now. We've implemented horizontal and vertical collisions, but what if we're falling or jumping fast at an angle? Nothing is checking when both our x and y speeds are at high numbers and collide simultaneously with a solid. The solution: diagonal collision checking.

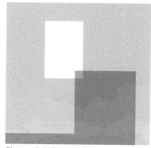

Figure 9.3 Corner issues

Beneath the horizontal collisions add another if check, this time checking for both x and y speed with objSolid. Inside the if, write another while loop that checks the sign of x and y speed, and then moves Pinky's x and y by the sign of each. After the while loop set both speeds to 0. Overall, it should look like this:

```
//Diagonal Collisions

if (place_meeting(x + xSpeed, y + ySpeed, objSolid) == true) {

    while (place_meeting(x + sign(xSpeed), y + sign(ySpeed), objSolid) ==
    false) {

    x += sign(xSpeed);

    y += sign(ySpeed);

    }

    xSpeed = 0;

    ySpeed = 0;

}
```

Figure 9.4 Hovering Issue

All stuff we've done, just adding a check for both at once. Now run the game and try to collide with a corner. No more getting stuck! We're knocking out these issues slowly but surely!

The other small problem you may have noticed is Pinky sometimes, when jumping up onto the ledge and coming down, will be ever so slightly above or inside of a solid **(Figure 9.4)**. It doesn't hinder movement or jumping but does look weird. Why is this? It comes down to math. Our gameGravity variable increases by .25 every frame we're in the air, and sometimes when Pinky begins the vertical collision checking, her ySpeed isn't a whole number (like 1, 2, 5). So, when we move flush against a solid, we're moving 1 pixel at a time. If our y was 93.5, it will stay 93.5, just half a pixel above or inside a solid, enough to look odd but not affect the bounding box and collisions.

The simplest and most effective fix for this is to round our y coordinate when we're on the ground. GameMaker has many rounding functions, and the one we want is simply called round. At the place where we're checking if Pinky is on the ground, add this code in the if check:

```
y = round(y);
```

Take out the draw event, then run your game and test it out. No more floating or dipping glitches. The round function simply takes the number and rounds to the nearest whole number, based on its decimal position. GameMaker also has a floor and ceil function, which rounds the number down or up, respectively. I'm going to add a comment as to why the rounding function is there, and I suggest you do the same, as it's easy to forget why it's there after a few days **(Figure 9.5)**.

```
31   //Checking if player is on the ground
32   if (place_meeting(x, y + 1, objSolid) == true) {
33       y = round(y); //Prevents hovering or dipping into a solid
34       ySpeed = 0;
35       if (keyboard_check_pressed(vk_space)) {
36           ySpeed = jumpSpeed;
37       }
38   }
39   else { //Applying gravity while player is in the air
40       ySpeed += gameGravity;
41   }
```

Figure 9.5 Rounding

So, are we ready to move on yet? Almost, but in fixing these glitches we've found yet another one. It might seem amazing that with only around 60 lines of code we already have so many problems, but don't be surprised. Coding well and bug free is difficult, sometimes an impossible task. Remember to visualize it as a challenge, a puzzle to solve, maybe even a mini game. Debugging isn't what you sludge through to get to the fun part of game development, it is the bulk if making a game. Brainstorming the game and mechanics is easy, getting them implemented correctly is not.

The new glitch we've uncovered is when we try to jump next to a wall and then immediately move away from the solid. Pinky drops down like a sack of rocks, losing all momentum. It happens on either wall. But why? Pinky's not

glitching into the wall, we fixed that problem by setting the collision mask manually right? Well, almost.

This glitch stems from Pinky's sprite not being perfectly centered. Open sprPinkyIdle. The origin is set to Middle Centre right now, which is usually fine, but look closely at how Pinky is standing. Her sprite is just slightly more on the right than the left. This isn't a problem, usually, but since we've inverting the image_xscale when we move left and right, it's flipping the collision mask as well. When we're flush against a wall and move the opposite direction, for just a frame we're inside that wall. The fix is to move the origin over one pixel to the left. It will now say Custom on the top right, indicating we've moved, and that's what we want **(Figure 9.6)**.

Figure 9.6 Custom

Now when we move left or right, the collision mask will be center, instead of moving ever so slightly. Run the game and see for yourself. Move against a wall, jump, and move away. No more jump glitches there!

We've now fixed all the bugs and glitches in our game and have the basics of a platformer up and running, way to go! Next, let's get jumping feel exactly right by allowing the player to cheat just a little bit.

I Totally Jumped There!

Now, when I say cheat what I mean is allowing the player to jump even when they're not on a ledge. We want to do this because it will feel better when playing. The human brain is great at seeing things that aren't quite real, like believing they pressed jump on the exact edge of a solid when really, they were one pixel off. Falling to your death because of one pixel doesn't feel good and will often cause a player to quit playing. Unless you're aiming for a hardcore platformer, or exceedingly difficult game, that's not what you want.

Figure 9.8 Ledge Hover

So, we'll introduce a platformer concept called 'coyote time' (from Wile. E. Coyote and the Road Runner) that allows the player to jump even when they're not a ledge, but only for a few frames after they've just left the ground. Let's return to the create event in our player and add two new variables. The first will be called maxJumpBuffer and set it equal to 5. Then create one called jumpBuffer and set it equal to maxJumpBuffer.

```
maxJumpBuffer = 5;

jumpBuffer = maxJumpBuffer;
```

We'll begin counting down the jumpBuffer when we're no longer on the ground, and if it hasn't reached 0 before the player presses jump then they will jump. I've found 5 to be a good number, but you can change it if you want to be more generous or strict, the larger the number the more amount of coyote time they get. By setting jumpBuffer equal to maxJumpBuffer, they'll both start at the same value, and to change them both we only need to alter one value.

Move into the Step event and find our ground checking code. When we're on the ground, we want to reset jumpBuffer to maxJumpBuffer. Add that in now. Then, when we're not on the ground, we want to subtract 1 from jumpBuffer. Add that in now. Finally, we need to take our whole jump code out of our if check and move it below (if you move it above you won't be able to jump anymore). If we want to be able to jump while not on the ground, we can ether duplicate the code to check outside of this if check and check against the jumpBuffer or move it out. I opt to never duplicate code when possible, as it makes it more prone to bugs and errors.

Now add an and operand (&&) to the key check for space that checks if jumpBuffer > 0. And lastly, when we jump, set jumpBuffer to 0. That's everything we need to do. We're now checking against the jumpBuffer, instead of being on the ground, to see if we can jump. When we're not on the ground, jumpBuffer decreases rapidly, and once we jump it gets set to 0 **(Figure 9.7)**.

```
31  //Checking if player is on the ground
32  if (place_meeting(x, y + 1, objSolid) == true) {
33      y = round(y); //Prevents hovering or dipping into a solid
34      ySpeed = 0;
35      jumpBuffer = maxJumpBuffer;
36  }
37  else { //Applying gravity while player is in the air
38      ySpeed += gameGravity;
39      jumpBuffer -= 1;
40  }
41
42  if (keyboard_check_pressed(vk_space) && jumpBuffer > 0) {
43      ySpeed = jumpSpeed;
44      jumpBuffer = 0;
45  }
```

Figure 9.7 Coyote Time

I know that was a lot, so be sure to check your code against **figure 9.7**. But if you think you got it all, then run your game and test it out! A buffer of only 5 is small, but still significant. If you want to really see it in action, and do some serious coyote time, set maxJumpBuffer to 50. That will give you almost a full second to jump after leaving a solid. Experiment with the number and find one that you like and that feels good. I'm going to reset mine back to 5.

Fair Hit Boxes

The last thing we're going to tackle today is making the game feel better. Right now, Pinky's collision mask is covering all of her, which makes sense. However, it doesn't feel particularly good, or look particularly good, in practice. To see what I mean, jump up to a block and inch towards the ledge **(Figure 9.8)**. Notice how you can get several pixels away from the solid and still be standing there. It's not our collision code, it's that the bounding boxes are larger than the feet.

To remedy this and make it feel better, open sprPinkyIdle and expand the Collision Mask section. Change the Mode from automatic to manual. Again, you get to decide what feels good and fair to you, but as for me I'm going to bring the collision mask in several pixels on both sides. I'm also going to bring it down a few pixels **(Figure 9.9)**.

Figure 9.9 Manual Colision Mask

This collision mask will also dictate damage when we add in spikes and an enemy. I don't want any player to get hurt from a collision mask that's too large because that doesn't feel good, even if it is technically fair. Once you've set the collision mask, run your game, and see how it feels. If you brought it in too much Pinky will be inside of the solid when right next to it. If you expanded the mask, you won't be able to get close to the walls at all. Try and find the right spot.

Conclusion + Challenge

And that's it! We've covered a lot today, fixed a load of bugs, and added a new feature. All in all, it was a great day.

The challenge for today is to play a platforming game. It could be Mario, Super Meat Boy, or a thousand others. Since we're creating a platformer in this book, it would be good to have some play time with one. Even if it's not your favorite genre, give it a real go. And while you're playing, think like a game developer about what makes the game feel good or bad. Did they use coyote time? Do they have other little tricks that help the game feel better? Hit me up on Twitter @_aaron_lltt and let me know.

Tomorrow we'll tackle tile sets and begin level design!

PRO TIP

What to Do When You Feel Overwhelmed or Inept

Aaron Craig | Let's Learn This Together

LetsLearnThisTogether.com

Have you ever been assigned a task or job that you felt completely unqualified for? You know that feeling when you've gotten in so deep that you can't see a way out? I've been there. A lot. School assignments, jobs from my boss, and personal projects I thought I could handle but turned out to by way harder than I expected.

We've all felt overwhelmed at some point. Maybe the task was beyond your skill level, or you had so many things to do that you thought you would never even accomplish one. What do we do when we begin to feel that way when making games? Because trust me, you'll feel that way at some point. Even if you start small, you'll encounter something that is daunting and challenges you to the point of breaking. But don't give up.

The key to overcoming how you're feeling is the same way you make a game. By breaking it down into small, manageable chunks. Every task, no matter the size, can be broken down into bite sized pieces. Just

like putting together a puzzle, you do it one small piece at a time. When making a game, your task isn't to 'make the game', it's to get the player moving. Then you get the player animating. Then you get the player attacking. And then and then and then, it just goes on. It's not one giant task, it's a dozen, or even a hundred, small ones that all build up to accomplish that ultimate goal.

This is one reason I think everyone should be a programmer. Programming isn't about making an application or game, it's about the little things. It's solving how to pass information from one page to the next, and how to get an enemy to bounce back when it takes damage. It's all these little things that you put together, that eventually come together to create something awesome.

So, the next time you're feeling overwhelmed, take three steps back. Break down whatever's causing that feeling. Then begin to tackle it one task at a time.

Day 10

Designing Your First Level

All About Tiles

How was your time playing a platformer? I find it crazy there are so many different styles to the one genre. You've got Mario, which I bet you're familiar with, which is fun and easy. Then you've got precision platformers like Super Meat Boy which are intensely tough and can make you rage quit after 10 minutes. It just goes to show that even in a genre, like platformers, you can have a wide variety of gameplay styles that give the game a totally unique feel.

But now it's time to turn our attention to the basics of level design and the workflow that GameMaker uses. For the most part it's awesome, as GameMaker has some great tools to use when creating levels. Before we dive into those, however, let's learn what Tile Sets are and how to get them into our game.

In the Assets folder, open the folder labeled Tile Sets. In there you'll find a file called Forest. This is all we're going to use to design the layout of the level itself. Just one image. You can import it the same way you do a sprite, because it starts its life as a sprite. For me, I'm going to drag it into the Tile Sets folder in GameMaker and rename it sprForestTiles **(Figure 10.0)**. The properties of this sprite are inconsequential as we won't be using it as a sprite, so ignore all the speed, origin, and mask settings we've usually tweaked.

Once the sprite is inside our game, right click on the Tile Sets folder and create a new tile set. This opens the Tile Set Editor where we can control all the properties of the tile set, how it appears, and how we'll work with it **(Figure 10.1)**. Click on Select Sprite or drag the forest

Tile Sets

Tile sets are a special set of sprites that contain individual frames that can be used to design anything. Tile sets range from house interiors to space stations, and they're an efficient and quick way to design a level with infinite variety and minimal overhead.

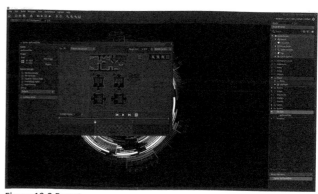

Figure 10.0 Forest

85

Figure 10.1 Tile Set Editor

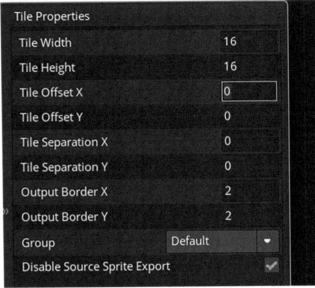

Figure 10.2 Width and Height

Figure 10.3 Tile Lyear

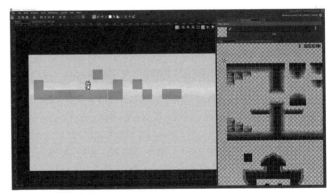

Figure 10.4 Work Area

sprite into the middle of the editor. Now our tile set knows which sprite it's using. From here we need to set the appropriate tile set properties.

Tile sets can come in many shapes in sizes, the most common being 8x8, 16x6, and 32x32. Our tile set is 16x16, which is the default setting in GameMaker. The first property is the width and height of the tiles, but we don't need to change it at all **(Figure 10.2)**. The next two options, offset x and y, move where the beginning of the grid is at. Separation x and y adjust the separation, like when we converted our sprite sheet to frames. Output border doesn't matter to us, so let's ignore it. The group being default is fine, and you can leave the Disable Source Sprite Export checked.

Now to use a tile set in our game, let's move over to our room. We need to add a new tile layer to our Layers, by using the tile layer icon **(Figure 10.3)**. With that layer added, we can now use our tile set to start designing. On the right, a new tab has appeared next to Assets called Room Editor. Well, I suppose there's already one called Room Editor, but this is a different Room Editor tab. In it, we can select a tile set to use. Choose our forest tile set.

When designing in GameMaker, I tend to minimize the left tab and enlarge the right to give me more space to see all the tiles. Then I zoom in on the area I want to work on, because you design one section at a time **(Figure 10.4)**. This tile set has quite a few different styles you can use, and I encourage you to experiment with them and see which ones you like the most. I'm not actually going to tell you how to design, instead I'm going to teach you how to use the tile set, what they can do, and then let you at it. So, today's chapter will be a little shorter than the others, but the challenge will take longer.

Designing The Level

The primary tool we'll be using will be the basic Tiles tab, which holds the sprite we brought in and allows us to

pick a 16x16 tile and then place it in the room. You can select multiple tiles at once, such as a big chunk of ground or wall, and slap that into the room, too. The black and white checker in the top left of the tile set is a blank tile, you can use to erase, but mostly it's because GameMaker needs it there. Let's go ahead and try laying some tiles.

Select the first chunk of ground with the stones sticking up and place it into the top left area of the room. Left click and hold down, and then drag until you've got your entire selection. Then select just a bit of the ground without the stones and extend the ground outward **(Figure 10.5)**. Now we have a stage to run around in.

To make it all look and feel right though, we need to move just a few things around. First let's move the tile layer beneath the instances layer so the solid blocks appear above

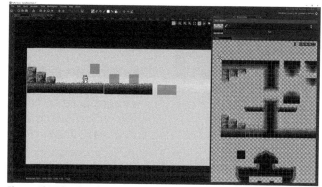

Figure 10.5 First Level

our tiles. Now arrange the solid squares to fit with what we've created. The trick I use when doing this is to stretch the solid when it needs more than one. This cuts down on how many objects are in the level making it easier to manage. You may also need to change the grid snap to 16x16 instead of the default 32x32 **(Figure 10.6)**. For the smallest steppingstone, you'll need to shrink the solid to half its size. My final product looks like **Figure 10.7**.

Before running the game, let's turn the solid objects invis-

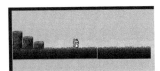

Figure 10.7 The First Level

Figure 10.6 Grid Snap

Figure 10.8 Too Large

Figure 10.9 Grid Snapping Icon

ible to make our game look nicer. Open the objSolid object and untick the Visible check box. Now run your game and move around. It feels like we're really playing a game now! The power of tile sets gives your game a beautiful look and combining it with the solids give a nearly finished look to the game. Of course, there's still plenty to do, but be sure to take a break and celebrate how far you've come. When you began 10 days ago you knew little about programming or game development, and now you've created a beautiful platformer that feels fun to run around in. Way to go!

You may find the solid object is slightly larger than the tile set in some areas **(Figure 10.8)**, but you can easily change the size of each solid in the level to conform to the tile sets. Uncheck the grid snapping system completely, the small grid icon we clicked on earlier **(Figure 10.9)**, and you can now move objects around without any snapping. This also allows for easy resizing to fit it perfectly with whatever tile set you use.

Conclusion + Challenge

Now I've got two homework assignments for you. The first is to explore the world of 2D level design in platformers, or any kind of game, to get inspired and see what others are creating. Do a search of 2D level design or visit some indie dev websites to see what they're creating.

Once you have a good feel for level design, put it to the test! Use the tile set we've been using or add some new ones and create the first level for your platformer game. Start small here, don't try and create a huge level that's 3000x3000 pixels or anything. The room size we have now of 1366x768 is a good start, but you can go even smaller if you don't want to include falling or jumping up too much. Really spend some time on your level, experiment with the tile sets, experiment with jump distance and feel.

I'm going to also create a simple level which I'll show you tomorrow. Don't look ahead and just copy me though. You can create and design levels, even if you're not an artist. Don't believe you can only program, or you're not talented enough to do level design because that's a lie. It's one I believed for a long time and it held me back. Don't let it do the same to you. You can create an awesome level. You will create an amazing level!

See you tomorrow!

Day 11

Upgrading Pinky

Homework + Level Design Recap

How did your time designing your first level go? I hope it was good. For some of you I'm sure it was a breeze, being a creative and artistic type already. For others of you, it may have been an exercise in frustration. Wherever you fall on that spectrum, just remember that everyone has a different set of skills, but we can all learn new ones, too. Don't give up because it was hard, and don't just relax because it was easy, there's more for you to learn and improve upon even if you have some natural talent starting out.

My first level is quite simple, and you can see it in **Figure 11.0**. I changed my room size to 640x368, the same size as the background I'm using. I put a border on the left so I can't wander off that ledge, and I created the first obstacle we'll overcome today, a jump barrier. From here on out, or games will probably look a lot different, and that's perfectly fine! Everyone has their own opinion on what looks good, and many games require specific level design to work well. The important part is the reason behind why I do certain things, and how I do them, not how it looks. Don't try to imitate my level, embrace your own.

Adding A Power Up

Today we'll be adding a jump powerup our hero can collect. It will allow them to get past the first obstacle. If you don't have a height barrier in your game, try and add one now. You don't need one, but it may be easier to follow along with the code, if you can see what we're trying to do.

Open up objPlayer and go into the Create event. We currently have a jumpSpeed variable that directly controls how high our little hero can jump. The goal today is to add another variable that influences jump and can be upgrad-

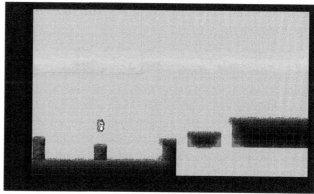

Figure 11.0 My First Level

ed as we collect them. This specific implementation can transfer over to every other element in your game and is commonly used in RPG's. We'll only be affecting our jumping power, but once you understand how we do that, adding it to run speed, attack power, and anything else you can imagine will be easy.

First, create another variable and call it jumpPower, setting it equal to 1. We'll be multiplying this jumpPower variable by our jumpSpeed, so it needs to start at 1 and not 0, otherwise it will make our jumping effectively none. Now go into the Step event and locate where we apply our jumpSpeed to our ySpeed, which for me is line 43 (I'm sure yours isn't the same, and that's fine). Alter the line to now read like this:

```
ySpeed = jumpSpeed * jumpPower;
```

And that's really all we need to do in the players code. The system is now in place so when we increase our hero's jumpPower, we'll jump higher. Simple, right? Our goal now is to add in a powerup in the game that we can collect, have it increase jumpPower, and then be destroyed so it doesn't infinitely increase our jumping ability.

Navigate to the Assets folder and open Sprites. There's a sprite in here labelled Power up; drag it into the Sprites folder in your game. It comes in as a single sprite, but it's more of a sprite sheet, so we need to cut it up. We've done this several times already, so all I'll tell you is they are 16x16 pixels.

Once you've got it converted, trim the frames down. Now let's rename the coin to sprPowerUp. The default speed is much too fast, so change it to 6, or whatever you feel looks the best. You're at the point now where you can tell when an animation looks good or bad, so be sure to trust your instincts. This coin needs an object, so create a new object in the Objects folder and name it objPowerJump, assigning this sprite to it.

Inside objPowerJump add a create event and a collision with the player event. In the create event make a new variable that will hold how much this coin will increase the jumping power of our player. I've named mine power-Level and assigned it a value of 0.25 **(Figure 11.1)**. We've got that figured out and made it so we can change it dynamically in the level (which I'll show you later), so now we need to fill out the collision event.

Figure 11.1 Power Level

Jumping Higher

In this event, I'm going to introduce several new concepts. Each one builds upon the other, so how we'll do this is start with the simplest one and get the code working the way we want. Then I'll discuss whether it works the way we really want it to or if we need to change it.

The first new concept is dot notation. Dot Notation is the ability to access other objects data from anywhere, such as our objPowerJump and influence our player's code. It is literally a dot, or a period, which then grants access to all the variables and data of that object you called it upon. It

Dot Notation

Dot notation is the most common way to access other objects data in programming. It's used in every language I've used, which is quite a few, and is essential to change objects' data in game.

looks like this:

```
objPlayer.jumpPower += powerLevel;
```

Add that line of code to your collision event, and then call instance_destroy() after it **(Figure 11.2)**. When our hero collides with the power up, it will find the player and increase their jumpPower by the powerLevel variable we created. Then it destroys itself. Let's test it out. Place a power up in the level and see if it allows you to get over your first obstacle.

```
⊿ objPowerJump: Events
Create                    ×  objPlayer            ×
   1 /// @description Increase Jump & Die
   2 objPlayer.jumpPower += powerLevel;
   3 instance_destroy();
```

Figure 11.2 Collision Event Take 1

Viola! It does for me. If your obstacle is taller than the largest steppingstone the powerup may not have been enough. Try adding a few and play around with how high you can jump. It gets pretty crazy pretty fast.

So, it seems to be working, right? The powerup is destroyed, our hero's jumpPower has increased and all is right in the game world. Except it only seems that way. To visualize the problem we have, add another player object into your level. Position one of the players on top of the coin so they gain the powerup immediately, and the only a few squares to the right **(Figure 11.3)**. This way one hero gets the powerup while the other doesn't. Run your game and try to jump.

What happened? Did the one who gained the powerup jump higher? No, they both jump at the new upgraded height, even though only one gained the power. Why? Dot notation is enormously powerful, and useful, but must be used correctly. In our code we are accessing

Figure 11.3 Two Player

objPlayer itself, not a specific instance of objPlayer like we want to do. That means whatever we say to do to objPlayer, it applies to every instance of it in the game. There are many times you may way to do this, such as removing all enemies from a level, or slowing the speed of all projectiles to enable a bullet time look. And even in our case, it doesn't really break our game since we only have one player. But what if we wanted to enable multiplayer? Then we'd have a problem. And besides, it's better to always code as correctly as possible to eliminate future bugs from popping up.

So, if we want to access only the player who collides with our powerup, we need to specifically increase that instance's jumpPower, not every single objPlayer. Fortunately, there's a keyword just for doing so in a collision event; it's called other. The Other instance keyword gives you the ability to access whatever object just collided with us. No longer do we need to know which object it was, or change all instances of an object type, we can use the keyword other to only change one instance in our level. The code looks like this:

```
other.jumpPower += powerLevel;
```

It's not a huge coding difference, but it does make a huge change in what's happening. Make the change now and

Other

Other is a special instance keyword, like all, which can be used in a collision event or combined with the with statement. It specifically refers to whatever the other object is, depending on context. In a collision event, other refers to whatever just collided with the object that has the code. You can use other combined with dot notation to access that specific instance in the game.

then run your game and try jumping, you'll now see only the player that collided with the powerup received its power. Perfect! Now it works as expected without any weird side effects.

Delete the second player from your level, we only need one (unless your game idea involves operating two players simultaneously, which does sound interesting). We're not totally done with the powerup yet, as it still needs a bit more to be complete. It should come with a message to the player telling them what's happened upon collection, which we'll tackle in a few days. The other thing to make it better, I think, is a little sound effect.

Playing Sound Effects

In the Sounds folder in our Assets find the one labelled Power Up and drag it into the Sounds folder in GameMaker. GameMaker may produce a popup, just click save and continue. Adding an audio file opens a whole new looking window called the Sound Editor **(Figure 11.4)**. Rename this sound to sndPowerUp and lower the volume to 0.5. Press the small play button and you can now hear it. There are several more options you can change, but we don't really need to change any of them. There is an Output option which is currently set to Mono, but in GameMaker Mono doesn't mean only play in one speaker, it means play the same sound in both speakers. Stereo would be important when the audio file has different levels or sounds in the right vs left, which is unusual for sound effects and video game music. You would choose 3D for Output if you're using audio emitters in your game, which we aren't.

Let's return to the collision event of objPowerJump and play our new sound effect when we collect it. Before we call instance_destroy use this function:

```
audio_play_sound()
```

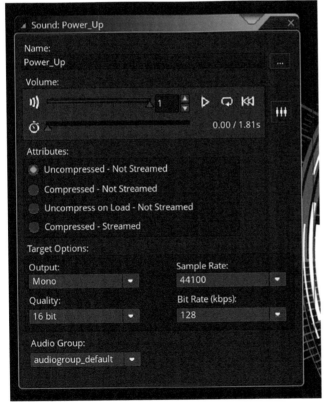

Figure 11.4 Sound Editor

Sound Editor

The Sound Editor is where you can name, listen to, and alter the qualities of all sounds in your game. The main attribute to change in this editor is the volume, as it will change the volume of the sound in game as well, unlike the playback type or playback location.

It accepts 3 arguments. The first is soundid, which is the resource you want to play, in our case sndPowerUp. The second is priority, starting at 0 and going to 100, with the higher number being the one with higher priority. When there are many sounds to be played, the higher priority will take precedence. Personally I've never had an issue with the sounds not playing or a priority being the wrong number, but I still put in music as being more important than sound effects. And lastly is loop, a Boolean indicating if it should loop or not.

For our code, we want to play our powerup sound, give it a priority of 10, and tell it not to loop. If you set it to loop, it will play forever, or until you tell it to stop.

So, now let's test out our game with sound effect in place. If you didn't move your hero off the powerup then you heard it just as the game began. Otherwise, it works as expected and sounds good. There are functions for controlling sounds in GameMaker, such as pausing, resuming, stopping, fading, and many more. Right now, we don't need them, but if you want to experiment with adding your own music or different sounds, go for it.

Remember how I mentioned 3D sound and emitters? Even though we won't be using them in this game, I want to mention them because they are important. GameMaker has a system for placing sound emitters in your game to emulate sound coming from a certain direction. Imagine a waterfall off in the distance, the player can hear it faintly in their right ear, so they wander off in that direction. As they get closer, the sound grows louder and louder. That's what an emitter is and how it works. They're cool, although beyond the scope of this book. I just want to tell you about them so you can keep them in mind for future projects.

Game Music

In the assets folder, you'll find game music. There's music for the menu and main game. To use it, it's the same process as playing sound effects, which you now know how to do. To add some fun music into our game, import Main Game Music from the Assets folder into sounds. Rename it sndGameMusic and set its volume at 0.1. I prefer the background music to not be too overwhelming, and this music can get a little loud.

And now in Pinky's create event, just anywhere, play our new music and set it to repeat. Test it out, and you'll now have music in your game!

Error Help

- If you don't hear anything for the music, or even the sound effects we played earlier, the problem may be in the device GameMaker is trying to play sounds through. Normally it chooses the right one, but sometimes it messes up. Click on File -> Preferences and select General Settings. The fourth option down is the Default Audio Device. Select your headphones or speakers on it and you should be good to go! Try restarting GameMaker if you still can't hear anything.

Conclusion + Challenge

You now know how to create powerups for your hero and improve upon their skills. We've transformed our simple platformer by adding some RPG attributes. Tomorrow we'll be adding a small puzzle to our game, to make acquiring the powerup not as simple as just jumping onto it.

Your homework for today is to play a recent, modern game. As you play, think about how many different genres are blended in that one game. It's becoming more and more common for games to not be restricted to a single genre, such as action, platformer, and puzzle. Instead, most games borrow from many different genres to create their own unique mix. See how many you can pull out and give some thought to whether they improve the game or are there simply because other games have done it before them.

Share your thoughts with me on Twitter @aaron_llt.

Day 12

It's Time to Rock!

My Thoughts on Genre Mixing

So, were you able to find any games with a mix of genres? I'd be surprised if you didn't, as these days almost all games borrow something from other titles. The most recent trend is for every type of game to incorporate RPG elements, like skill trees, into their game even when it's totally unnecessary. Skill trees can be fun and engaging, forcing the player to think about how they want their character to develop and what their playstyle is. Unfortunately, many games simply lock basic features behind a skill tree and then hand them out slowly over time. That doesn't make a game better, it makes it worse. Borrowing features from other genres isn't a good or bad thing in and of itself, it's all about execution; does this feature make our game more fun and engaging? If it doesn't, it's time for it to go!

Creating A Rock

But enough of my rambling, let's get down to business. Yesterday we added a powerup to the level and today we're going to block that powerup behind a small puzzle. It won't be complex, but it will teach you the basics of how to create puzzles, of which you can then create your own more varied and intricate puzzles.

Open the Assets folder and go intro Sprites, then click on Pinky. In this folder is a sprite labeled Rock1 and Rock2, we're going to use Rock2 since it's the larger one. Drag Rock2 into the sprites folder and rename is sprRock. We're going to make it so we can shove this rock around to get to the powerup. A basic premise in many puzzles is moving objects around to form a shape, open up a spot, or unclog an area, so you'll be able to use this mechanic in several varied ways.

Now, since the rock is a circle you may be tempted to change the collision mask from rectangle to ellipse. But we don't need to do that. Not only will ellipse run slower and cause

Scripts

Scripts allow you to write your own functions, a basic feature in every programming language. Custom functions allow you, the programmer, to implement code in a way that's reusable in both your current project and future games. Although don't spend too much time trying to write the perfect function, which is a pitfall I've fallen into many times, instead write a function which just works and slowly grow it as you use it more and more.

some strange collision issues, it also doesn't provide any advantages. Our object can have a rectangular collision mask and still function like a circle. This is a little game designing trick you should add to your arsenal. Just because a sprite is a certain shape doesn't mean its mask needs to match. We'll play around with this concept a little later.

Next, create an object for the rock. Name it objRock and assign our sprite to it. We'll need two events for this rock, the Create and Step events. Go ahead and add them now. In the create event add an x and y speed variable, setting both to zero **(Figure 12.0)**. This rock is going to move in a similar fashion to Pinky, including checking for collisions like our player. The big difference is it will only move when Pinky pushes against it.

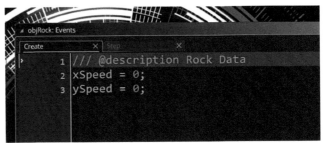

Figure 12.0 Rock Data

To that end, we're going to need a collision system for our rock so it knows when it can move and when it should stop. We have a good system in our player object right now, should we just copy and paste it over to our rock? Absolutely... NOT! I've talked a little about copy and paste coding and how terrible it is. For a few small things, like movement, it can be ok since it's just saving you time. But if you ever come up against a problem where the solution is some code you've already written, copying it isn't the right answer, a function is.

Scripts and Custom Functions

We've been using functions since day two, so by now you're familiar with them. But today we're going to create our own functions, expanding the possibilities of what you can create tenfold. In GameMaker functions used to be called scripts just a version ago, which is why they have a Scripts folder in the Asset Browser. It wouldn't surprise me if they removed that folder sometime in the future, but for now we'll use it. The Scripts you can create in Game-Maker now are containers for functions that we write, so each script can have an unlimited amount of functions, although I'll be grouping similar functions together.

Right click on the Scripts folder and create a new Script asset. Depending on which version of GMS you're using, you may see a message like in **Figure 12.1**. Let's delete that comment, as I've already explained what scripts are now. Then let's rename our script (the one in the Asset Browser) to Collisions. And inside the Collisions script, rename the Script1 function to CollideWith. We now have our first function which we can call anywhere in our game, just like GameMaker's functions. Of course, it doesn't do anything just yet, but we can remedy that!

Figure 12.1 New Script Message

Find inside objPlayer where we're doing all the collision checking. There should be collisions for vertical, horizontal, and diagonal. Select all of that code and cut it out (Ctrl+X or Cmd+X). Then paste it all inside our script CollideWith (Ctrl+C or Cmd+C). Most of it won't be indented properly, so select all the code that isn't indented and then press tab. Now it should all be aligned properly **(Figure 12.2)**.

```
function CollideWith(){
    //Vertical Collisions
    if (place_meeting(x, y + ySpeed, objSolid) == true) {
        while (place_meeting(x, y + sign(ySpeed), objSolid) == false) {
            y += sign(ySpeed);
        }
        ySpeed = 0;
    }

    //Horizontal Collisions
    if (place_meeting(x + xSpeed, y, objSolid) == true) {
        while (place_meeting(x + sign(xSpeed), y, objSolid) == false) {
            x += sign(xSpeed);
        }
        xSpeed = 0;
    }

    //Diagonal Collisions
    if (place_meeting(x + xSpeed, y + ySpeed, objSolid) == true) {
        while (place_meeting(x + sign(xSpeed), y + sign(ySpeed), objSolid) == false) {
            x += sign(xSpeed);
            y += sign(ySpeed);
        }
        xSpeed = 0;
        ySpeed = 0;
    }
```

Figure 12.2 Collide with Script

You can ignore the yellow warning; it's telling us we haven't called this anywhere. Although it also thinks our function is a variable, so it may be a bug in my version of GMS which you won't have in yours. Either way, we've now created our script. Hooray! But how do we use it and how does it work? Well, we can use it the same as GameMaker scripts. Return to where we cut out all that code from our player and call our script there **(Figure 12.3)**.

```
41
42  if (keyboard_check_pressed(vk_space) && jumpBuffer > 0) {
43      ySpeed = jumpSpeed * jumpPower;
44      jumpBuffer = 0;
45  }
46
47  CollideWith();
48
49  x += xSpeed;
50  y += ySpeed;
```

Figure 12.3 Calling our Script

Run your game and notice how there's no difference. Our script is executing just like all that code was still in our player because that's how functions work. When you call a function, GameMaker goes to where that function is stored and executes the code. When calling a function inside of an object, that function can also read that objects data.

For example, if we were to change the x and y inside of our CollideWith script, it would move objPlayer's x and y since it's the object *calling* that script. This has immense possibilities, which we'll continue to explore as we build more scripts, but for now just keep it in the back of your mind.

So, now that we have our own function that controls what we collide with we can use that in the rock. Open the rock's step event and call our new function, and then after it increase the x and y based on the x and y speed variables, just like in our player **(Figure 12.4)**. It also saves a lot of lines of code, since we can call one function instead of having 25 lines of code each time, we want an object to collide with something. It also decreases the number of bugs in

```
▲ objRock: Events
  Create            ×  Step           ×
▶  1 /// @description Move Around
   2 CollideWith();
   3
   4 x += xSpeed;
   5 y += ySpeed;
```

Figure 12.4 Rock Step Event

our game, because if something's wrong with our collision code we only must change it in one location instead of many.

One last side note about scripts and functions: you can name them however you want. If naming your functions with underscores (_) helps you because then they look just like GameMaker's, go for it. I use Pascal Case simply to iden-tity they're my functions, but it doesn't change how they work. The important part is to pick a naming convention and then stick with it. I'll show you later, when we create more custom functions, how to add your own arguments and special comments to your functions.

So, right now our script is being called in the rock, but we have no way of pushing it around right now. Let's get to fixing that!

Local Variables

Local Variables are data that's created and then discarded shortly after. They're immensely useful inside loops and functions when you need to store data but don't want it sticking around to clog up your programs. When created in object events, they're only accessible in that event, and are discarded at the end of it. So, a local variable in the create event cannot be accessed in the step event. This also means you can have local variables named the same in different events, since they never interact.

Pushing the Rock

To push the rock itself, we need to know when Pinky is colliding with the rock and which direction she's trying to move. This code could be in either the rock or Pinky, but to avoid future problems, let's put it in objPlayer and I'll explain why later down the road.

Let's return to where we called our CollideWith script in objPlayer and write the code to push the rock immediately above it. What we need to check for is if we're colliding with the rock based on our x and xSpeed, and if we're trying to move left or right. If all those things line up, then we'll move the rock based on which direction we're going.

From this point on I'm going to describe what we want with code and then give you the chance to solve it yourself. The description will be in a custom style to make it easily identi-fiable. Take the opportunity to do so, as discovering the solution on your own will not only leave your feeling proud, but the solution will also stick with you far longer than if I just told you what to type.

The code we need is in **Figure 12.5**. We're checking if we're colliding with the rock and if we're trying to move in either direction. This works, but personally I'm getting tired of typ-ing out the entire keyboard_check function and arguments every time we need them. So, let's get lazy! Jump to the top of objPlayer's step event and make a few blank lines. We're going to create some variables to store our key checks in, so we can reference those vari-

```
47 if (place_meeting(x + xSpeed, y, objRock) && (keyboard_check(vk_left) || keyboard_check(vk_right))) {
48
```

Figure 12.5 Colliding with the Rock

ables instead of typing out the entire function each time.

Add this line of code up at the top:

```
var left = keyboard_check(vk_left);
```

You'll notice that our variable turns yellow instead of blue like normal. And what's up with the var keyword we used in front of it? This is how you create a local variable. Local Variables are data that get created and then discarded at the end of their event, function, or loop. They don't stick around for long and are perfect when you just need some data for a little while but not forever. In this case, we only need to know if the left key is being pressed in the step event, we aren't checking it anywhere else. So why would we want to keep that variable around, persisting and taking up space, when we never use it elsewhere? The answer is we don't, and local variables are the perfect way to fix that small issue.

Now go through wherever we have the function keyboard_check(vk_left) and replace it with the variable left. This saves us a lot of space in our code and will save us time from typing out an entire function in the future, since we can just use this local variable instead. Replicate this functionality for the right key and the shift key **(Figure 12.6)**. If you're feeling really motivated, you could also replace the jump key and shift released check with local variables. However, since we've only used them once right now, I'm going to let them slide. If we add more checks in the future, I will replace them.

Error Help

- If you test your game now and find you cannot move, you may have replaced the key checks for released left and right when changing to the idle sprite of Pinky. You can undo that or change it to what I did in **figure 12.7**.

```
 2
 3    //Keyboard Input
 4    var left = keyboard_check(vk_left);
 5    var right = keyboard_check(vk_right);
 6    var run = keyboard_check(vk_shift);
 7
 8    if (left) {
 9        sprite_index = sprPinkyWalk;
10        image_xscale = -1;
11        xSpeed = -walkSpeed;
12    }
13    if (right) {
14        sprite_index = sprPinkyWalk;
15        image_xscale = 1;
16        xSpeed = walkSpeed;
17    }
18    //Sprinting
19    if (run) {
```

Figure 12.6 Local Variables

One thing to note here is that even though shift is the key we press to run, I named my local variable run instead of shift. This isn't a big deal, but in my brain, it makes more sense to name the variable what it does instead of the key it's checking for.

With that detour complete, our code to check if we're colliding with the rock is much shorter and, in my opinion, easier to read. Now, inside of the collision with the rock we need to begin moving the rock itself. Yesterday we saw the pitfalls of calling out an object specifically and changing its data. So, we don't want to just increase objRock.xSpeed, because if we ever added more than one rock it would affect all of them! Instead, we can use the function instance_place to get the id of the rock we're currently touching and change its properties. To do that, the code looks like:

```
var rock = instance_place(x + xSpeed,
y, objRock);
```

Hey, look! It's another local variable. This variable will only exist inside of this if statement, then disappear. It has an extremely limited Scope, but it's still especially useful. We can

Scope

Scope, when referring to variables, is the range in which their influence extends. Local variables have the smallest scope, as they can only be used in their event, statement, or loop and then vanish. Instance variables have a larger scope and can be accessed inside of an object, from any event. Global variables have the largest scope and can be accessed from any object or function in the game.

now modify the rock we're colliding with using this local variable, without worry about changing other rocks. Let's now move the rock by modifying its xSpeed against the sign of ours. I would suggest dividing that by 2 so it isn't too fast **(Figure 12.7)**.

```
31  if (!left && !right) {
32      sprite_index = sprPinkyIdle;
33      xSpeed = 0;
34      alarm[0] = 1;
35  }
```
Figure 12.7 Idle Check

Test out the game. If our goal was to create a rock sliding on ice, then we succeeded! The nice part is it does stop against the stone, so its collision code is working properly. But now the problem is it moves on its own, which isn't what we want in this specific instance. So, let's add an else statement after this if check, and tell that rock to stop moving. Your initial attempt at doing so will probably fail, and that's in part due to GameMaker.

```
rock.xSpeed = sign(xSpeed) * 2;
```
Figure 12.8 Moving the Rock

Look at **figure 12.8** and notice how there are no errors on my screen. GameMaker's telling me my code is flawless. But try to run this code and it immediately crashes the

```
53  if (place_meeting(x + xSpeed, y, objRock) && (left || right))
54      var rock = instance_place(x + xSpeed, y, objRock);
55      rock.xSpeed = sign(xSpeed) / 2;
56  }
57  else {
58      rock.xSpeed = 0;
59  }
```
Figure 12.9 Is This Flawless?

game telling me an unknown built-in variable hasn't been set before reading it. Again, I think this is a specific version bug and will hopefully get fixed soon. The problem here is I'm trying to access a local variable that *doesn't* exist in the else statement. The scope of local variables is limited, and the local variable rock only exists in the if portion of our check, not the else. GameMaker *should* recognize that and throw an error, but it doesn't.

Since we can't access rock in the else, we need to find another way to set the rock's xSpeed to 0. However, this is trickier than at first glance. Our else statement will trigger every time our if check fails. That means we must think about several things, including if there even is a rock in the level, as trying to set a rock's xSpeed when there is no rock will crash our game. And what if we do want our rocks to slide like they're on ice, we can't just set every rock's xSpeed back to zero when we're not colliding with one.

Conclusion + Challenge

How do we deal with all of this? I'll show you tomorrow. In the meantime, I want you to think on it, and attempt to solve it yourself. There isn't one correct way, which means your solution may not be mine, and that's alright! While there can be more *efficient* code, there isn't a *righter* kind of code, unless you're getting into security issues, which we aren't. So, play around with pushing the rock and see what you can do. If you get ambitious, import the push animation for Pinky and get that implemented, too.

Best of luck!

PRO TIP

Scope Screep

Benjamin Anderson | uHeartBeast

HeartGameDev.com

Scope is the size of your project.

Scope creep is when the size of your project gets slowly larger and larger across its development cycle.

In my experience there are 2 main sources of scope creep: idea scope creep and problem scope creep.

First, idea scope creep. Idea scope creep happens during the initial planning phase of your project. You come up with a core design mechanic and get excited about it. As you plan, you start to imagine all the features that will make it "amazing".

As a solution, those ideas can be put into an "idea" document but shouldn't be considered until the core of the game is complete. Worst case scenario, you can make a sequel or add DLC.

Second, problem scope creep. Problem scope creep happens as you run into design or technical issues in your project. You see a problem with your current game and you come to the conclusion that you "need" such and such new feature to solve it. The hard thing here is that sometimes the new feature is a really good idea. I've been there. I've struggled with this while working on my current game, Demonlocke.

The thing I've learned is that small teams that finish games, most often, figure out how to solve problems within the constraints of their current project scope

I truly believe that when it comes to game design, less is more. Look at Mario: when they added enemies to the game, Miyamoto didn't go, "hmmmm, in order to kill these enemies we better give Mario a sword". Instead, he chose to give Mario the ability to defeat enemies using an existing feature--jumping! That existing feature also happened to be the core design mechanic for the game.

Here are my steps for avoiding scope creep:

During the planning phase focus on the core design mechanic (like jumping in Mario).

When you run into design or technical problems during development ask yourself, "What features are already available in my project that can solve this?"

I'm confident that if you implement these steps, they will help you mitigate the amount of scope creep in your projects and you will get much better at finishing them!

Day 13

Coding Like A Pro

Solving Yesterday's Challenge

How much were you able to figure out yesterday? How much did you try? That second question is really the more important one. In my personal life, I find myself trying many different ideas looking to solve a problem. Sometimes I do get it solved, but many other times I fail, repeatedly. It isn't until I take a break, let my mind stew on the problem in the background for a while, that I finally discover the solution. So, it's not about getting it right away, or even getting it at all. It's about the persistence of effort and not giving up. Remember that as you go forward, it will aid you immensely.

But now let's get down to business and get this rock moving in the right way! If you were able to solve it, then compare your code to mine, I would bet big money we didn't do it the same way. There are several ways we could solve this, each one with its own strengths and weaknesses. I am going to solve this under the assumption that there could be a range of zero to any number of rocks in any given level. That means we must have a system for accessing the rock nearest us and not any other. We must also not try to access a rock if one doesn't exist.

And, wouldn't you know it, GameMaker has a handy function for getting an instance based on where it's at in relation to another instance. The function we want to use right now is called instance_nearest, and it gets the closest object to the one calling the code. We can use this function to only touch the rock closest to us, and check against what it returns to see if there are any rocks at all! The function takes three arguments, x, y, and obj. The x and y we'll use are our own coordinates, since we want the rock closest to our player, and the object will be the rock.

If you open the manual **(Figure 13.0)** for this function you can see it returns the instance ID or the keyword noone. So, the plan is to call this function and save the result in a local variable and use it to determine collisions. Create a local variable named rock and save the result of the function call **(Figure 13.1)**. Do this outside of our if statement we created yesterday, as we'll want to check this in both the if and else portion. Delete our other assignment of rock.

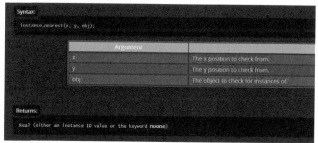

Figure 13.0 Instance_nearest Function Docs

```
53  var rock = instance_nearest(x, y, objRock);
```
Figure 13.1 Saving Rock

```
58  else {
59      if (rock != noone) {
60          rock.xSpeed = 0;
61      }
62  }
```
Figure 13.2 Else Code

Now, inside of the else statement we need to check if our variable of rock does not equal noone, and if that's true, then we set the rock's xSpeed to 0 (**Figure 13.2**). We must check if rock is a valid instance, because if it isn't and we try to access its data then our game will crash. Checking rock against noone ensures we only modify it if it exists. Run your game and try it out. The rock now moves only while we are colliding with it, and you can add more rocks or remove them all and it works. Of course, it's not working exactly how we want yet, but we're getting close.

The next step is to slow down the player's movement when they're colliding with the rock. This way we'll move at the same pace as the rock. In the if check after we set the rock's xSpeed, set the player's xSpeed to match (**Figure 13.3**). Then Pinky will look like she's pushing against the rock and won't move through it, at least until it hits a stone. It's looking better! Remember how I mentioned we had a pushing animation for Pinky? Let's bring that in and set it while we're colliding with the rock, it will look ten times better.

Figure 13.4 Pushing the Rock

```
55  if (place_meeting(x + xSpeed, y, objRock) && (left || right)) {
56      rock.xSpeed = sign(xSpeed) / 2;
57      xSpeed = sign(xSpeed) / 2;
58  }
```
Figure 13.3 Slowing Down Pinky

Image Angle

Image angle controls the rotation of a sprite. This is a powerful built-in property. For more symmetrical sprites, like rocks and explosions, spinning them around can look nice and it doesn't require drawing any additional frames. When changing the image_angle, however, the mask_index also shifts so be wary of using it when also checking against collisions.

Navigate through Assets, Sprites, Pinky and find Pink_Monster_Push_6. Bring it into Pinky's folder in GameMaker and do the usual converting to frames and trimming down. Rename it to sprPinkyPush and find a good playback speed, I like 8 fps. When you're done, return to objPlayer's code of pushing the rock and, while Pinky's colliding with the rock, set her sprite_index field to sprPinkyPush. Now run your game and move the rock. It looks a lot better, yeah (**Figure 13.4**)?

The last big change we need to make is rolling the rock while we're moving it. To affect the angle of an image, we can use the built-in property of image_angle. The Image Angle of a sprite controls how rotated it is. It begins at 0 with the image looking how it does default, and each increase rotates it slightly counterclockwise. So, let's try to use this alteration while moving the rock to get it to spin.

After setting Pinky's xSpeed, increase the rock's image_angle by 1 each frame.

```
rock.image_angle += 1;
```

Run the game and let's see if it's working!

If you're pushing your rock to the right, then you'll need to decrease image_angle by 1 instead. In just a bit I'll show you how to get it working in either direction.

Woah hold up. What just happened? Pinky just went through the rock instead of pushing it **(Figure 13.5)**. The rock began to rotate on my screen, but not very much at all. What's going on now?

Figure 13.5 The Mask Changes

Advanced Drawing

Well, if you read the little description I put of image_angle you'll remember the note about how image_angle changes the collision mask of that object. So, when we increase the image_angle of the rock it changes the mask which in turn causes Pinky to not collide correctly and screws the entire process up. I wanted to show this to you because it's a mistake I've made many times and has caused me lots of headaches.

To really understand what it's doing though, let's get a visual representation of how the collision mask changes. Open up objRock and add a Draw event. This time don't add draw_self. Instead, we're going to draw the bounding box of the rock to watch it change as we rotate its image_angle. Use this code:

```
draw_rectangle(bbox_left, bbox_top, bbox_right, bbox_bottom, true);
```

The bbox properties are where the bounding boxes are in the level. You can draw each one with this function to see them in action. Now run the game again and you'll see just an outline of a square. Try to push it and watch what happens. The square grows and shrinks depending on how much you collide with it and where. Our code expects it to be directly in front of us, and when it grows, we're now inside of it causing issues.

So, instead what we want to do is give the rock the illusion of rotating without actually rotating the mask. We can do this with the function draw_sprite_ext, where ext stands for extended. It's a function with many arguments, giving you full control over every aspect of the sprite you draw, including rotation. With this function, let's draw our rock just like it was.

```
draw_sprite_ext(sprRock, 0, x, y, 1, 1, image_angle, c_white, 1);
```

The last two arguments are for the color, which you can blend different colors with sprites, and the alpha, or transparency. Setting the color to c_white will not blend the sprite, and 1 is at fully visible. If you run the game now, everything will look and act the same. But we can fix all our issues with one small change. Instead of modifying the image_angle itself, let's put a variable in for the rotation. That way the rock will still rotate, but the mask won't change and cause us problems.

In the create event for the rock, add a variable called angle and set it to zero. Then in the draw event, replace image_angle with that variable. And lastly, in objPlayer replace the increase of image_angle with the variable angle **(Figure 13.6)**. Now at last, it works!

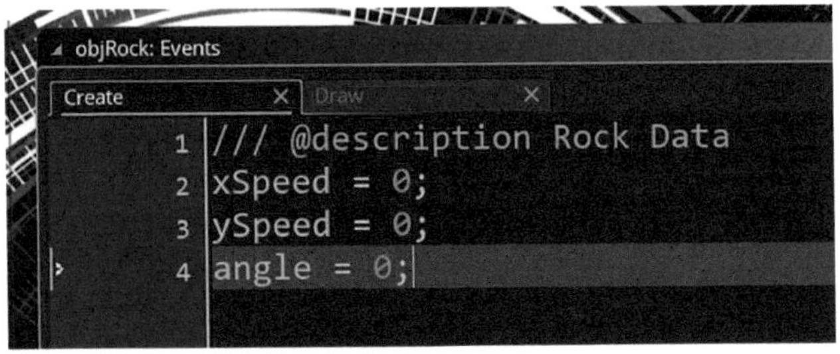

```
▲ objRock: Events
  Create          X   Draw          X
    1  /// @description Rock Data
    2  xSpeed = 0;
    3  ySpeed = 0;
  ▸ 4  angle = 0;
```

Figure 13.6 Part 1 Rotating the Rock

```
: Events
      X   Draw          X
    1  /// @description Drawing The Rock
    2  draw_sprite_ext(sprRock, 0, x, y, 1, 1, angle, c_white, 1);
```

Figure 13.6 Part 2 Rotating the Rock

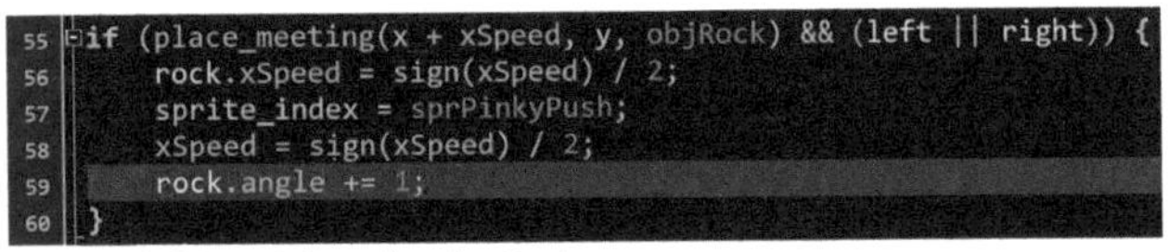

```
55  if (place_meeting(x + xSpeed, y, objRock) && (left || right)) {
56      rock.xSpeed = sign(xSpeed) / 2;
57      sprite_index = sprPinkyPush;
58      xSpeed = sign(xSpeed) / 2;
59      rock.angle += 1;
60  }
```

Figure 13.6 Part 3 Rotating the Rock

The only issue you may have found is that because we're increasing the angle it only works pushing the rock to the left. We can fix this by changing that line to instead decrease the angle by the sign of xSpeed. Do that and then it will rotate correctly whether you push it right or left **(Figure 13.7)**.

```
59      rock.angle -= sign(xSpeed);
```

Figure 13.7 Correct Rotation

Pulling the Rock

Now, depending on how you've set up your puzzle, you have probably run into the issue where you can push the rock into a stone that isn't the one holding the powerup. When that happens all, you can do is restart the game. That's not ideal in the slightest, at least not for our game. I do remember some puzzles in games that you could leave the room and it would reset, but that's not our goal here. The best way to fix this is to enable to player to pull rocks as well, enabling them to move the rock both ways.

The idea behind pulling is the same as pushing, except Pinky needs to look one way and move the opposite. This little detail creates a surprising amount of problems when coding. How do we know, with our code, which direction Pinky is facing? How can we tell if there's a rock right next to us? We have all the data and variables we need already, so let's put it into practice!

Underneath the code to push the rock, create another if check to see if there's a rock in front of the player. Inside here we want to check if we would collide with a rock 5 pixels in front of us, which we can determine based on our image_xscale. One is to the right; negative one is the left. And then if a key is being held, I've decided to use the tab key, but it doesn't matter which one. Then inside this if check we need to change our sprite and check if left or right is being pressed, and then execute code to pull the rock in the correct direction.

Now that's a huge coding challenge, so think about it for a few minutes. Check out my solution in **figure 13.8**. If you coded with just a check for left or right, then you probably repeated a lot of code. My goal is to eliminate redundant code, but it's also not a requirement. Many awesome games have sloppy code. When starting out, the goal is to create your game, not spend forever on writing the best code.

If Pinky changes sprites but then reverts when you press left or right, check your image_xscale and what you're

```
69    //Pull The Rock
70    if (place_meeting(x + (6 * -image_xscale), y, objRock) && keyboard_check(vk_tab)) {
71        sprite_index = sprites[hero][2];
72        if (left || right) {
73            xSpeed = sign(xSpeed) / 2;
74            rock.xSpeed = sign(xSpeed) / 2;
75            rock.angle -= sign(xSpeed);
76        }
77        if (left) {
78            image_xscale = 1;
79        }
80        else if (right) {
81            image_xscale = -1;
```

Figure 13.8 Pulling the Rock

setting it to. When going left it needs to be 1, when moving right it needs to be negative one.

Another glitch happens when we try to pull the rock and encounter a solid behind us. The player will continue to pull the rock on top of them, causing them the get stuck and unable to move. This looks odd and isn't what we want. The reason for it is we're setting the xSpeed of the rock based on our xSpeed before we do any collision checks. The quick way to fix this is to call CollideWith before the code to pull the rock. Just call the function there and it will work perfect.

And the last glitch I've discovered occurs when we've pushed the rock all the way against another solid and then try to pull it back. Doing this warps the player to the closest solid away from the rock, sometimes a rather large warp. The reason for this issue is when we pull the rock away from another solid, it gets pulled closer to us just a bit faster than expected because of its own collisions, causing it to collide with us. Then, because we're colliding, our horizontal collision kicks in, and because we're moving away from the rock, it warps us to the nearest solid in the direction we were just moving. To fix it, add an if check at the end of pulling the rock to see if we're colliding with the rock, and if so, move our x coordinate the amount of sign of xSpeed **(Figure 13.9)**. This code will only trigger the one time we're colliding with the rock, not the entire time we're pulling it.

```
108        //Prevent weird warping when pulling rock when it's up against a wall
109        if (place_meeting(x, y, objRock)) {
110            x += sign(xSpeed);
111        }
112    }
```

Figure 13.9 Final Glitch Fix

What Did I Inherit?

We've done a lot already, but we're missing a crucial piece of this entire puzzle: the ability to jump on the rock! Without that, being able to push the rock around is pointless. GameMaker has an awesome system called inheritance that we can use to make multiple

Inheritance

Inheritance is a programming paradigm in object-oriented languages. It allows one object to inherit the properties and code of another, sometimes explicitly, sometimes more as a promise. In GameMaker inheritance can be used to have one parent object and many children, such as a parent collision object with dozens of others inheriting that collision check.

objects share attributes. This is a huge part of programming languages, and a feature that is going to make your life so much easier!

Inheritance is a way to share code and properties among objects. The way we're going to use it now is to create a parent for collisions. We'll change our code to look for that parent and all its children. This allows us to use the same code we have; with only a slight modification of which object we're looking for. Many of the functions in GameMaker respect inheritance, such as when checking for a collision with a parent it will also check all the possible children, too.

It's a concept that's easier to understand with an example, so let's do that now. I would recommend you revert your code to how it was yesterday to avoid any unexpected errors. Once you've done that, let's create a new object. In the System folder, create another group called Parents and create the object inside of there, naming it objSolid-Parent. We'll have a couple of different parent objects in this game, so it makes sense to group them together. In that objects properties, click on the Parent button **(Figure 13.10)**.

This opens a new window labeled Parent. Inside you can select a parent for this object or set children of this object. We want to set its children, which can be done in a few different ways. The first is to click on the little plus circle and select objSolid **(Figure 13.11)**. objSolid then appears in the children section. Other methods for setting children are to

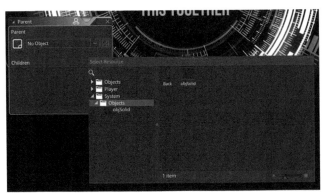

Figure 13.11 Selecting a Child

Figure 13.10 Parent Button

drag the object from the Asset Browser into the Children section or opening the Parent window in objSolid and selecting the parent from there. However, you do it, the result is the same: objSolid now has a parent! Choose one of those methods and add the rock as a child, too **(Figure 13.12)**.

But what does that do and how can we use it? The easiest way to show off the power of inheritance is to open the CollideWith function and replace all instances of objSolid with objSolidParent. With that simple change run the game and you'll now see that the rock reacts just like a solid! The function place_meeting is checking for objSolidParent and all of its children, so when it discovers any of them, it returns true.

There's no limit to the number of children an object can have, so using this system we can create a thousand different rocks, and other objects to jump and collide with barely any effort. GameMaker takes care of all of that for us. Awesome right? The other neat part of inheritance is the parents share code with their children.

To see that it in action, add a destroy event to objSolidParent, you don't need to add any code. Close the window for objRock and then re-open it (This is a small quirk in GameMaker), and you'll see the parents event in the child's event list **(Figure 13.13)**. If you double click on it, the event will open and show you what's inside, which is currently nothing. Also take note of the small lock icon on the tab of that event, indicating the code can't be altered from here, it can only be changed from the parent. Now we have a system of adding a score to our game where every enemy can increase it by just using the code from their parents destroy event.

Figure 13.12 Both Children

Figure 13.15 Powerup Placement

Figure 13.14 Inheriting Code

Figure 13.13 Parents Event

The possibilities are virtually endless when it comes to inheritance, and it's a system I use in every game and prototype I create. It speeds up production, saves time because you can share code among objects, and opens up new possibilities for how to interact with objects. The last thing I want to note about inheritance for now is that code doesn't have to be shared among related objects. Right click on that destroy event in objRock, and you'll notice we have several options **(Figure 1.4)**. We can inherit the event or override it, allowing us to make this object's event unique, or bring in our parents code and add some on top of it.

That ladder option is how I tend to design my enemies and objects in games. I set up all the variables, like health and movement speed, in the parent and then inherit that code into the enemy while also adding unique data on top of it. To inherit the code, you call the function event_inherited and then can run that objects specific code before or after it.

For now, though, we don't need to inherit any code. Return to objSolidParent and delete the destroy event.

Finishing the Puzzle

So now that we've got our rock that we can push, pull, and jump upon, let's move the powerup to the higher ledge. In this way it makes it obvious what they're supposed to do and sets up that this game will have puzzle elements throughout. I'm going to put it up just high enough that they player also needs to jump when they're on the ledge to reach it **(Figure 13.15)**. The reason for this is later we'll create a message box to display information to player, and it will pause everything in our game, and that effect will be a little cooler if the player is in mid-air.

Using More Keys

Right now, we only use four keys in our game, left, right, space, and tab. But already I've found myself pressing the up-arrow key to jump on many occasions. Perhaps you've tried to use the a and d keys to move left and right, as that's traditional in many games, too. In many games there are ways to set key binds within the menu, allowing for total customizability when it comes to control. Game-Maker also has this ability, but it goes beyond the scope of this beginner project. Instead, I want to show you a quick way to enable the use of more keys without writing a lot more code.

GameMaker has an awesome function called keyboard_set_map and it allows us to set all the code linked to one key, such as the space bar, and link it to the up-arrow key. Then GameMaker will check both keys and if either are pressed the code for jump will activate. Let's give it a try in the create event of objPlayer, since it only needs to be

```
10
11  //Keyboard Customization
12  keyboard_set_map(vk_up, vk_space);
13  keyboard_set_map(ord("A"), vk_left);
14  keyboard_set_map(ord("D"), vk_right);
15  keyboard_set_map(ord("W"), vk_space);
```

Figure 13.16 Multiple Keys

called once.

The function takes two arguments, and in my opinion, is one of the worst written argument names and manual entry in the entire manual. Personally, I have a difficult time discerning which key should go where, so I just put them in and test it out. I just did that in fact to ensure I would be telling you the right order. The first argument is the new key, and the second is the key the code is already written for, so to add the up-arrow key would look like this:

```
keyboard_set_map(vk_up, vk_space);
```

Add that into your game and then test it out. You can use the up arrow and the spacebar to jump. Now let's add the same for moving left, right, and jumping with the w, a, and d keys **(Figure 13.16)**. Later, we'll be adding in the ability to attack with the mouse, so the letter keys make more sense to set up as the primary key configuration. But this allows for variety and play choice, which players always appreciate.

One important side note is that this function specifically deals with the keyboard keys, it cannot map mouse keys. With a name like keyboard_set_map that might seem obvious, but I haven't found any other way to do mouse to keyboard mapping, or vice versa, with a simple function like this one. If that's your goal, then you'll need to come up with your own function.

Conclusion + Challenge

That's all for today! Parents are also an abstract concept to wrap your brain around, and I've found the more time given to process abstract ideas, the better. We'll continue to use parents and inheritance, and I want you to keep thinking about it and how the system can be used in the games you want to make.

The challenge for today is to come up with a real-world example of inheritance. Go beyond the simple example of you and your parents and dig deeper into what things out there share similarities. How much do they share? Is it to their benefit or detriment? Sometimes an inheritance can also be negative. Tweet me at Aaron_LLTT with what you find!

Day 14

More Heroes, More Data

Arrays!

Did you discover any interesting examples of inheritance? Either way, I hope thinking about it for a day helped solidify the idea for you. Now on to another powerful concept, although this one isn't as abstract, in my opinion.

Today we're discussing arrays. Arrays are a list that can be accessed via index, such as 0, 1, 2 or 3. In GameMaker they can hold any other kind of data type, such as integer, string, resource, and so forth. In many other languages, arrays are only able to hold one kind of data. We'll be implementing an array today to hold the different animations of all the fluffy heroes so we can bring in more characters. Arrays are one of the most useful and powerful tools at your disposal, but they can also be a little confusing at first, so let's break it down.

An array is a data type, just like the other ones we've seen in our game. They are also declared as a variable that we create. The main difference is an array can hold many pieces of data and are accessed with square brackets ([]) after the name of the variable. It looks like this:

```
playerInventory[0] = objHealthPotion;
```

The variable has a name, playerInventory, and it's holding onto data. Then the brackets and 0 indicate we're accessing the first entry in this array, as arrays start at zero. We then assign that index to hold a reference to objHealthPotion. How much it can hold depends on the language you're using, but in GameMaker it can hold tens of thousands of entries. I've never gone above a few hundred, but you can!

Arrays

Arrays are a powerful data type in all programming languages. They are like a list, where each item has an index that can be accessed by a number. They're great for storing long lists, and when combined with loops can do incredible things! Arrays begin counting at 0 and can never be negative.

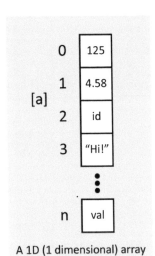

A 1D (1 dimensional) array
Example: array [3]= "Hi!"

Figure 14.0 1 Dimantion Arrays

	0	1	2	3	4
0	4	3	6	4	4
1	5	3	7	0	4
2	0	4	5	1	4
3	4	8	2	9	1
4	2	2	0	2	2

Figure 14.1 2 Dimention Arrays

The syntax for creating and using arrays is like what we've already been using, it's the idea of why we'd want to use and how to best utilize it that gets a little more complicated. Fortunately, I've got a great example ready for us to build that will show off the power of arrays! But before we get to it, let's talk multi-dimension arrays.

You can imagine an array, or more specifically, a 1-dimension array as a list **(Figure 14.0)**. Each item is in order, can be moved around, and you can put anything in there. I'll say it one more time since it's so important, array's begin at 0! So in the picture, the first item has an index of 0, and when you want to see what's inside that spot, you call the variable name followed by square brackets, and the number you're checking.

Now when it comes to 2-dimension arrays, imagine it like a list that's holding another list **(Figure 14.1)**. The syntax for that looks like:

```
playerInventory[0][0] = objHealthPotion;
```

See how it stacks? And it can go infinitely deep, although in practice I've only ever gone three layers deep. 1-dimension arrays are super useful in their own right, they can hold a hand of cards, the enemies to spawn in a game, the instructions for a script to execute and so forth. But 2-dimension arrays are where things really start to shine. With 2 dimensions, you can store huge amounts of information, like entire inventories, a list of every enemy in every level, and so forth.

What we're going to do is create a 2-dimension array that will hold all the sprites for each hero we can play as, and then set our sprite_index to the correct sprite based on who the player is currently. Let's give it a go!

More Fluffy Heroes!

There are two other fluffy heroes I want to bring into our game for the player to be. They've got the same sprites as Pinky, so it's just a matter of importing the sprites, converting them to frames, and naming them. Let's do that part first.

In the Sprites folder of Assets, locate Dude and Owlet, they have their own folders, just like Pinky. To save some time, I'm going to bring in their entire folders into the Player section in GameMaker **(Figure 14.2)**. There will be a lot of extras in here, some of which will be challenges for you to implement but having a little more is better than not having enough. Now it will have opened up windows for every single sprite we just brought in, so let me show you a little trick to decluttering the workspace. Right click on the top of any window and click 'Close All But This', and then close that window. Viola, all windows are now closed **(Figure 14.3)**.

Right now, we just need the same sprites we've already got, which are idle, walking, and pushing. Find those sprites in Dude and Owlet and get to work! Don't forget to set their speeds as well. Idle is at 9 fps, walk is at 10 fps, and push is at 8 fps. Be sure not to trim the heroes after converting them to frames, otherwise it will cause some weird issues. We want each frame to be 32x32 pixels, and trimming them would break that.

Figure 14.2 All the Heroes

Once you've got the rest of the sprites finished, we can start the process of being able to swap between heroes whenever we want. As we add more sprites, it will just be a matter of adding a few entries into an array. And speaking of that array, let's create it now. In the create event for objPlayer, create a new variable like this:

```
sprites[0][0] = sprPinkyWalk;
```

Figure 14.3 Choosing Windows

So, the first index of both dimensions holds the sprite for walking as Pinky. When working with 2d arrays it's important to decide how you'll view them in your head, because that's what the code is going to reflect. Examine **figure 14.4** for the two different ways to imagine the 2d array. Neither is more correct, but you don't want to confuse the two otherwise your code will not work correctly.

As for myself, I prefer to imagine the first index like x coordinate in a graph, and the second dimension as the y coordinate. So when I code the array to hold the sprites, the first index for all of Pinky's sprites will be 0, like so:

```
sprites[0][0] = sprPinkyWalk;

sprites[0][1] = sprPinkyIdle;

sprites[0][2] = sprPinkyPush;
```

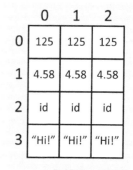

	0	1	2
0	125	125	125
1	4.58	4.58	4.58
2	id	id	id
3	"Hi!"	"Hi!"	"Hi!"

array[1][2] = 4.58
array[1][2] = id

Figure 14.4 Thinking about 2D Arrays

And then for the next fluffy hero, whichever one it is, will be accessed with 1 while keeping the second dimension the same for all the sprites **(Figure 14.5)**. Replicate this code for yourself now.

With all of that in place, we're close to being able to swap heroes. We need some way to know which hero the player has selected, so let's create a variable called hero and set it equal to zero. Then in the step event we're going to locate every time we set objPlayer's sprite_index and replace it with our 2d array. I know this may be a little confusing but follow along and you'll get there.

The first instance of changing objPlayer's sprite for me is on line 9 when the player moves left. Alter the code to now read this:

```
sprite_index = sprites[hero][0];
```

```
17  //Sprite Animations
18  sprites[0][0] = sprPinkyWalk;
19  sprites[0][1] = sprPinkyIdle;
20  sprites[0][2] = sprPinkyPush;
21
22  sprites[1][0] = sprDudeWalk;
23  sprites[1][1] = sprDudeIdle;
24  sprites[1][2] = sprDudePush;
25
26  sprites[2][0] = sprOwletWalk;
27  sprites[2][1] = sprOwletIdle;
28  sprites[2][2] = sprOwletPush;
```

Figure 14.5 Sprites Array

```
90  if (keyboard_check(ord("1"))) {
91      hero = 0;
92  }
93  else if (keyboard_check(ord("2"))) {
94      hero = 1;
95  }
96  else if (keyboard_check(ord("3"))) {
97      hero = 2;
98  }
```

Figure 14.6 Changing Hero

Let me explain how this line works. It first looks on the right-hand side at our array and fetches whatever's inside of it. Before it can do that though it needs to learn the value of our variable hero. Right now, it's 0, so GameMaker looks at the first index of both dimensions in sprites and sees that it's sprPinkyWalk, and then sets the sprite_index accordingly. When we change hero to a different number, it will find a different sprite to assign.

Now let's go through the rest of the step event and replace all the times we assign Pinky's sprites to fetching the value from our array. Remember that walking has a value of 1 in the second index and pushing has a value of 2.

Once you've finished that, the last thing to do is set up a way to change our hero variable. At the bottom of the step event, add some if checks for the numbers 1, 2, and 3. When 1 is pressed hero becomes 0, when 2 is pressed hero becomes 1, and when 3 is pressed hero becomes 2. Even though our array begins at zero, our system shouldn't as it would confuse most players. Instead we say 1 is the first player in the interface and set the code to 0.

Here's how I have it set up in **figure 14.6**. You could also use the keyboard events, but I prefer to put it all in the step event. With that last change our game is now ready

to run. Test it out and change heroes in the game. You'll find it works great!

This is why we created an object called objPlayer instead of objPinky in the beginning. It's better to have one object that can change sprites than multiple objects. It makes sharing data easier and switching simpler in the long run. Imagine having three player objects, ensuring the health and score was always the same would get tough.

Organizing Your Code

The last thing I want to introduce you to today is regions! Regions are a fantastic way of folding up code and organizing it so it's easier to read and find the specific section you're interested in down the road. I use them all the time to organize my projects.

Regions in GameMaker begin with the pound symbol followed immediately with the word region, like so:

```
#region
```

Everything after that keyword on that line is a comment, so you can label each region with what it is. Then go down a few lines and add this:

```
#endregion
```

Now you'll notice a minimize button appear on the line

```
12  #region Keyboard Customization
13  keyboard_set_map(vk_up, vk_space);
14  keyboard_set_map(ord("A"), vk_left);
15  keyboard_set_map(ord("D"), vk_right);
16  keyboard_set_map(ord("W"), vk_space);
17  #endregion
18
19  #region Sprite Animation Array
20  sprites[0][0] = sprPinkyWalk;
21  sprites[0][1] = sprPinkyIdle;
22  sprites[0][2] = sprPinkyPush;
23
24  sprites[1][0] = sprDudeWalk;
25  sprites[1][1] = sprDudeIdle;
26  sprites[1][2] = sprDudePush;
27
28  sprites[2][0] = sprOwletWalk;
29  sprites[2][1] = sprOwletIdle;
30  sprites[2][2] = sprOwletPush;
31  #endregion
```

Figure 14.7 Create Event with Regions

```
1   /// @description Player Logic
2
3   #region Keyboard Input
8
9   #region Walking && Running
40
41  #region Checking if player is on the ground
57
58  #region Rock Collisions
91
92  CollideWith();
93
94  x += xSpeed;
95  y += ySpeed;
96
97  #region Change Heroes
```

Figure 14.8 Step Event Folded Up

with the word region. Press this button and the code will fold up, leaving just the region line with your comment. I use this in the step events to organize input, movement, states, and so much more. It is a feature that was only added recently, but most other languages and IDE's have had it for years. It allows long events, like our step event, to be shrunk down and find what's important quickly and easily.

Let's go through our code now and add regions where they make sense, such as the sprites and variables in the create event, and collision checking in the step (Figure 14.7). If you've been adding comments to your code, you can probably just take that comment and use it for the region comment.

You'll probably now also notice those same little boxes on the if statements. They can also be collapsed! Here's how I folded up my code in the step event (Figure 14.8).

Conclusion + Challenge

Well that's arrays and a great way to use them. We'll continue to use arrays all over the place, so take some time and play with them a bit more. The challenge for today is to use arrays and discover some of their unique properties. I've already told you they start at 0 and can't be negative, but what else? What happens when you create an array and set index 10 to a value, but don't set the others? What if you try to access a value you haven't set yet?

Explore these ideas and hit me up on twitter if you have any questions!

Day 15

What State Are You In?

Arrays Once More, With Feeling

Yesterday I gave you the challenge of experimenting with arrays more. How did it go? I want to break down the properties of arrays one more time, as I don't think it can be done too often when starting out.

- Arrays are a data type, and are created just like any other variable
- Arrays begin at zero and cannot be negative
- Trying to access an index beyond what has been set will crash your game
- GameMaker sets any indices in an array to zero by default
- Arrays can hold any kind of data
- Arrays can be multiple dimensions

Some of these properties are specific to GameMaker, such as setting all indices to zero by default. Other languages may set it to null. Some languages also require a size when creating, but not GameMaker, they make it easy to use.

The reason I harp on this so much is arrays are the backbone of so many more complex structures in game dev and programming in general. We'll go over more uses for them, especially in conjunction with the for loop, but just know their power is nearly endless.

Time to Jump

There's still one more animation for our characters we need to add, the jump. Right now, we can jump in the game, but we don't change sprites at all. That's a little odd, so let's get that fixed. Our sprites have jump sprites already, but we're not going to use them as

Figure 15.0 Jumping Frames

they are. Instead, we're going to cut out just two frames from the jumping animation, and then set one for when we're going up, and one for going down.

The primary reason for this is creating an entire jump sequence is a little tricky and for our game unnecessary. We don't need a build up for the jump unless you want to have some kind of ability to jump higher after holding the jump button for a second. That's a cool idea, but not what we're aiming for. Maybe try that as a challenge.

First, let's find the rest of Pinky's animation's we'll be using and add them to her folder. Navigate to Assets, Sprites, Pinky. Then grab Attack1, Hurt, Jump, and Throw. We won't prepare all these sprites right now, but since we have all the other characters sprites already in our project, it makes sense to bring in Pinky's, too.

Now open the jump sprite and let's pick out the frames we want to use. Let's go ahead and convert it to frames to make it easier. Then keep only the 4th and 5th frames **(Figure 15.0)**. Repeat the process for Owlet and Dude and giving the sprites the appropriate names. Once that's complete, let's add the jump animation to our sprites array, making it the third index in the second dimension **(Figure 15.1)**.

```
19  #region Sprite Animation Array
20  sprites[0][0] = sprPinkyWalk;
21  sprites[0][1] = sprPinkyIdle;
22  sprites[0][2] = sprPinkyPush;
23  sprites[0][3] = sprPinkyJump;
24
25  sprites[1][0] = sprDudeWalk;
26  sprites[1][1] = sprDudeIdle;
27  sprites[1][2] = sprDudePush;
28  sprites[1][3] = sprDudeJump;
29
30  sprites[2][0] = sprOwletWalk;
31  sprites[2][1] = sprOwletIdle;
32  sprites[2][2] = sprOwletPush;
33  sprites[2][3] = sprOwletJump;
34  #endregion
```

Figure 15.1 Sprites Array with Jump

You may start wondering if there's a more memorable way of accessing the sprites array, because soon it will be a lot larger and difficult to know which index belongs to which sprite. And wouldn't you know it, there is! We can create a Macro to hold the name of our character and which sprite they're on. To make a macro, use the pound symbol (#) followed by the word macro, then give it a variable name and a value. But they don't use equal signs, and you can't add a semi-colon at the end. To create one looks like this:

> #macro Pinky 0

Figure 15.2 Macros

Macro

Macros are like variables; except they have hard-coded values that cannot be altered during the game. They're constant throughout your game, and are great for holding information that many objects need to access because they're global in scope.

Macros are a bit odd at first, and trying to use the traditional programming techniques, like assigning the value, will cause an error. Trying to change the value later will also cause a crash. So, with all the strangeness about them why would we use them? Well, they're global in scope which means any object or script can access them, and they initialize before the game begins, so even if we access a macro in the create event of our very first object, that value will be there. This is different compared to global variables.

GameMaker uses macros for many built-in constants as well, such as noone or undefined. We can do that same thing to make our array significantly easier to read. Let's add a few right before our sprites array and see how helpful they can be. Create macros for Pinky, Dude, and Owlet, setting their values to the first index of where their animations are at in the array. Then proceed to create macros for walk, idle, push, and jump, again setting their values to the second index of where the array has them located **(Figure 15.2)**.

Ignore the warnings for now, they're just saying we haven't used them anywhere yet. When I create macros, I capitalize them, the same thing I do for global variables. This is a normal convention when working with variables in a global scope, as it immediately identifies them as different from all other variables. You don't have to follow me in this practice, but I would suggest you do.

Next, replace all the numbers in our sprites array with the macros we just created. It will make the code a little longer, since we're using words and not numbers, but much more readable and easier to work with **(Figure 15.3)**. And then in the step event, do the same thing everywhere we're using the sprites array. Then run your game and see it in action. Granted, if it's working nothing will have changed in the gameplay itself, but it's still a good idea to test your game frequently when making coding changes.

```
28  #region Sprite Animation Array
29  sprites[Pinky][Walk] = sprPinkyWalk;
30  sprites[Pinky][Idle] = sprPinkyIdle;
31  sprites[Pinky][Push] = sprPinkyPush;
32  sprites[Pinky][Jump] = sprPinkyJump;
33
34  sprites[Dude][Walk] = sprDudeWalk;
35  sprites[Dude][Idle] = sprDudeIdle;
36  sprites[Dude][Push] = sprDudePush;
37  sprites[Dude][Jump] = sprDudeJump;
38
39  sprites[Owlet][Walk] = sprOwletWalk;
40  sprites[Owlet][Idle] = sprOwletIdle;
41  sprites[Owlet][Push] = sprOwletPush;
42  sprites[Owlet][Jump] = sprOwletJump;
43  #endregion
```

Figure 15.3 Sprites Array with Macros

And now finally, we can add in the jump sprite when we're jumping and falling. We can do this without needing to refer to our sprites array, because we know exactly which number is the jump sprite, it's our macro. With just four sprites, this can seem a little silly, but imagine a game with 50 different sprites and how much time it would save to be able to type out the sprite as a macro, instead of scrolling through a huge array every time.

When we press jump is where we want to change our sprite to the jumping animation, but only the first frame. So, let's set image_index to zero, and sprite_index to jump where we're checking for the space key **(Figure 15.4)**. Run the game and try jumping. It doesn't work, does it? The sprite changes for just one frame, then reverts to idle or the walk sprite if we're moving, even though we're in the air, clearly *not* being idle or just walking on the ground.

The issue right now is the rest of our animation code is overruling our jumping sprite. Look at where we're setting our player to change to idle. If we're *not* pressing left or right, the player changes to the idle sprite. This has no checks to see if we're in the air. Same goes for walking, at any time if we press left or right, the sprite will change. We need some additional checks before changing our player's sprite, such as if we're in the air or not.

```
66 ┌if (keyboard_check_pressed(vk_space) && jumpBuffer > 0) {
67 │    image_index = 0;
68 │    sprite_index = sprites[hero][Jump];
69 │    ySpeed = jumpSpeed * jumpPower;
70 │    jumpBuffer = 0;
71 └}
```
Figure 15.4 Jumping Sprite

Conclusion + Challenge

That's going to be your challenge for today. It's a little tougher of a challenge, but I think you're ready for it. But I won't leave you without any help. Use this line of code at the top of your step event:

```
var onSolid = place_meeting(x, y + 1,
objSolidParent) == true;
```

That checks if the player is on a solid object. With that line of code, you can then get your hero jumping properly. I'll leave my answer in tomorrow's beginning section, but I encourage you to fiddle around with it first. Try it for 20 minutes, then take a break and come at it again later. Many times, the secret to unraveling a problem is to let your brain sit on it a while and try again at another time.

So, get to it!

PRO TIP

What is programming?

John Watson
Developer of Gravity Ace

GravityAce.com

Let's start with what programming is not. It isn't memorizing magic words and the order they go on the screen. Programming isn't typing things into a computer. Rather, programming is a creative process by which you make a computer do what you want it to do. Every computer program solves a problem. And problem solving requires logic, planning, and the ability to break big problems down into smaller problems. In short, programming is thinking.

One of the most important skills in programming is the ability to think about how to solve a problem in the most basic terms. That's because computers only do exactly what you tell them to do. That requires breaking big problems down into a set of smaller problems or steps that you can solve one by one. Those steps often need to work in a particular order and later steps often depend on earlier steps. How those steps are performed does depend on the programming language you're using. But that's at the end of the process — the easy part. Figuring out the problem and how to solve it is the hard/creative part. From there it's just a matter of converting your thoughts into code. And let me tell you a secret: most programmers "cheat". I've been a professional coder my entire career. I'm very good at it. And I search the internet for solutions and code snippets all day long.

Now, it is true that learning a computer programming language is necessary. But don't think of it like learning a spoken human language. Programming languages only have a few tens of words and the syntax is usually very simple and regular. But knowing the syntax and vocabulary of the language you are using won't help you at all if you don't know what you are trying to say. You've got to solve the problem logically in your mind first. Typing it in is just a way of validating your thought process.

Day 16

Enemies

Challenge Review

I left you with a big challenge yesterday, to get the animations transitioning correctly when jumping, idle, and walking. **Figure's 16.0** and **16.1** show my code and my solution. Wherever I'm setting the sprite_index of objPlayer, I first check if they're on the ground, and if so, they can change to idle or walking. Then, if they're in the air, I keep the image_index set to either 1 or 0 depending on if they're going up or down.

```
49  #region Checking if player is on the ground
50  if (onSolid) {
51      y = round(y); //Prevents hovering or dipping into a solid
52      ySpeed = 0;
53      jumpBuffer = maxJumpBuffer;
54  }
```
Figure 16.0 Checking if on Solid

The other problem is when we're checking if the player is on the ground, where we're setting ySpeed to zero and rounding our y, that if check is only looking at objSolid. We can alter the object it's looking for, or just use our local variable, onSolid, which is what I'm going to do **(Figure 16.2)**.

The only issue that you might encounter with my system, and possibly yours, is when colliding with the rock. So far, all our rocks have been on the ground, that's the way we have it set up. But if you ever created a floating rock, or some other object that can be pushed, it would prioritize the pushing sprite over the jumping one. To fix that, move the pushing and pulling of the rock code above the jumping code. However, this won't be a problem for the game I'm making, so I won't worry about it. But I thought you should know; in case you go further with Fluffy Heroes.

```
 9   var onSolid = place_meeting(x, y + 1, objSolidParent) == true;
10
11  #region Walking && Running
12  if (left) {
13      if (onSolid) {
14          sprite_index = sprites[hero][Walk];
15      }
16      image_xscale = -1;
17      xSpeed = -walkSpeed;
18  }
19  if (right) {
20      if (onSolid) {
21          sprite_index = sprites[hero][Walk];
22      }
23      image_xscale = 1;
24      xSpeed = walkSpeed;
25  }
26
27  //Sprinting
28  if (run) {
29      image_speed = 1.5;
30      if (left) {
31          xSpeed = -walkSpeed * 2;
32      }
33      if (right) {
34          xSpeed = walkSpeed * 2;
```

Figure 16.1 Part 1 Correct Jumping Animations

```
40  if (!left && !right) {
41      if (onSolid) {
42          sprite_index = sprites[hero][Idle];
43      }
44      xSpeed = 0;
45      alarm[0] = 1;
46  }
47  #endregion
48
49  #region Checking if player is on the ground
50  if (place_meeting(x, y + 1, objSolid) == true) {
51      y = round(y); //Prevents hovering or dipping into a solid
52      ySpeed = 0;
53      jumpBuffer = maxJumpBuffer;
54  }
55  else { //Applying gravity while player is in the air
56      ySpeed += gameGravity;
57      jumpBuffer -= 1;
58      //Sets the jump sprite when jumping or falling
59      if (ySpeed > 0) {
60          image_index = 1;
61      }
62      else {
63          image_index = 0;
64      }
65  }
```

Figure 16.2 Part 2 Correct Jumping Animations

Remember, whether you solved the puzzle alone, with some help, or by copying my code, it's about the effort you made. If you're not trying to do this, if you're not getting a little frustrated now and then, you won't remember the code you're writing near as well. Game dev and programming isn't inherently frustrating, but it often is anyway, and that's ok. Take a break, let your brain break down the problem in the background while you do other things. The next time you try it, you'll be surprised how easily it comes to you.

The First Bad Guy

Artificial Intelligence

Artificial Intelligence is the logic computers use to pretend to think. AI can be very complex, such as machine learning, or very simple, like goombas from Mario. Any computer-controlled object that reacts to stimuli has artificial intelligence, and in video games, that AI should prioritize fun and challenge for the player.

Today's topic is going to be enemies and their logic, or Artificial Intelligence. AI (artificial intelligence) is one of my favorite topics, as I find it fascinating, not just in video games, but in every realm it touches. Video game AI is a unique field of AI, as you don't want the enemy, or even the ally's, to be truly intelligent. Imagine a game villain that knows where you always are, knows instantly what button you press, and can dodge every attack you throw because it has lightning fast reflexes. People would drop that game like a hot potato!

Instead, the goal with video game AI is to create the illusion of intelligence by limiting what the computer knows, how fast they can respond, and above all, make it enjoyable for the player. If your game is supposed to be challenging, then the enemy can be tough. But, if your game's goal is a fun party time with friends, the AI should be simpler and play into that theme. It's up to you, as the designer, to match the AI to the game.

With that little spiel out of the way, let's bring in our first, and only, enemy! You can find our enemy in the Assets folder under Sprites, Enemy. I chose this enemy because it fits our look and style, but also because its sprite sheet looks a lot different than the ones we've been using. If you recall, I've mentioned how sprite sheets can come in many different shapes and sizes, some good, some terrible. This one falls in the middle. It's evenly spaced, but it's all one long line which isn't very convenient. The walk animation is also separated, if you want to use the individual images to make that sprite.

The way I'm going to do it now is bring in the sprite sheet, and duplicate it three times, so we'll have the sprite sheet the number of different animations for the enemy.. But first, let's create a new folder called Enemy's and inside that a folder called Biter. To duplicate an asset in GameMaker, press Ctrl+D or Cmd+D, or right click and duplicate.

Don't forget, on these sprites we're creating from the sprite sheet, don't trim them down otherwise you'll have problems. We'll alter the collision masks to ensure they're fair, but if you trim them down, the origins of one may be different than another, so when transition from walking to attacking, it will warp in a weird way, causing glitches. A little excess space on a sprite doesn't hurt anything, so long as the collision mask is set appropriately.

The first animation we want is idle, which is the first 10 frames of the sprite sheet. It's 32x32 pixels, so just bring in the first 8 frames and rename it to sprBiterIdle. Change the fps to 10 and it's all done.

Next is walking, which is 8 frames and begins immediately after the last idle frame. To ensure we have the same frame sizes for our enemy, change the Horizontal Pixel Offset to 320 **(Figure 16.3)** and it will begin at the right spot. Change the amount to bring in to 8 and the fps to 10. Rename it to sprBiterWalk.

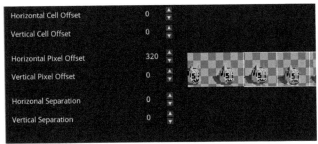

Figure 16.3 Changing Horizontal Pixel Offset

The attack animation begins at 576 pixels offset and has 9 frames. Change this animation to 10 fps as well and rename it to sprBiterAttack. And the last animation is biter getting hit, which begins at 864 and has three frames, although selecting more frames than there is sprite sheet doesn't do anything at all. Change the fps of this animation to 10 and rename it to sprBiterHurt.

With the sprites created, we now need the enemy object. We could take the same approach as we did for the player and have one enemy object, but I don't think that's a good idea. Enemys tend to vary greatly from one another, which is what makes it fun to play against them, which means their code will be vastly different. It's possible to create one enemy object and have different sections of code based on which sprite it's wearing, but that will be more work than it's worth. Objects are cheap, in terms of memory and processing power, so it has zero impact on our game by having a few dozen, or even hundred,

different objects.

In the Enemy's folder, create an object called objBiter and assign the idle sprite to it. The goal with biter is to have a roaming enemy that, when it sees the player, will charge at them and attack when it's close enough. After attacking it will resume it's walking until it spots the player again. It's a simple system but it will cover the basics of creating an AI that can be used in all future enemies.

The Enemy's Logic

When designing the AI for something, in this case Biter, remember you must tell it what and how to do everything. Nothing will be built-in, there is nothing so obvious you don't have to code it. If biter is walking and there's a ledge, unless you tell him to turn around, he'll continue walking right off the ledge. Just as in coding for the player, we must come up with every situation biter can be in, and how he should respond.

So, the first thing we'll do is have biter be idle. Let's add a Create event and a Step event to biter. In the Create event, add the variables we need to have biter be able to move, such as moveSpeed, xSpeed, and an idleTimer that we can use a timer **(Figure 16.4)**. The values in these variables are yours to set, use mine as a baseline. If you want your enemy to be more sporadic, lower the idle timer. If you want him to be a quick little biter, ramp up that moveSpeed variable. These little changes can make each enemy feel different, offering unique challenges to the player.

I would encourage you not to just change the color of biter and spawn multiple enemies with only slightly different traits. Players quickly see through this strategy and will then be more likely to drop your game in favor of one that did take the time to make unique enemies. Each encounter should offer something new for the player.

```
/// @description Biter's Data
moveSpeed = .75;
xSpeed = 0;
idleTimer = 90;
```

Figure 16.4 Biter's Data

Now, move into the step event and let's set up a countdown for biter, that when it ends it will begin wandering around. There are two ways we can do this: the first is to set an alarm equal to idleTimer, and when it triggers to have it change a Boolean in biter. The second is to manually decrease idleTimer in the step event and check when it reaches zero, and then perform some new chunk of code. Neither one is right nor wrong, it mostly depends on your preference.

Personally, I like to have total control over what my code is doing, and if I set up the idleTimer to decrease in the step event, I can easily pause it and check where it's at. Of course, you can also do that with an alarm, so again, choose which way you prefer. The deeper you get into programming, the more you'll discover there are dozens of ways to perform the same action. Many are almost the same, with one maybe being easier to use, one being faster, and the other offering some other kind of benefit. All of that to say, do what works for you!

My code looks like this:

```
idleTimer -= 1;

if (idleTimer <= 0) {

xSpeed = moveSpeed * choose(1, -1);

}

x += xSpeed;
```

I decrease the idleTimer by 1 until it's at zero, then I set the xSpeed to either positive or negative and biter will begin to move. The choose function selects one of the options inside of its brackets. You can put in as many arguments as you want, and the arguments can be anything, not just numbers.

If we run the game now we'll find that after the timer reaches zero, biter begins to move. However, the if statement will be forever triggering because the timer is still at or below zero, so biter wiggles back and forth, sometimes going further one direction than another, but clearly not moving the way we intended.

The solution for this would be to add some more if statements to only select a direction if one hasn't been selected, or possibly reset idleTimer back to its original value after a direction has been chosen. Whatever the case is, it will need several if checks to work properly, and this is only the idle code. When we add in movement, charging, attacking, taking damage, and dying it will become exceedingly difficult to read or get biter to do exactly what we want. We need a better solution.

And that's where a state machine comes in! What is a state machine? You'll find out tomorrow!

Conclusion + Challenge

Before I introduce you to state machines, I want you to try your hand at creating biter's AI with just the knowledge you have now. It isn't impossible, and you may be able to figure out some elegant solutions that I haven't thought of. Either way, it will be a good exercise to try using the tools you know to create something complex. Because then when I show you a more advanced tool, you'll really appreciate its power.

It's a little like power tools vs hand tools. If you never struggle with the hand tools, you'll never appreciate the power ones. So go struggle a bit, and tomorrow I'll change your life.

Day 17

Let's Switch States!

Reviewing Biter's AI

Well, how did creating your first enemy AI end up? I'm curious to see what you made and how well it worked, so send me some snapshots or a video of your enemy on Twitter @ Aaron_LLTT.

My guess is it got complex and difficult to sustain, and the idea of adding in more behaviors didn't sound appealing. That's not what we want when designing. It needs to be flexible, and able to adapt to new ideas. Game dev is all about experimentation, following the fun, and reacting to surprising bugs and glitches. If any of our objects is so complex it can't be tweaked on the fly, there's something wrong with it (at least in smaller projects).

The Mythical State Machine

Now onto State Machines. State machines are only one of many different, and equally viable, methods of creating AI. They're a little stiff in the sense that we'll still be coding exactly what they should do, just limiting what they're allowed to do by the state they're in.

Think of a state as a current way of being. What state are you in right now? You're probably sitting down, with a computer in front of you, maybe a drink or snack off to the side. That state you're in would be focused or studying. In this state you can read, listen to music, talk to someone next to you, etc... To leave your state you might stand up and shut your computer, moving into a more active state where you exercise, or go drive to visit a friend. Human states are a little more fluid, as we're capable of doing so many things wherever we are, but when it comes to AI the states will be much more fixed.

We want biter to start out being idle, which we'll be making into a state. Another state will be patrolling. While in idle, biter can listen for queues that can change him to patrolling,

> ## State Machines
>
> *A state machine, also known as a finite state machine, is a layer of abstraction used to create a complex set of behaviors. It's finite because there is a limit to how many states it can have, although you'll never reach that maximum number. In games, it's used for players, enemies, allies, and more, to limit the code that can run to only the appropriate state, such as walking, or death.*

Enum

Enum, or enumerator, are constants like macros. The difference is they can only hold numbers as values, and there can be many values connected to one enum. They're useful for state machines, or in other systems where you need a range of values that are all connected and are easier to type out with auto complete.

such as the timer reaching zero or spotting the enemy, and he can change into the hurt state if he's attacked. Each of these queues we'll program into the state, creating a transition from one to the next. In that transition we can execute code that triggers only once, solving the problem we ran into yesterday.

State machines are awesome, and we're going to use them both in biter and in our player as we add in more code, but they're just one tool. There are more advanced methods of creating AI, but the bigger tool isn't always the best. You don't need an industrial jackhammer to snap a twig in two, that would be overkill. The same principal applies to programming and game dev, use the right tool for the job, not the most fancy or powerful.

The first part of the state machine we'll create are the different states. We'll do this by using enum's. An Enum stands for enumerator, and it's a way to create our own data type consisting of integers. We'll be using them to switch between the logic in our enemy. Here's how you create an enum:

```
enum EnemyState {

idle,

walking

}
```

The values of idle and walk are 0 and 1, respectively, because enum's always begin at 0. You can manually set the value by assigning it a number, but for our state machine there's no need. If you try to use the variable Idle, with a capital I, it will produce an error because Idle is a macro we already have which doesn't contain an integer value. Enum's are pre-compiled and global in scope, which means we only need to write them once to use everywhere.

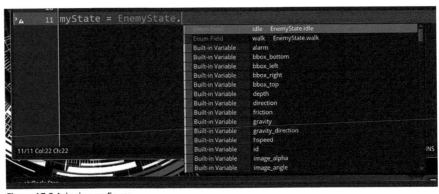

Figure 17.0 Asigning an Enum

To use an enum, you type out the name of the enum, which is EnemyState, and use the period to begin the auto complete functionality and find the specific enum you want **(Figure 17.0)**. Open objBiter's create event and create the enum from before, and create a variable called myState and assign it to EnemyState.idle. This will be the beginning state for our enemy, and while they're in the idle state, only their idle code will run.

Then add the rest of the states we'll be using for our enemy, and those are: charging, attacking, damaged, and dead. That's all we need to do in the create event for now, so let's move to the step event and begin creating our state machine.

Using A State Machine

There are two ways of selecting different paths in Game-Maker, and that's using an if check, which we've done many times now, and the Switch Statement. They are remarkably similar in functionality, but do look different, and the switch statement has a hidden superpower as well. The primary reason I want to introduce you to switch statements now is they'll help our state machine look better, which in turn makes it easier to read and edit as it grows. It's also good to know they exist, because many programmers prefer one over the other, so to fully prepare you for the real world, you need to know how to read and write them.

Switch Statement

The switch statement is similar to the if / else checks we've been doing, but do hold a few key differences. The first difference is, the checks are compared against a value, such as the enum we've created, not a statement like someVar == 5. Second, multiple parts of a switch can execute together, giving it a little more power and flexibility than if / else.

The syntax of a switch statement looks like this:

```
switch (myState) {

case EnemyState.idle:

//Code goes here

break;

}
```

Error Help

There are a lot of ways to make a mistake in a switch statement, so be patient when starting out with them. Here's what to double check when using switch's:

- Use a colon, not a semi-colon at the end of the case

- Don't forget the break at the end of the case, otherwise you may have multiple cases trigger simultaneously

- Don't try to use curly brackets in the case code like in if checks, it all goes between the colon and break (you can of course use curly brackets inside there, such as in if checks or other things)

When the game comes to the switch statement it will get the value of the variable it's checking against, in this case myState, and then check each of its cases for a match. When it finds a match, it will execute the code inside, then continue looking for more matches. That code inside ends at the break statement, so if our state was idle and we forgot the break, it would execute the idle code *and* all code after idle until it found a break. There's a lot of ways to use that power effectively, but it can also cause big issues if you forget the break keyword. That's why I almost always type out the case and the break at the same time, to avoid that future error.

Let's move our current idle code into the case for being idle **(Figure 17.1)**. If we run this now, nothing will have changed, and the biter will still behave super oddly. But now we're in a place to fix that behavior rather easily. In the if check on line 7, we can now add a line of code that changes the variable myState to walking, since biter is now done being idle. That will make the if check only execute one time, since after it leaves this chunk of code, it won't come back to it because it's in a new state **(Figure 17.2)**.

```
 3  switch (myState) {
 4      case EnemyState.idle:
 5          idleTimer -= 1;
 6          if (idleTimer <= 0) {
 7              xSpeed = moveSpeed * choose(1, -1);
 8          }
 9
10          x += xSpeed;
11      break;
12  }
```
Figure 17.1 Idle Case

```
if (idleTimer <= 0) {
    xSpeed = moveSpeed * choose(1, -1);
    myState = EnemyState.walking;
}
```
Figure 17.2 Changing States

Now let's create the walking case inside our switch statement. Take the x += xSpeed code from the idle state and put it in the walking case, as we don't want biter to be moving while in idle anyway **(Figure 17.3)**.

```
11      case EnemyState.walking:
12          x += xSpeed;
13      break;
```
Figure 17.3 Walking State

When it comes to where to put the cases and how to separate them, it's all up to you. You can have lines between each case, you can put the cases in the switch statement in any order, they'll still work correctly. What I prefer to do is use regions inside of my switch statement to allow for easy collapsing, because the states can grow large very quickly **(Figure 17.4)**. Try using regions and see how you feel about them. Whatever you decide, just stick to it wherever you use state machines to make it easy to navigate them.

```
 3  switch (myState) {
 4      #region Idle State
13      #region Walking State
14      case EnemyState.walking:
15          x += xSpeed;
16      break;
17      #endregion
18  }
```
Figure 17.4 Switch Statement with Regions

Try running the game now and you'll find biter transitions into the walking state from idle exactly as we want. The only thing is his sprite remains as idle, not walking. Where do you think the best place is to fix that issue? Because changing the sprite for biter is something that only needs done *once* it's best to do it immediately before changing states. So, return to the if check where we change states, and somewhere in there change the sprite for biter to sprBiterWalk. This way our code is not running more than it needs to, and our sprite will be changed right as biter begins to walk. But don't forget to also change his image_xscale to match his moveSpeed, or he'll be doing a moon walk half the time.

Conclusion + Challenge

Biter's logic in the walk state needs a lot of work, as he'll currently move through any solid object and ignore the player, but it's a good start. Hopefully now you can see the power and benefit of using a state machine. It logically separates our code, only runs the appropriate logic for the state, and provides an easy way to execute code only once when moving from state to state. The difficult part is ensuring you've got all your transitions covered in each state, but that comes with practice and testing.

Today's challenge is to wrap up the state machine cases for biter, and to try your hand at implementing the logic to keep him from walking through walls and off cliffs. What I mean by wrapping up the state machine cases is not to code everything, just add the remaining cases to the switch statement and wrap each one in its own region, so we can jump between them easier in the future **(Figure 17.5)**.

```
 3  switch (myState) {
 4      #region Idle State
15      #region Walking State
20      #region Charging State
25      #region Attacking State
30      #region Damaged State
35      #region Dead State
40  }
```

Figure 17.5 Organized Switch Statement

And as for the correct collision challenge, remember you've already got a script checking for collisions in the player. Can you re-use that, or modify it, to fit our enemy? Give it a shot and see what you can do.

Day 18

Building a Better Biter

Challenge Review

How's biter looking in your game? Is he functioning properly and working the way you want? If not, do you have an idea as to why? If you've got the collisions working as expected, then check your code against mine and see how it differs or is similar. If your code isn't working then delete it and follow along, I'm sure you'll see what went wrong and how to fix it after today.

Getting Biter on the Ground

The first thing I want to do is ensure this enemy is always on the ground. Biter won't be jumping anywhere; all he's doing is patrolling the ground he can already access. It sounds boring, but it's important to start simple and work up to more complex enemies. With that in mind, we should add a check outside of biter's state machine to see if he's on the ground, and if not to set him there. The reason we'd want to put this outside the state machine is it should happen no matter the state he's in. It also makes spawning biter's in while the game is running easier, because then you just need to spawn them in above any solid object, and it will automatically put them where they should be.

So, above our state machine, add a while loop that checks if biter is on a solid or not, and if he's not then move him down until he is. If you put biter in a place where there is no solid underneath, this could cause issues. To fix that, you can either always be sure to spawn them in correctly, destroy biter if there's no ground underneath, or do a little more work and find the nearest solid even if it's to the side. Let's walk through those options.

The first option, to always spawn biter in the correct place, would require checking if there's a solid underneath where you want to spawn biter. And since we're not dynamically spawning him, I'll leave that one for you to figure out when the time comes.

The second option of destroying biter would be the easiest if there wasn't a weird programming issue where you can't destroy an instance while it's running a while loop. In **figure 18.0**, I have the code to find the next solid underneath biter, and if there is no solid, it destroys him. The weird catch is you *must* have that break keyword in that if statement, otherwise the while loop will continue forever, and it won't destroy the instance. That's something I had to figure out as I was writing this, which just goes to show there's always more to learn.

```
3   while(place_meeting(x, y + 1, objSolidParent) == false) {
4       y += 1;
5       if (y > room_height) {
6           instance_destroy();
7           break;
8       }
9   }
```

Figure 18.0 Destroying Biter

The third option of finding the nearest solid, even if it's off the side, can be done with the function instance_nearest. This function returns the instance id of the object closest to the x and y that you pass in. The function is simple, but to get biter in the correct spot is a little tricker, because you   must account for the different sizes and offsets of both biter and the ground. The code I got to work is in **figure 18.1**. It sets biter in the middle of whatever solid is closest, accounting for the height of that solid and the height of biter. Remember both those origins are in the center, so dividing by half gets us the correct amount to move up.

```
12  //Locates nearest solid and gets set there
13  if (place_meeting(x, y + 1, objSolidParent) == false) {
14      var ground = instance_nearest(x, y, objSolidParent);
15      x = ground.x;
16      y = ground.y - ground.sprite_height / 2 - sprite_height / 2;
17  }
```

Figure 18.1 Locating Closest Solid

Whichever of the three methods you choose is fine by me. You may not even need one if you set every biter in the game by hand, ensuring they're already on the ground. I just wanted to show this to you to open up more options in designing this game. I'm going to leave my code where it finds the nearest solid and sets biter there, as I think it's the most versatile option.

The Walk State

Now let's move into the walking state so we can get biter colliding with walls and responding to ledges. I had suggested that you could use the CollideWith script yesterday, but if you attempted that you would have encountered some errors. Biter has no ySpeed variable, so it can't be used with him. And that's fine! Not every script we write will be compatible with every object we have, there are many times you'll need to write a custom function for something.

In this case, we want to write some code that will check if there's either a solid in front of us, or a ledge, and in either case turn around and walk the other way. Since we've only got this one enemy, let's go ahead and write the code in the walk state itself, instead of a function. If you add more enemies, you'll be able to pull this code out and create a function for multiple enemies to access, but right now that's a bit overkill.

In the walk state create two local variables called atLedge and atSolid. The atLedge variable will look like this:

```
var atLedge = place_meeting(x +
sign(xSpeed) + 16, y + 1, objSolidPar
ent) == false;
```

This variable checks if there's a solid 16 pixels out in front of the way biter's walking and compares it to false. That last part is helpful, because we can now call atLedge and it will be true if we're on a ledge, and false if we're not, making it easier to read and write those if statements. The reason for the 16 pixels is that it's half the width of biter's sprite, so when he's halfway off the ledge with his bounding box it will turn around. That looks much more natural than all the way off the ledge, plus if you kept the code for placing biter on the nearest solid, only checking one pixel it will cause him to warp back to the center of the nearest solid. But it's almost always better to use built-in values over hard-coded numbers, so in this case replace the 16 with sprite_width / 2. This way, if you re-use the code on another enemy, or change biter's sprite size, it will still always look good.

And the reason we can use sprite_width like this is because when changing image_xscale, sprite_width changes from a positive value to a negative value. If it didn't do that, we'd have issues where it's always adding either positive or negative.

Now underneath this variable we can write an if check to see if biter's at a ledge, and if so, then change directions **(Figure 18.2)**. I really like how this if check reads like a normal sentence, which happens because we named it atLedge, and because that variable already holds a true or false. This is purely a preference thing, but it's one I'd recommend continuing as it adds to the readability of your code for yourself and others.

```
32      case EnemyState.walking:
33          var atLedge = place_meeting(x + sign(xSpeed) + sprite_width / 2, y + 1, objSolidParent) == false;
34          if (atLedge) {
35              xSpeed *= -1;
36              image_xscale *= -1;
37          }
38          x += xSpeed;
39      break;
```

Figure 18.2 Changing Directions at a Ledge

The other thing we must check against is if biter will run into a solid object, and if so, reverse course yet again. Try writing that code out yourself, just like how we did atLedge. You can even use the same if statement, just add an or check in there against your new Boolean variable. Check out my code in **figure 18.3**.

```
34          var atSolid = place_meeting(x + sign(xSpeed) * 6, y, objSolidParent) == true;
35          if (atLedge || atSolid) {
36              xSpeed *= -1;
37              image_xscale *= -1;
38          }
```

Figure 18.3 At Solid

Does your code look like mine? Perhaps the only difference is that times 6 I have. I know I was *just* talking about not hard coding in numbers, but there are also times when you should do it. That 6 is there for two reasons:

Firstly, if you don't add a little bit of wiggle room biter gets stuck in the solid when turning around. Secondly, it *looks* better at 6 than any other number I tried. And that's the key difference, it's a number that looks good only on biter. If we were to create a script for other enemies, I would make that number an argument you could pass in to get each enemy looking their best when colliding with a wall. When dealing with looks and how something feels, it's fine to use hard coded values, because those values are only for that object and should be unique to it.

I'm Done Walking

So, we're not totally done with the walk state yet, but we're getting close. The next thing to work out is which other states can biter move into from walk. The ones that make the most sense to me are idle, charging, and damaged. Biter can return to idle after walking for a while, or begin charging if he see's the player, or take damage if the player attacks him).

Let's first tackle returning to the idle state. We need another timer to know when to return to idle. We could use the idleTimer variable we already have, but I think it would be more interesting if it was a new random value each time biter began walking. So, create a walkTimer in the create event and set it between 100 and 200 using the function random_range. Each time we enter the walk state from idle, we want to set this value once again, so do that when transition from idle to walk. Then in the walk state, decrease the timer just as in idle, and when it reaches zero return to the idle state **(Figure 18.4)**.

```
21    case EnemyState.idle:
22        //Reduce timer to change to walking state
23        idleTimer -= 1;
24        if (idleTimer <= 0) {
25            xSpeed = moveSpeed * choose(1, -1);
26            myState = EnemyState.walking;
27            sprite_index = sprBiterWalk;
28            image_xscale = xSpeed;
29            walkTimer = random_range(100, 200);
30        }
31    break;
32    #endregion
33    #region Walking State
34    case EnemyState.walking:
35        //Reduce timer to return to idle state
36        walkTimer -= 1;
37        if (walkTimer <= 0) {
38            myState = EnemyState.idle;
39            sprite_index = sprBiterIdle;
40        }
41
42        //Reverse direction when at a ledge or a solid
43        var atLedge = place_meeting(x + sign(xSpeed) + sprite_width / 2, y + 1, objSolidParent) == false;
44        var atSolid = place_meeting(x + sign(xSpeed) * 6, y, objSolidParent) == true;
45        if (atLedge || atSolid) {
46            xSpeed *= -1;
47            image_xscale *= -1;
48        }
49        x += xSpeed;
50    break;
51    #endregion
```

Figure 18.4 Walk to Idle Code

I recommend commenting the blocks of code that transition biter from one state to another. It really helps later when you want to add a feature or fix a bug to know exactly where the code is switching states.

Now try out your game and see if biter is transitioning states as expected. Depending on the random values you've got, you may see biter change direction mid stride, but you'll certainly see him not going idle. Now why's that? The reason is we haven't reset our idleTimer, so even though biter does go to the idle state, he comes out of one frame later, barely enough to notice. We can resolve this by resetting the idleTimer either when moving out of the idle state or moving into it. One way isn't necessarily better than the other, so just choose one and add that code in. I put mine in moving from walking to idle.

And now we've got a walking, idling biter! The last transition we'll setup today is moving to the charge state. For this I'm going to introduce you to some more advanced collision functionality in GameMaker.

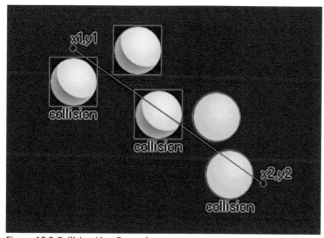

Figure 18.5 Collision Line Example

Advanced Collisions

Up until this point we've been using functions to check for collisions at one specific point, such as place_meeting. But what if we want to check a larger area, like a line or big circle? GameMaker has functions just for that!

The first function we'll explore is collision_line, a function that checks for a collision against an object in a straight line (when I say straight, I mean from point a to point b and the line could go diagonally, up or down, left to right) **(Figure 18.5)**. The collision_line function accepts 7 arguments, the first four are the x and y's of the line, and then the object you're looking for a collision with, whether you want it to be precise or not (usually we don't), and if we are excluding the instance calling the code. The last one is kind of confusing, but because the collision line can be anywhere in GameMaker, it could also overlap with the object that's calling it, and many times we don't want to include the object calling in that collision check, so there's an option to turn it on and off.

This function will return an instance or the keyword noone, which makes for an easy check: if it's noone then it didn't find the player. What we're going to do is use this line as a line of vision, where it extends from biter a certain amount out depending on what way he's facing. Let's give it a try!

```
var canSeePlayer = collision_line(x, y,
    x + (image_xscale * 60), y, objPlayer,
    false, true) != noone;
```

This local variable tells us if biter can see the player in front of them. It starts the collision line in the center of biter and extends out 60 pixels left or right, depending on his image_xscale. We're looking for the player, not concerned with precise collisions, and ignoring ourselves. Now to use this variable, we'll add an if check to see when it's true, and when it is change to the charge state. For now we'll just increase the xSpeed of biter, and deal with the logic of the state later on **(Figure 18.6)**.

```
52    if (canSeePlayer) {
53        myState = EnemyState.charging;
54        xSpeed *= 2;
55    }
```
Figure 18.6 Changing to Charge

If you run this and biter sees you, he'll stop moving. We don't have any logic in the charge state, so even though we increased the xSpeed, we have no code moving biter according to his xSpeed. This is both great and a little annoying. It means that each state is completely separate from the others, but that separation means repeating some code, like the x += xSpeed. You can write it outside of the state machine, as we did in the beginning of the chapter, but I would warn you not to do that too much, lest you cause more problems than you solve.

For now, I'm going to leave the charge state empty, we'll deal with it another day. Before we end though, I want to show you a really helpful trick when working with the advanced collision functions.

To help visualize this collision line, and to show you how to do so for future uses, let's add a draw event to biter. Often times I have tried using collision lines, circles, or whatever shape, and discovered they aren't working properly. The reason is because I'm not using the correct arguments, and it's easiest to spot that when you draw the shape you're using. In the draw event add the function draw_self, and then beneath it, draw_line. Inside draw_line put in the same arguments we have in collision_line. Now run the game and you'll see a line originating from biter, going in the direction he's facing **(Figure 18.7)**.

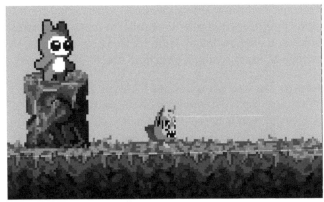
Figure 18.7 Drawing the Collision Line

I find this trick extremely helpful whenever I use the collision functions. It's so easy to forget image_xscale, or input the wrong coordinates, but when you can visualize the collision, it shows what you may have done wrong. Now delete the draw event.

Conclusion + Challenge

Tomorrow we're going to begin setting up the player's state machine. I want you to begin thinking about what states the player's going to have, and how the code we already have in objPlayer can be broken up into the different states.

Talk with you tomorrow!

PRO TIP

Sharing Your Games with Friends & Family

Aaron Craig | Let's Learn This Together

LetsLearnThisTogether.com

Sharing what you create with your friends and family can be tough! The more intimate that creation is the harder it becomes to share. That's never been truer when creating games. Making a game takes a long time and is often a passion project. Sharing that with anyone is hard because what if they don't understand it? What if they don't like it?

Those fears are valid, and I've been there, too. It's easy to close yourself off from criticism and feedback, especially when it's about projects you're deeply invested in. But I'm here to tell you, you can't do that anymore, especially with your games. Video games need feedback to live and grow, to become the best they can. Creating anything, but especially a game, in a bubble usually results in a less than stellar outcome.

Feedback helps our creations change into the best they can be. You may not want to hear your game is slow, boring, doesn't feel right, etc., but without hearing those things your game won't improve. Would you rather create the game of your dreams and have it turn out terrible or create a game with feedback and have it be awesome?

Now there are times when the feedback you receive won't be valid. Maybe the person you're getting from has an awfully specific taste in something that most people wouldn't agree with, and that's ok. Getting feedback doesn't require you to change anything, it simply informs you and can help guide your game. Use that knowledge, but don't let it control what you do.

And the last thing I'll note is you want to do this as early as you can. Don't wait until you're almost done. The very moment you have a game that you can do something in, begin sharing it. Most people will be extremely supportive, giving you encouragement to continue. And the sooner you begin discovering that something is awesome or terrible, the quicker you can double down or tear it out.

The goal is to fail fast, so you can achieve the best down the road.

Day 19

Upgrading Our Player

Setting Up the Player's State Machine

Let's dive right in to creating our player's state machine and see if the ideas you pondered yesterday come true. The first thing we'll need to do is create the enum for the player's states and the myState variable in our player object. Up till this point we've been creating enums and macros in the events of our player and enemy, but this is actually a terrible practice. Recall that both enums and macros are global in scope and pre-compiled before the game even begins, allowing them be used everywhere. Well, because of that, it's best practice create a script and create all enums and macros in it, to both consolidate them into one place, but also to not re-initialize them during the running of the game.

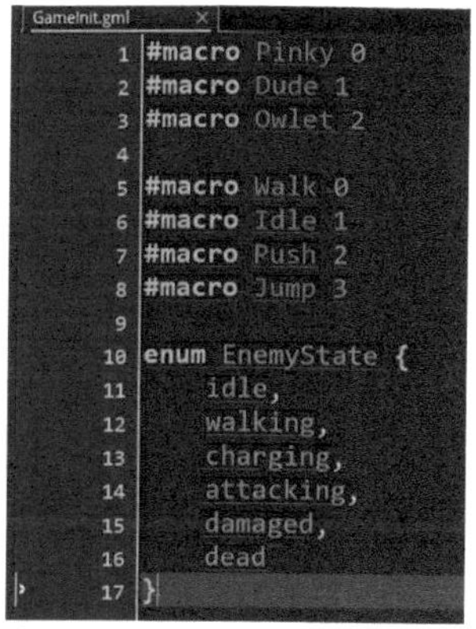

So, create a new script and call it GameInit, which stands for initialization. This is the script that will hold all the things we need to be compiled before the game begins, and it will only ever get run once. Erase everything in the script, as we don't need a function for the enums and macros to run, they run automatically when the game begins to compile.

Figure 19.0 GameInit Script

Cut out the macros from objPlayer and place them in this script. Then grab the enum from objBiter and place it here **(Figure 19.0)**. Next, we need to create an enum for the player to use. If you wanted to reduce the amount of code you're typing, you could rename EnemyState to just State, and then use that for both the enemy and player states. This isn't a bad idea, but I prefer to have separate enums for my objects, it helps me process them better, especially when they're interacting. But your code won't suffer or break if you use just one enum, so I'll leave that call up to you.

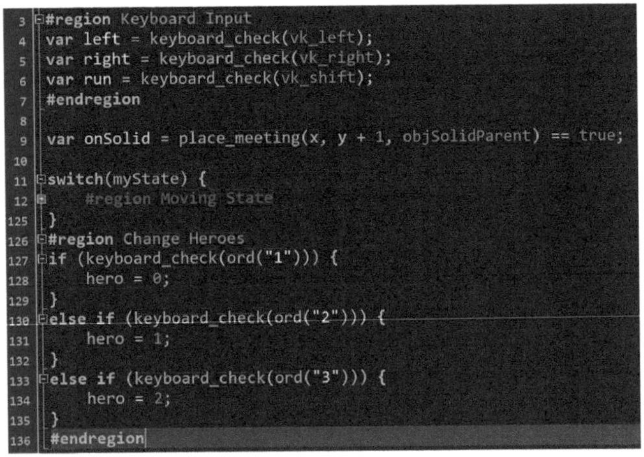

```
3  #region Keyboard Input
4  var left = keyboard_check(vk_left);
5  var right = keyboard_check(vk_right);
6  var run = keyboard_check(vk_shift);
7  #endregion
8
9  var onSolid = place_meeting(x, y + 1, objSolidParent) == true;
10
11 switch(myState) {
12     #region Moving State
125 }
126 #region Change Heroes
127 if (keyboard_check(ord("1"))) {
128     hero = 0;
129 }
130 else if (keyboard_check(ord("2"))) {
131     hero = 1;
132 }
133 else if (keyboard_check(ord("3"))) {
134     hero = 2;
135 }
136 #endregion
```

Figure 19.1 Moving State

Either way, we'll need a few more states for the player. I'm going to create a new enum and call it PlayerState and include these states in it:

- moving
- attacking
- damaged
- dead
- dialogue
- changingRooms
- mainMenu
- gameMenu

There are many here we'll tackle over the next few days, but it doesn't hurt to have them all in place now. I have the advantage of following a project I've already created, as do you, but in your personal games don't worry about thinking up all the states up front. There's nothing wrong with starting with just a few and adding as your game grows.

You may have also noticed that we have no idle state here. Again, this is a personal preference. We've already got the code for moving into an idle sprite in our player, and I see no benefit of creating an entire state for those few lines of code. If you had an idea to do more while idle, such as slowly healing, it would make sense to add the idle state, but for our simpler game I find it to be overkill.

Incorporating the State Machine

So now we've come to plugging in the state machine to code we've already written. Our player can walk, jump, idle, and push and pull objects. Fortunately, I think that all fits nicely into the moving state, making it easy to start out. The only sections of code I would exclude are the input, as we'll use them in several states, and the changing of the heroes, because I want them to be able to do that in every state.

So, starting from where we check for left and right, down to increasing x and y, wrap that all up in the case for moving. You'll also need to add the switch statement and the region so fold all that code up **(Figure 19.1)**. There's over 100 lines of code in that state, which is impressive! You've come a long way on your journey to being a game developer, be sure and celebrate that today!

Next, add the remaining states as cases so we can quickly move from to the other. This will take a few minutes. A little time saving trick is to create the outline of one of the sections, then copy and paste them many times **(Figure 19.2)**.

And finally create the variable myState and set it to moving. After that, we're ready to start filling in the states!

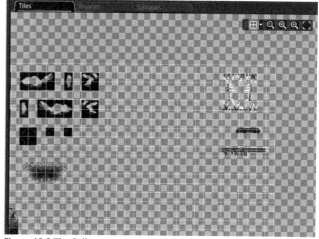

Figure 19.2 Generic Case + Region

Taking Damage

Now that we've got the states set up, we can begin filling them in. From here though you can go whatever route you want to take. We'll tackle the damage state of the player first, but there's no reason you can't begin else-where.

So, let's open the damaged state up and think about how we can both get into this state and get out of it. The first question we must answer is, how do we get hurt in this game? I've got two ways that can happen. The first is when biter attacks us, and the second is some spikes we'll set up throughout the level. Because getting biter to attack means filling out another state, let's instead get the spikes set up.

Figure 19.3 The Spikes

The spikes themselves are part of the tileset we've been using. Open the tile layer in your room and go to the top right of that sprite, you'll see a set of spikes **(Figure 19.3)**. These are the ones we'll be using, but we should create another tile layer before doing so, otherwise the spikes will override some of the grass/tiles we already have in there.

Create a new tile layer and put it *above* Tiles_1. This is important, because the depth of the layer is determined by where it's at in this list (at least by default, you can change it in the editor and through code). Select the same tileset we've been using and put one of the ground spikes in your room where you can jump onto it **(Figure 19.4)**.

Figure 19.4 Spike in the Room

The reason we added a second tile layer is you can't place more than one tile in a square in a tile layer. Go back to Tiles_1 and try placing a spike somewhere else in your room and you'll notice that part of that tile disappears, or maybe all of it. The tiles with just a hint of grass don't look awful being erased by the spike, but it's a good practice to get into of having multiple tile layers when you want to have some sort of depth. It's not uncommon to have a dozen tile layers for more intricate levels.

Figure 19.5 Damage Sprite

Because the spike is a tile, we can't collide with it. But we can do the same thing we did with the ground; create an invisible object that does damage. There are ways to collide with tiles, but again that's beyond the scope of this book. I'll leave it as a challenge to you to try and implement if you're up for it.

Open the System folder and create a new object in Objects, calling it objDamage. Then make a new sprite for this object, just as we did for objSolid. I'm going to create mine black with a crying face, to show it hurts when you touch it, and call it sprDamage. **(Figure 20.5)**. Don't forget to change it to 16x16 pixels to fit our tiles and put it in the System folder.

Now put that object over the spike in our game. We'll look for objDamage, and if we ever collide with it, we'll transition into the damage state and fling the player away from that damage. Return to objPlayer and at the top, underneath keyboard input, create another local variable that holds if we're colliding with damage. It's outside the state machine, so we can use it in multiple states.

For more complex state machines, like our player will be, I like to group all the transitions (into and out of that state), together for easy navigation. If I know all the places I can get into and out of the moving state, then if there's ever an issue where I'm *not* doing that correctly, I know where to look. I'm going to go to the bottom of the move state and begin putting the check for damage there under a comment **(Figure 19.6)**. I use the multi-line comment and all caps to draw attention to it, it serves no other purpose than to catch my eye.

```
125    /*INTO AND OUT OF MOVE STATE*/
126    if (gettingHurt) {
127        myState = PlayerState.damaged;
128    }
```

Figure 19.6 Into Damaged State

So, what are all the things we should do with the player when they get hurt? Depending on your game, that answer will vary greatly. If your game is going for brutal and tough, you may want to kill them at their first mistake, which in that case you probably don't need a damaged state at all. But for Fluffy Heroes, we're going to use a heart system, where each time the player gets hurt, they lose one heart. That means we need to introduce some health variables, so let's do that now.

In the create event, add two new variables to hold the current and max health. Don't use the built-in health variable, as it's only around to support older games that used it and will be deprecated eventually. **Figure 19.7** shows the system I like to use. It's simple and easy to use and doesn't allow for errors since you're setting the players current health to

```
12   maxHealth = 5;
13   currentHealth = maxHealth;
```

Figure 19.7 Health

its max upon startup.

Now that our player has health, we should display that somewhere, so the player also knows that. To inform the player of their health, I've got a great heart sprite we'll show for each point of health they have. Open the Sprites folder and find Heart, then drag it into the Player folder. It is related to the player, so it makes sense to put it there. However, I don't want it just floating around, so let's create a sub-folder in Player called Related and stick it in there. Rename it to sprHeart.

Drawing the Player's Health

With those variables and that sprite, we can now display how much health the player has. And we're going to do with a for loop, an incredibly powerful loop that I use all the time. For loops look very confusing at first because they have several parts that are required in a certain order for it function at all. Let's break down those parts now.

```
for (<assignment>; <expression>; <operation>;)
    {
    <statement>;
    }
```

The assignment section is where you set a variable to a number. You want to use a local variable here, and traditionally a lower cased I is used in for loops. There's no real reason you must use i, except everyone else will be confused if you don't. Then you set an expression, like that inside of an if check. This expression is checked every time *before* the for loop executes, and if it's ever true, the for loop is done. If you write your expression incorrectly, the for loop may not trigger at all. And lastly, you've got the operation, which usually is ++i. That increases i by one each time the loop runs and should make your expression eventually true.

And now that you're thoroughly confused, let me show you how we're going to be using it to display hearts, as a practical example should clear up a lot of the confusion. First

For Loop

The for loop is a special loop that looks intimidating at first, but I'm confident you can master. To use a for loop, you initialize a variable to a starting number, tradition called i and starting at 0. Then you tell that loop when it should stop with a statement, such as i < 10. Then lastly you perform an operation, usually increasing i by an amount, so that the condition will eventually be met.

though, consider how to display the health of the player on the screen without a for loop. We could write a switch or if statement, drawing the correct number based on currentHealth. But this is tedious and doesn't scale. What would happen if we started with five health, but could grow to 19? Would you have to write 19 different if statements to draw the correct amount of health? Yes, you would.

Instead, the for loop allows you to execute code a fixed number of times, and that fixed number can be the amount of health the player has. Here's the code we'll be putting in our game shortly:

```
var width = sprite_get_
width(sprHeart) / 2;

for(var i = 0; i < currentHealth; ++i) {

draw_sprite(sprHeart, 0, width + (i *
10), width);

}
```

We first get how wide the heart is. I do have other hearts you can use in the Original Assets folder, or maybe you want to find your own. This variable holds half it's width. Then the for loop. We set a local variable to 0 (so that it scoped to this loop), then tell it to continue running until i is less than our currentHealth. And finally, we increase i by one each time the loop runs.

Then inside the loop we execute just one line of code, but in that line of code we are accessing that local variable i. And that's where the real power of for loops comes into play. The i variable is increasing each time the loop runs, so if the player has five health, the loop runs five times. The first time we draw the heart, i (which is 0), multiplied by 10 is still 0. But the second time, that equation becomes 10, so we draw the second heart 10 pixels to the right, and repeat until the end of the loop.

So, with just a few lines of code, we can now draw an in-

finite amount of hearts on screen, moving each one over so they don't overlap. Go ahead and copy this code into your game, putting it in a Draw event for the player. Don't forget to add draw_self somewhere or the player won't show up. Try running it and see how it looks.

Nothing shows up. What's up with that? Well look at **Figure 19.8**, the hearts are in there, but why aren't they in yours? The reason is the coordinates where we're drawing them is at 0, 0 + a little bit. That means the hearts will be in top left corner of the game. I changed my camera to view the entire room, but that's now how the game should look. We want the hearts to be in the top left cor-

Figure 19.8 Hearts in Game

ner for our player, no matter where they are in the room.

There are two ways to fix this, the first taking multiple functions to figure out where the camera is at, then drawing the sprites there. This works, and I've got several tutorials on how to do exactly this on my channel. However, there's a much simpler way that almost doesn't involve any extra coding, and that's using the Draw GUI event.

Take the code in the draw event, except for the draw_self function, and put it in a new Draw GUI event in the player. You can delete the previous draw event. And now, run the game and see the hearts in the top left wherever you move. They are quite small, but we can fix that!

The reason the hearts are so small is they're only 16x16 pixels, which is small, but not that small, so something else is off. Well, by default the GUI in GameMaker is 1919x1080, modern HD standards. And even though our window is 1919x1080, our camera is no-where near that size, recall it's 256x144. So by using the function display_set_gui_size, we can tell GameMaker that our GUI should only be 256x144, and then the hearts will display at their proper size.

So, in the player create event (since we only need to call this function once), call dis-play_set_gui_size and pass in the camera dimensions. Then run your game and check out this big, beautiful hearts! Those are the correct size. However, I think they may be even a little too large. We can fix this by shrinking our hearts, which isn't ideal, or bump up the gui size. Go ahead and multiply the arguments by 2, and then run it again.

Now you'll see the hearts look good and are in the correct place. Awesome! Does it still work when we change our currentHealth? Try it. You can put any number in there, except less than 0, and the hearts will show up exactly as we want. That's the power of for loops!

Draw GUI Event

The draw gui event is different from the normal draw event. It draws things onto the screen based on the window, not the room. This means you can draw something at 0, 0, and it will always draw that thing in the top left corner of game. This event is fabulous for UI and GUI elements, hence the name.

Conclusion + Challenge

Well, we went off on quite a rabbit hole, didn't we? Instead of coding the player's dam-aged state, we brought in a heart, learned about for loops, and changed the gui of our game. But that's how game dev goes a lot of the time; you try to add a new feature only to discover you need six other features in place first! And that's one of the things I love.

The challenge for today is to not do any more coding. Take a break. For loops are amaz-ing, but they are also very confusing, and often where beginners quit because they can't understand them. If that's you, put this book down and take a break for the day, let your mind work on them in the background. Repeat today if you need to, there's no shame in that.

Tomorrow we'll pick up in the damaged state!

Day 20

All About That Damage

Running Away Bravely

Today is a little bit longer of a day, but it all meshes together well. So, stick with it, you've got this!

Normally I don't condone hurting others, but in this case, I'll allow it. It's time to make Pinky (or whomever is on screen), feel some pain! Yesterday we started to code the damaged state and got distracted with health and for loops, today we get back on track. If you're still struggling with how a for loop works, don't worry! We'll use them a little more in this game, and I'll explain it again each time.

For now, however, let's return to our move state and where the player is colliding with the spikes we've got set up. Right now, all that code is doing is changing the player's state to damaged, which then results in a weird glitch of continuing to animate while staying in the same spot. What we need to do next is take damage, fling the player away from the damage source, and then get out of the damaged state after a few seconds.

Let's start with the losing health, as it's the simplest. In our if check of getting hurt, subtract one from the player's currentHealth variable. And that's all there is to it.

Next, we need to bounce away from whatever hurt us, be it spikes or biter, or something else you create in the future. This is more of a preference, there's no rule saying you must get tossed back when taking damage, but it is a quite common thing with solid reason behind it. If we're fighting an enemy, then being flung away gives us time to reconsider our strategy while not still being in range of their attack.

So, the first thing we need is the instance that did the damage, which we can get with the function instance_place, which takes the same arguments as place_meeting, but returns the instance id of what we're colliding with, instead of true or false. Create a local variable called damageSource and set it to what instance_place returns **(Figure 20.0)**. We can be assured that this function will return an instance id instead of noone (which it does when there is no collision), since this code is only running when we've already verified there is a collision. If it weren't in this if statement, I would recommend checking damageSource doesn't equal noone before doing anything with it.

```
if (gettingHurt) {
    myState = PlayerState.damaged;
    currentHealth -= 1;
    var damageSource = instance_place(x, y, objDamage);
}
```

Figure 20.0 Damage Source

We know the id of what's hurting us, and with that information we can then determine where it is in relation to us. Another super helpful function is point_direction, which takes four arguments, two sets of coordinates, and returns a number between 0 and 359. The number returned is the direction from point to point b in Gamemaker, with 0 being right, 90 being up, 180 being left, and 270 down. Call point_direction now and save its result in a local variable called position. The first set of coordinates is the players, and the second set is the damageSource's x and y.

Then we want to check the location to determine if we're flinging the player to the right or left. If position is greater than or equal to 90 and it's less than or equal to 270, we know we got hurt by something to our left, otherwise it's to our right. We must include the equal to checks for these numbers, because if we do take damage from something exactly at 90 or 270, we're still including those numbers in our checks. We also need to set our ySpeed to a number, and I'll just use jumpSpeed since we have it and it works well **(Figure 20.1)**.

```
var position = point_direction(x, y, damageSource.x, damageSource.y);
if (position >= 90 && position <= 270) {
    xSpeed = -walkSpeed;
}
else {
    xSpeed = walkSpeed;
}
ySpeed = jumpSpeed;
```

Figure 20.1 Thrown Back

And for now, that's all we need to do to move into the damaged state. Later, we'll check if we have no health left, and if so, move into the dead state instead of damaged. But right now, we need to code the damaged state because it still isn't doing anything. The first thing to do is to move our player since we just set their x and y speeds. So, in the damaged state increase the x and y by their speeds.

It stands to reason if we're throwing the player around in the damaged state, we also need to be checking for collisions, and you're right! But we can't just use the collision script we already have, because the collisions in damaged look a little different, and we need to be applying gravity. So, let's first create all the code we need in the damaged state, and then if we need to make a script, we will.

The first thing to add is gravity, just like how we have it in our move state. We have the onSolid variable we can use and just check if it's false, like so:

```
if (!onSolid) {

    ySpeed += gameGravity;

}
```

You could also write out if it's equal to false, but the exclamation point does the same thing. Do what's easiest for you to read and understand, there isn't a right or a wrong way for this.

Next, we'll check if the player has reached the ground. Again, this code can be copied right out of the walk state. Then we'll check horizontal collisions, but instead of coming to a stop when colliding with them, let's have the player slightly bounce off them, like a trampoline. Each bounce will slow the player down, so they'll come to a stop eventually.

This code will be like the horizontal collision code in the walk state, so go ahead and copy that over, too. Then change the setting of the xSpeed from 0 to multiplying it by negative .5. This will cause the player to bounce a little each time they collide with an object. If you don't like this effect, then change it until you do, or keep it setting xSpeed to 0, this is your game after all.

And underneath all that use this code to slow the player down over time:

```
xSpeed -= xSpeed / 100;
```

Now we're almost done, we just need a way to transition back to the moving state. Find where we're adding gameGravity to our player. That if check is only functioning while we're in the air, and it makes sense to me that when we're finally on the ground we would return to the move state. So, add an else here that sets our xSpeed to 0 (so we don't continue flying around), and changes our state to move.

Alright, that was a lot of code we just wrote! You can compare yours against mine **(Figure 20.2)**. And it's usually a bad idea to write a lot of code without testing it along the way, but it's also sometimes necessary. Go ahead and run your game and give it a go. You should find the collisions function as expected, with a little more bounce this time around. You can move into and out of the damaged state, and you lose health each time. The only issue is, depending on where your spikes are located, is you can enter a damage loop where you get bounced back into them multiple times and lose all your health very, very quickly. This is not fair or fun, so let's fix that.

```
148    //Apply Gravity
149    if (!onSolid) {
150        ySpeed += gameGravity;
151    }
152    else {
153        myState = PlayerState.moving;
154        xSpeed = 0;
155    }
156    //Stop moving once we're on the ground
157    if (place_meeting(x, y + ySpeed, objSolidParent) == true) {
158        while (place_meeting(x, y + sign(ySpeed), objSolidParent) == false) {
159            y += sign(ySpeed);
160        }
161        ySpeed = 0;
162    }
163    //Slightly bounce off horizontal collisions
164    if (place_meeting(x + xSpeed, y, objSolidParent) == true) {
165        while (place_meeting(x + sign(xSpeed), y, objSolidParent) == false) {
166            x += sign(xSpeed);
167        }
168        xSpeed *= -.5;
169    }
170    //Slow the player down
171    xSpeed -= xSpeed / 100;
172
173    x += xSpeed;
174    y += ySpeed;
```

Figure 20.2 Damaged State

The only thing we need to do is check if we're colliding with another damage source inside of the damaged state, and if so, bounce away again without taking more damage. This should eventually get the player out of harms way and onto solid ground.

Beneath the horizontal collisions let's add an if statement to check if we're colliding with a damaged source, and if so, bounce away some more! Copy the code from the move state where we're setting the x and y speeds based on the damageSource. With that done, try out your game. You should now be able to bounce on the spikes, get tossed around, even land on more spikes, and not take more damage.

The only issue you may find is you lose two hearts sometimes. That sometimes happens when you're walking into spikes instead of landing on them. This happens because of the way our code is set up. We transition from the move state to damaged without moving our player at all, so if we were on the ground in the move state, we're still on the ground in the damaged state. Then the first thing that's checked is if we're on the ground, change back to move state, and the process happens again, so we take more damage. But after the second time moving into the damaged state, our ySpeed has been set, so we begin to fly away, and then the damaged states collision code triggers properly.

To best see what I'm describing, put a breakpoint on the transition code into the damaged state and follow it through. You'll see the player move into damaged state, then immediately out of the damaged state, and then immediately return to it. We don't want this, as it hurts the player more than it should.

How can we fix this? The simplest solution is to take the moving of the player, where we change the player's x and y, and put it before the check to change back to the move state. But that causes some issues where we're changing our ySpeed but then not moving until the frame after, so we could get stuck in the ground. So, in this case, the simplest

solution isn't the right one.

Instead, we can turn some of code into scripts, such as the collision code in the damaged state and the launching of the player away from a damaged source, which we can then call in a better order and elsewhere, to eliminate this issue. So, let's do that!

Wrapping Up the Damaged State

Our main problem stems from how we're moving back into the move state from damaged. It's currently checking if we're on the ground, and then transition back into the move state. But if we were on the ground when we moved into the damaged state, nothing has moved the player, so it's going to continue the cycle for at least 1 time, doing more damage than it should. Find the section of code that bounces the player away in the moving state when transitioning to damaged. Cut out everything after creating the local variable damageSource.

Then open the Collisions Script and create a new function called BounceBack which takes one argument called damageSource. In that function paste the code you cut out. Format it properly, for me I had to shift+tab most of the code back two times. This script is what we'll call to set our player's ySpeed based on whatever damage source we collide with **(Figure 20.3)**.

```
29  function BounceBack(damageSource) {
30      var position = point_direction(x, y, damageSource.x, damageSource.y);
31      if (position >= 90 && position <= 270) {
32          xSpeed = walkSpeed;
33      }
34      else {
35          xSpeed = -walkSpeed;
36      }
37      ySpeed = jumpSpeed;
38  }
```

Figure 20.3 BounceBack Function

Then return to the transition code and call our new function, passing in that local variable damageSource. We're not quite ready to test it yet, as all we've done is take the code and turn it into a script. What we still need to do is move the player and check for collisions. This collision checking is similar to our movement, so you may be tempted to call CollideWith, but there are a few key differences we need to maintain when bouncing in the damaged state, such as we want to bounce more than just fall or stop when running into a wall. For these reasons, we're going to create another script to handle the collisions in our damaged state.

Return to the Collisions Script and create another function called DamageCollisions with no arguments. For this script, copy everything inside the CollideWith script and paste it inside. And then wherever xSpeed is being set to 0, instead set it equal to -.1. This will bounce the player off the wall they collide with, slowing them down and eventually stopping them. And then, at the bottom of DamageCollisions, add this line:

```
xSpeed -= xSpeed / 100;
```

This will slow the player down and eventually stop them bouncing. Below that line, increase the x and y of the player by their xSpeed and ySpeed values, as we want this function to move the player around, instead of only check for collisions. And lastly, at the top of this function, check to see if the player is on the ground, and if not increase their ySpeed according to our gameGravity variable:

```
if(!place_meeting(x, y + 1, objSolidParent)) {

    ySpeed += gameGravity;

}
```

And that's all we need for that function. Now we need to sort out the rest of moving into the damaged state. Currently, our collision checking and movement all happen before we check if we're getting damaged, which isn't exactly what we want. The collision checking part is fine, as it just ensures we don't fall into the floors or walls, but by moving the player before calling BounceBack, it can create a runtime error and crash our game.

The error happens because of how we're getting damage-

Source and passing it into BounceBack. The local variable damageSource is created by a meeting function, and it's possible that our player got hurt, moved out of that object's collision, and is then trying to find that object with the collision function. It won't crash your game all the time, but even sometimes is too much. We're going to fix it by moving the code that increases our x and y below the check of being hurt.

Keep CollideWith above the code moving into the damaged state, just move the x += xSpeed and y += ySpeed code to the very end of our case. That will fix any of those errors from cropping up. Then we can move into the damaged state, and with our new functions, simplify the code we have there immensely.

In fact, it will be easier to start from scratch in the damaged state than try to modify it. So, go ahead and delete everything in this case. Now, check if the player is on solid ground, and if so change back to the moving state and set the player's speed to 0. If they're not on solid ground, if they're still colliding with a damaging object, and if so, bounce them away from it. Then under it all, call DamageCollisions() **(Figure 20.4)**.

```
case PlayerState.damaged:
    if (onSolid) {
        myState = PlayerState.moving;
        xSpeed = 0;
    }
    else if(gettingHurt) {
        BounceBack(instance_place(x, y, objDamage));
    }
    DamageCollisions();
break;
```

Figure 20.4 Damaged State 2.0

And that's all we need. It takes the damaged state from 30 lines of code to 8. And if there's anywhere else we need to collide with hurtful objects, or get thrown back from something, we have scripts for that. We can use BounceBack anywhere, not just with something that hurts us. It's versatile and general, a great ideal to strive for when creating functions. Of course, not every function needs to be written like that, nor should every function. But when you can, think about how to write a function so it can be used elsewhere in your game, or other projects even.

The last thing to do is add in the hurt sprite for each of our characters and assign our player to the sprite when getting hurt in the move state. The sprites are already in the project, so find and convert them to frames for each character. I'm setting the FPS to 15, but select what you think looks best. Then in objPlayer, add this new animation to our sprites array. And then add another macro with a value of 4 called Hurt. Finally, when our player gets hurt in the move state, change their sprite to this new hurt sprite, and we're all done! Try it out and see how it looks and feels.

> ## Error Help
>
> - If you find your player getting stuck in a loop of bouncing off a nearby wall and falling back onto the spikes, you may need to adjust your BounceBack function. I found this to be the case when I had a value of -0.5 in Bounce-Back, and so adjusted it several times to find the best value. It's impossible to test every scenario of your game, but if you find that a spike a certain distance from the wall causes issues, then don't place a spike there, or continue to adjust values in BounceBack, maybe flinging the player further away, or changing the value to a random value each time so it can't get caught in a loop.

No Time to Die

Well, actually, we need to find some time to die. We've got our damaged state all set and working properly. The next logical step is to do the same with our death state, as we now take damage and display that to the user. We already have a dead state ready to be filled out, and this time it won't take as long as the damaged state.

There are two ways to go about dying. The first is to check the health of the player when moving into the damaged state and, if we have 0 or less, then proceed to the dead state immediately, bypassing the damaged state entirely. The second approach is to check at the end of the damaged state if we have 0 or less health, and then move into the dead state. Personally, I think the first approach is the best, as it saves time for the player, and makes more a little more sense, at least to me. Once the player is dead, why fling their body around instead of just moving into the death state immediately?

This time around, let's set up our sprites first and then move into code. We don't have the

Pinky death sprite, so pull that in from the Assets folder. I'm setting the animation speed to 6, as I really like the animation and want to see it play out. After you've converted them to frames, add the new animation to the sprites array and add a macro for it.

Now return to our players states and where we transition into the damaged state. Move the subtraction of currentHealth to the top, and then wrap the rest of the code in an if check. If our players health is above 0, run that code, otherwise move into the dead state and begin playing the death animation. And don't forget to set image_index to 0 to ensure the animation starts at the beginning **(Figure 20.5)**.

```
if (gettingHurt) {
    currentHealth -= 1;
    if (currentHealth > 0) {
        myState = PlayerState.damaged;
        var damageSource = instance_place(x, y, objDamage);
        BounceBack(damageSource);
        sprite_index = sprites[hero][Hurt];
    }
    else {
        myState = PlayerState.dead;
        sprite_index = sprites[hero][Dead];
        image_index = 0;
    }
}
```

Figure 20.5 Moving to Dead State

And since we never added a damage sound when working in the damage state, now's a great time to add it. We want to play it every time we get hurt, so we can call it right after subtracting some health from our player. In the Assets folder, open Sounds, and find Hurt. Bring it into the project and rename is sprHurt.

In the dead state, we want to check when the animation will be done playing and then restart the game. Later on, once we implement a start screen, we'll return to that, but for now a restart will suffice. There are a couple of ways to determine if an animation is about to end, each with their own strengths and weaknesses. We're going to use the simplest method, but I'll also explain the other ways so you can decide which one you want to use.

The easiest way to determine if an animation is about to end, is to check if the image_index is greater than or equal to the image_number, the number of frames in a sprite. Remember the image_index stores which frame we're currently displaying, so if the frame we're on is the last frame in the animation, it will be done in the next step. It looks like this:

```
if (image_index >= image_number) {
    game_restart();
}
```

This, logically, looks like it will work. And sometimes it will! Reduce your players health to 1 and give it a try, you'll find the game restarts and works as expected.

However, this only works when the animation is both slow and you're starting at 0, like we are here since we set our image_index to 0 right before playing this animation. To show this doesn't always work, change the FPS of the animation to 24 and run the game again. This time you'll find it plays in a loop forever. But why?

The math! To understand exactly why let's look at some math, but I promise we won't go too in-depth. Recall that FPS stands for frames per second. So, when we set our death animation to 24 FPS, it roughly equates to 24/60, or adding 0.4 every step to image_index. But a weird thing about numbers, especially decimals, is that they're rarely that even. I won't get into why, but 24/60 isn't 0.4 to GameMaker, it's actually 0.400000005960464 **(Figure 20.6)**. And

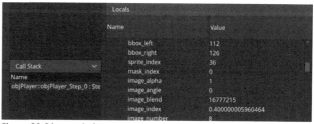

Figure 20.6 image_index

now that goes up every step, until it eventually reaches 8. something, and instead of triggering our if check, it then goes back to 0 and adds whatever is over 8 to the start. GameMaker doesn't show this, and I'm not sure why, but our if check will probably never trigger, unless you let it run for a long time and those fractions eventually add up to a whole 8.

The key thing to remember here is that faster animations trigger this problem, while slower ones do not. If you have a faster animation you need to check, you still can with this method. Subtract 1 from image_number in the equation, and it will still work for faster animations, like our death animation at 24 FPS. The downside to this is you'll lose part of the animation, since we're now checking if our image_index is more than image_number minus 1, so it won't play all the way to the end. It's not a huge deal for longer animations, but not ideal.

The other way to check if an animation is ending is the Animation End event in that object. This event triggers at the end of every animation, and so you can check if the animation ending is the one you're looking for, then trigger the code you want to run. In our case, it would look like **figure 20.7**. You can find Animation End in the Other events. This method is great for simple use cases, like restarting the game, but when you need to interact with other variables in your code, it causes issues because you're now in a different event.

Figure 20.7 Animation End

In this instance, our original code works fine at a speed of 6. If you're animating it quicker, then you may need to subtract 1 to ensure it picks it up. You can also use the Animation End event if you want. We will add more code to the dead event later on, but for the most part it won't grow too complex.

Conclusion + Challenge

As you learned today, even GameMaker has some weird quirks to it. It's a great game engine, but just like everything else out there, it's not perfect. But the more you know and experiment, the better you'll be at overcoming those problems. There are times it's the software, not the programmer, they're just few and far between, unless you're beta testing.

It was a long day today, so take a break and relax. No challenge today.

Day 21

Know Thine Enemy

Death Music

We can die now, but we need some cool music to go along with it. GameMaker is pretty easy to play sounds and music, but it has more functions that can also manipulate where an audio file plays at, how it plays, and more. Let's jump into that!

The first thing we need to do is bring in the game over music. Rename it to sndGameOverMusic. It's almost 9 seconds long, which is too long, but I know it gets good at the 4 second mark, so let's get it to start there. In the player's move state, when we transition into the damage state, we've already got a check if we're dead. In that else statement, when the player has no more health, let's play the audio and set it to start at 4 seconds **(Figure 21.0)**.

```
else {
    myState = PlayerState.dead;
    sprite_index = sprites[hero][Dead];
    image_index = 0;
    var gameOver = audio_play_sound(sndGameOverMusic, 100, false);
    audio_sound_set_track_position(gameOver, 4);
}
```

Figure 21.0 Playing Game Over Music

The local variable saves the ID of the audio asset playing, and then we can use that to set its play position. The manual's entry for audio_sound_set_track_position says that we can use that function to make all future plays of a specific sound start wherever we want. However, in testing this out I couldn't make that happen. This method though, of passing in the index of the sound being played, worked perfectly though. It begins playing the music at 4 seconds, skipping the beginning.

Once we get the audio playing correctly, we need to move into the death state. Inside here let's make it so the game will restart only after the music is done playing. However, doing that causes the death animation to loop, since the audio is longer. We can either slow the animation down, or stop it playing at the end. I'm going to choose to stop the animation when it reaches the end, as we've done that before. In the death state we need to add another if check and change the original **(Figure 21.1)**.

```
case PlayerState.dead:
    if (image_index >= image_number) {
        image_speed = 0;
    }
    if (audio_is_playing(sndGameOverMusic) == false) {
        game_restart();
    }
```

Figure 21.1 New Death State

The only issue with that is the last frame has some smoke effects on it, and stopping it there looks weird. So, let's add another frame to this animation, leaving it blank, and then it will look great!

Interacting with Biter

Now that we've got the damaged and dead state complete, we have everything we need to interact with our enemy, Biter. We created the scripts to bounce back from a damage source and to be able to collide around while in the damaged state, all things we'll need when taking damage from Biter. We could have done it the other way around, nothing says we have to code in a certain order, I just chose one I thought would be best for learning and went with it. After you've got the experience, feel free to code your games in whatever order makes sense to you.

Let's start by just making Biter an object that can hurt us, and we'll add an attack state for him after. I'm going to change my health back to 5 so I can more easily test out what we're working on. Then let's set objBiter as a child of objDamage. Run your game and test it out.

Bam! It just works. Pretty amazing if you ask me. Now this isn't the final solution, since having objDamage be the parent to our enemy doesn't make much sense logically. What if we want to add more enemies and use inheritance? We can't, at least not in a way that is easy to work with and remember. Instead, let's create a new parent and change up our code to look for that parent, instead of objDamage.

Open the Parents folder in System and create a new object, naming it objEnemyParent. Give this object two children, objDamage and objBiter. Doing this with objBiter will over-ride the inheritance from objDamage we set before. Now, let's open the Step event for objPlayer and at the top where we're setting the local variable gettingHurt to check for objDamage, change it to objEnemyParent. And then in the transition to damaged state, change the damageSource from objDamage to objEnemyParent. Finally, in the damaged state change the BounceBack function argument from objDamage to objEnemyParent.

And there we are! Now both the spikes and Biter are working as expected and we've got a system setup where we can easily add more enemies and damaging objects in our level. Fabulous!

Biter Getting Mean

Now let's add in some more states for Biter, including the charging and attack state. For the charge state, we've already transitioned into it, we just didn't fill out the state itself. Fortunately, the charge state isn't too complex.

Open Biter's Step event up and locate charging. Our goal here is to have Biter run faster directly at the player, and when it gets close enough, it stops and attacks. The other possibility to consider is the player runs away or jumps up high and Biter can no longer see the player, which then it will go back to walking around. Let's tackle that part first.

To determine when Biter should return to walking, it needs to have some number for its charging radius, or the distance at which it will stop chasing the player. In the Create event, add a variable called chargeRadius and set it to 60.

Now return to the charging state and let's add an if check to see where Biter is at in relation to the player. There's a handy function called distance_to_object which will tell us that exactly. Check that function against our chargeRadius variable, and if it's larger, Biter will go back to walking. And also add in the code to move Biter in the charging state, as it can't move right now. **(Figure 21.2)**.

```
case EnemyState.charging:
    if (distance_to_object(objPlayer) > chargeRadius) {
        myState = EnemyState.walking;
        image_index = 0;
        xSpeed = moveSpeed;
    }
    x += xSpeed;
```

Figure 21.2 Biter Charging

Run your game and test this out. Biter charges at the player just as expected, and we get tossed back, as expected. The problem arises when we're close to a wall and Biter will continue charging directly through that wall if we're on top of it, because we're still close to Biter. The code in

there now only switches it back to walking when we're far enough away, which isn't totally right. We also want Biter to revert when there's a wall or ledge in front of them.

We've already written the code to check both of these things, unfortunately they're local variables in the walk state. But we can fix that! Take the local variables atLedge and atSolid and move them to the top of Biter. They can still remain local, as we only need them in this step event. Then return to charging and check to see if either are true in our if check. If they are when Biter returns to walking, multiply its image_xscale by -1, or Biter will walk backwards for a while, which looks pretty funny **(Figure 21.3)**.

```
if (distance_to_object(objPlayer) > chargeRadius || atLedge || atSolid) {
    myState = EnemyState.walking;
    image_index = 0;
    xSpeed = moveSpeed;
    if (atLedge || atSolid) {
        image_xscale *= -1;
    }
}
```

Figure 21.3 Checking Other Cases

This works great when Biter is on our right and attacks but doesn't work as expected the other direction. The issue arises from the setting of xSpeed to moveSpeed, because when Biter is walking to the left, moveSpeed needs to be negative. Fortunately we already have a value we can check if moveSpeed should be positive or negative and that's image_xscale. So, let's set xSpeed after setting image_xscale and multiple moveSpeed by our xscale **(Figure 21.4)**.

```
if (distance_to_object(objPlayer) > chargeRadius || atLedge || atSolid) {
    myState = EnemyState.walking;
    image_index = 0;
    if (atLedge || atSolid) {
        image_xscale *= -1;
    }
    xSpeed = moveSpeed * image_xscale;
}
```

Figure 21.4 Changing xSpeed

With those two checks in place, run your game and try jumping up on a ledge or away from Biter and you'll see it returns to its walk state as expected. So, that takes care of getting into charging, moving as expected, and getting back out of it. Next, we'll tackle the attacking, which sounds like it's more complex, but in reality, only sounds that way. What we need to do is play a new sprite, then revert back when we're done. We have experience with that.

Biter on the Attack

Just like we needed a charge radius variable, we'll need one for the attack as well. How close you want Biter to be is up to you, although I've found that a distance of 4 works best. Otherwise, it's too close and the player will get hit just by Biter charging, and too far won't hit the player at all.

So, create a variable called attackRadius and set it to 4. Back in the charging state, create an if check just like we did for charging but this time for our attackRadius, except this time we want to execute the code when the distance to player is less than or equal to the attackRadius, and start playing the bite animation **(Figure 21.5)**.

```
if (distance_to_object(objPlayer) <= attackRadius) {
    xSpeed = 0;
    sprite_index = sprBiterAttack;
    image_index = 0;
    myState = EnemyState.attacking;
}
```
Figure 21.5 Moving to Attack

Then move into the attacking state and add a check if we're at the end of the animation, and when we are, we need to change everything back to the walk state. So, change the state first, reset the xSpeed, turn biter around by multiplying image_xscale by -1 (otherwise Biter will keep attacking forever), reset image_index, and set the

sprite back to walk **(Figure 21.6)**. Don't forget to do the same thing here with xSpeed as we did in the charge state, multiplying it by image_xscale. This is all the code we need in the attack state.

```
case EnemyState.attacking:
    if (image_index >= image_number) {
        myState = EnemyState.walking;
        image_xscale *= -1;
        xSpeed = moveSpeed * image_xscale;
        image_index = 0;
        sprite_index = sprBiterWalk;
    }
break;
```
Figure 21.6 Attack State

Try running your game and letting Biter charge and attack you. What happens? You get hit by the charge, right? You get flung away, he attacks, and then goes back to walking like he should. So, at least part of it is working correctly, but why are we getting hit before Biter actually attacks? The reason is the collision mask.

Open Biter's attack animation and you'll notice the collision mask is set to automatic rectangle, which creates a huge mask for all the frames. This isn't what we want! Instead, set it to precise per frame, and then notice how it will move the collision mask perfectly, fixing the issue of getting hit before Biter plays the animation.

Now try running your game again. Is it all working? Well, not quite. A pretty funny glitch occurs right when Biter starts attacking! It warps to the nearest higher ground and finishes the attack animation. What's up with this? It actually has to do with the code at the top of Biter's step event, the code that allows us to place Biter from the level editor and ensure that Biter is on solid ground when the game starts.

Return to the attack animation and look closely at the

second frame. Biter leaps into the air a few pixels, which means that it's no longer on the ground. And since it's not on the ground, that code looking for ground kicks in and warps it to the nearest highest elevation solid it can find. Needless to say, this isn't how we want it to work. The idea of a warping enemy that attacks from a distance and then appears next to the player is fascinating, but not what I intended.

To fix this, all we need do is add this code in the if check at the top:

```
&& myState == EnemyState.idle
```

That will make it so the code to place Biter won't run in the attack state. Add it in and then run your game again. Now it's all working as expected. Finally!

Conclusion + Challenge

That wraps up the charging and attack state for Biter, and we can now take damage from it. To add in more enemies, all you need is a new sprite and idea for how it works. You've got the parent set up, know how to change states and have it attack. There's still work to do when making enemies, but the foundation is set up and ready for you to work with. We won't be making more enemies for this game, but you certainly can!

Today's challenge is to start thinking about, and even attempting if you're up for it, how to implement the player's attack state. I'll let you know it will be a ranged magic attack, so when we attack it will shoot a projectile in a straight path. You can find the Ice attack in the Assets folder, or some other magic projectiles in the original assets.

What is the best way to make the attack state for the player? What are the things to think about? Give it some thought and we'll tackle it tomorrow!

PRO TIP

Difference between Game Designer & Programmer

Nick Dufault | Vimlark Games

Vimlark.itch.io

In the early days of video games there wasn't much difference between a game programmer and a game designer. As the industry and teams within it have grown, the roles split into more specialized fields. Designers are tasked with creating the experience the player will receive when interacting with a game, while programmers use technical knowledge to make those experiences functional.

From a focus perspective, a designer is concerned with relaying important game information to the player in a natural and easy to understand way. This will help them learn the systems and mechanics, allowing them to use that knowledge to take agency in their actions to experience the game as intended.

A programmer for that same game develops the systems and mechanics from a practical standpoint. Writing the code that tells the computer/console, when "x" happens then "y" should be the result. Having knowledge of how a system/mechanic works does not help unless it reacts the way the user is taught.

A designer is focused on the flow and moment to moment happenings of the player. If there is an enemy that shoots at the player, where do you place it? How often does it fire a projectile? How much health does it have? Those are just a sampling of questions a designer might ask.

The programmer on the other hand takes those questions and makes it possible to easily move the enemy. Creates a firing system that can be adjusted and triggered when needed. Builds the logic that keeps track of the health and what happens when it's gone.

While the two are very different disciplines, both are essential to make a video game and each require a different approach to solve the unique challenges that they face. Programmers tend to focus on the "how" while designers concentrate on the "why".

Day 22

Ready for Some Magic?

Getting Ready to Attack!

So, what thoughts did you get to thinking about? We've done many states at this point, and I believe you have a good idea of what it takes to add a new one, even if it does involve something new like creating a projectile and shooting it. Remember it's important to break big tasks down into smaller, more manageable chunks.

The first thing to tackle is what we'll need for the attack itself. And that's a new animation for the player, all three of them, the ice sprite, and the ice explosion sprite. Let's bring all those in now. The animations for attacking are already in our game, but we need to convert them to frames and rename them. I'll be using attack_1 for each animation, as attack_2 is longer and has two parts to it. It's clearly meant to be a melee attack, but we can make it work for what we want. If you want to make the attack melee instead of ranged, you'll be able to use a lot of the things we're doing in this section, so continue to follow along anyway.

I'm going to set the FPS at 15 for each animation and rename them to attack. Now hop into the player's Create evet and add in the attack animation to the sprites array for each character. Also add in the Attack Macro and set it to 6.

Then let's grab the ice attack and ice shatter sprites and bring them into the Related folder inside of Player. For the ice attack sprite, it's 64x64 pixels and has 30 frames in it. The ice shatter is 96x96 pixels and has 50 frames in it. The ice attack I'm leaving at 30 FPS, but the ice shatter I'm jumping up to 80, as it has a lot of frames and something shattering should go quickly.

And the last sprite we'll need is Biter's exploding/death animation, which can be found right next to the ice sprites. The Enemy Explode sprite isn't specifically for Biter but can

167

```
var attack = mouse_check_button(mb_left);
```
Figure 22.0 Left Mouse Check

be used on any enemy of similar size, which is cool. Bring in that sprite to Biter's folder and rename it sprBiterExplode. These frames are 80x80 pixels.

Part of the reason I left these sprites at different sizes is to show you how to work with different sized sprites that you'll find in the real world. No matter the case, you'll probably end up working with some assets you find by other artists, and they won't be the exact size and dimensions you'll want. But as a programmer, you can alter the playback, size, angle, and more with code. This means you can fit a square sized peg into a circle hole with enough patience and practice. The other reason is I'm lazy.

With all our sprites converted and named, let's get down to the business of attacking!

Call Me Elsa

The first thing to work on when adding a new state is how to get into and out of that state. For attacking, that will happen when the player presses the attack button, and when the animation of attack has finished playing. A couple of points to consider are when can we enter the attack state? Should the player need to be on the ground, or can they fire while jumping? How many times can they shoot in a given timeframe? If they're attacking, can they be knocked out of it another way, such as by taking damage?

How you answer these questions determines what will make your game unique. For instance, if you wanted your game to be more difficult and require precision, then only allowing the player to attack every few seconds encourages more thinking and planning. Whereas if the player can hold down the attack button and fire 20 ice blasts a second, it encourages a run and gun approach. Every design decision you make influences your game, sometimes

in subtle ways, and other times in huge ways.

I'd encourage you to follow along with me until the end of this book, and then if you want to turn the game into a totally different one, go for it. But first make sure you know how to make the pie before turning it into a cheesecake. I know that doesn't make any sense, but I really like how it sounds, so I'm going to keep it in here. Plus, I might be a little hungry.

Open the player's Step event and at the top let's make a local variable for attacking, just like we have for our other movement. Make the check for the left mouse button. Then in our section of changing states, below transitioning into the damaged state, add a check if we're attacking, and if we are, then change to our attacking state **(Figure 22.1)**.

```
141
142        //Attacking
143        if (attack) {
144            myState = PlayerState.attacking;
145        }
```
Figure 22. 1 Moving into Attack State

Inside here is where we'll create the ice attack, set it in the right direction, and change our sprite. Then we'll move to the attack state to wait until the attack is finished. This way we can control what the player can do in the attack state, such as only allowing them to collide and be affected by gravity. I will note here that it's possible to get away without using an attack state, depending on how you want your game to play, and if you don't mind a little extra complexity. As you'll see we revert back to our moving state after the attack animation is completed, but you could have that check be in the walking state instead of being in another one. Personally, I find using more states allows for easier debugging and coding overall, so that's what I prefer and what we'll be coding together.

The next thing we need to do is create our ice attack

object. Open the Player folder, then Related, and create a new object and call it objIce-Attack. Assign the sprIceAttack to this object's sprite. Then add a Create event and Step event, we'll focus on the Create first. Let's set the speed and direction of this attack here, using the built-in variables. We don't need to do anything super fancy with this attack, such as make it follow a flying enemy like a heat seeking rocket, so using the built-in variables works great. Set speed to 5. We will need to set the direction, but we'll do that when we create it because the direction changes whether we're facing left or right.

And now I find the size of the ice attack to be a little large, so I'm going to set the x and y scales to half. Decreasing the size through code gives a much better look than shrinking the image itself, so I'd encourage you to do that whenever possible.

Lastly, we're going to give this ice attack a life timer so it can't fly on indefinitely. Give it a variable called currentLife and set it to 0, and then a maxLife variable set at 40 **(Figure 22.2)**. Now let's go into the Step event and set it to eventually die if it reaches the end of its life, or it collides with a solid.

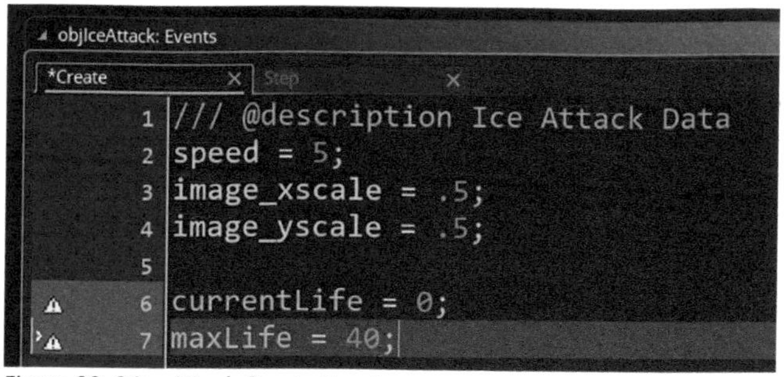

```
objIceAttack: Events
*Create                 ×   Step           ×
1  /// @description Ice Attack Data
2  speed = 5;
3  image_xscale = .5;
4  image_yscale = .5;
5
6  currentLife = 0;
7  maxLife = 40;
```

Figure 22. 2 Ice Attack Create Event

At the very top increase currentLife by 1. Then add a check if it's meeting with objSolid-sParent, or its currentLife exceeds its maxLife variable. In either of these cases, destroy this object **(Figure 22.3)**. We'll create another object later on, with the sprite of the ice blast disappearing, but for now just destroying the attack will work.

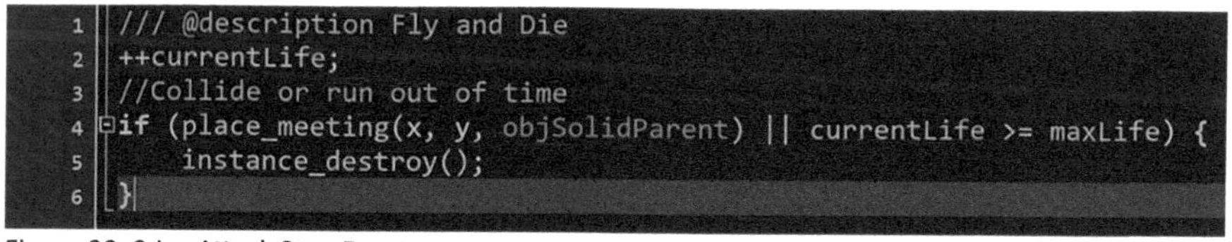

```
1  /// @description Fly and Die
2  ++currentLife;
3  //Collide or run out of time
4  if (place_meeting(x, y, objSolidParent) || currentLife >= maxLife) {
5      instance_destroy();
6  }
```

Figure 22. 3 Ice Attack Step Event

Now let's return to the player's step event and actually create the ice attack and set it off in the correct direction. First let's set the sprite to attack when we click the attack button and set the image_index to 0 so the animation begins at the beginning.

There are two primary ways of creating projectiles. The first is quite simple and what we'll be using in this game, whereas the second is more complex but offers a lot more flexibility in using many different projectiles of different shapes and sizes and different directions. I mention the more complex way because I have a tutorial on my channel that covers it in depth, which I encourage you to check out if you're going to be adding more attacks to this game, or think you'll be working with projectiles in your future titles (the tutorial is a little outdated, but the logic and code still function the same).

```
if (attack) {
    myState = PlayerState.attacking;
    sprite_index = sprites[hero][Attack];
    image_index = 0;
    var iceAttack = instance_create_depth(x + image_xscale * 15, y + 5, depth - 1, objIceAttack);
    if (image_xscale == 1) {
        iceAttack.direction = 0;
    }
    else {
        iceAttack.direction = 180;
    }
    iceAttack.image_angle = iceAttack.direction;
}
```

Figure 22. 4 Simple Method for Creating Attack

The method we're using is in **figure 22.4** and has us creating the ice attack at a fixed-point relative to the player. It's got hard-coded x and y coordinates and doesn't adapt to the sprite casting the spell or the spell itself. You can see the code changing the direction of the ice attack based on the way we're standing, and then setting the image_angle based on the direction. This setting of the image_angle is important because it's facing to the right by default but needs to be facing left when we fire it that direction. An important thing to note about projectiles is they should always be facing to the right in the sprite. If they're not, changing their image_angle at all becomes messy and doesn't work, but if it's facing to the right, you can adjust the image_angle to anything and it will always look great!

Give this a try and see what you think. Pinky, or whomever, will continue animating and you can only fire 1 attack right now, but it does spawn where you want it to, whether you're facing left or right. And that's all we need it to do, so let's call that good!

Now we need to handle the logic in the attack state and return to move when we're done. So, first check if the animation is done playing, and if it is, reset the sprite, image_index, and return to the moving state **(Figure 22.5)**. That's all we need to get back to moving, and then be able to continue attacking, but it isn't all we need in the attack state, however, because if we attack while in the air, we just hang there for a second, which looks and feels weird!

```
case PlayerState.attacking:
    if (image_index >= image_number - 1) {
        image_index = 0;
        sprite_index = sprites[hero][Idle];
        myState = PlayerState.moving;
    }
break;
```

Figure 22. 5 End of Atack Animation

The solution is to add gravity, collisions, and movement, just like in the damaged state. And that's today's challenge.

Conclusion + Challenge

We added in another state today and a projectile attack. It's looking good, but the attack state isn't quite finished. Your challenge for today is to finish the attack state's code, and to get it working and feeling good. We've done something similar in the damaged state, so look there if you get stuck.

Best of luck!

Day 23

Now We're Getting Somewhere!

Yesterday's Challenge

If you didn't attempt yesterday's challenge of coding the remaining attack state, I highly encourage you to do so. I know you can do it! The code I came up with is in **figure 23.0**. You may have also discovered a strange bug where Pinky slides across the ground when you attack while moving. The solution to this issue is to check if Pinky is on the ground when beginning the attack, and if so, setting their xSpeed to 0 **(Figure 23.1)**. You don't want to set it to 0 otherwise, since if they're in the air moving, they'll just drop like a stone.

```
if (attack) {
    myState = PlayerState.attacking;
    if (onSolid) {
        xSpeed = 0;
    }
}
```

Figure 23.1 Stop Sliding

```
#region Attacking State
case PlayerState.attacking:
    if (image_index >= image_number - 1) {
        image_index = 0;
        sprite_index = sprites[hero][Idle];
        myState = PlayerState.moving;
    }
    //Control Movement & Falling
    if (onSolid == false) {
        ySpeed += gameGravity;
        jumpBuffer -= 1;
    }
    else {
        ySpeed = 0;
        jumpBuffer = maxJumpBuffer;
    }

    CollideWith();

    x += xSpeed;
    y += ySpeed;
break;
#endregion
```

Figure 23.0 The Attack State

Shattering Ice

Now it's time to wrap up the ice attack and add some damage to it and Biter. Currently Biter can't take any damage because it has no health, but we'll get to that shortly. First, however, let's create one more object and call it objIceShatter, in the same folder with the ice attack. Add a Create and Animation End event. In the Create event, set the image scales to .35.. And in the Animation End event, destroy it. We've already set the speed we want this to play at, so all we need to do is create it, let it play, and then destroy it at the end.

Return to the ice attack object and add the Destroy event. Since we want to create the ice shatter object after the attack is dead, we can create it in the destroy event once, instead of needing to do it multiple times in the Step event. In here we want to create the objIceShatter object at a depth 1 under the ice attack and create it at the tip of the ice projectile, as it looks best that way. To accomplish that, we need to add 10 either right or left, depending on which way the ice attack is flying. The simplest method that comes to mind is in **figure 23.2**, giving dir a default value and changing it if it's not facing that way.

```
/// @description Create Shatter
var dir = -1;
if (direction == 0) {
    dir = 1;
}
instance_create_depth(x + (dir * 10), y, depth - 1, objIceShatter);
```

Figure 23.2 Ice Shatter

And finally, we need the sound that goes along with the ice shattering. It's in Assets, Sounds, labeled Ice Shatter. Bring it in and rename it to sndIceShatter. Set its volume to 0.25. Play it in the create event of the ice shatter.

With that code in place, run your game and try shooting an ice attack. The shatter effect now appears and, in my opinion, looks and sounds great! The primary reason we're using an object to do this in the first place, instead of just drawing this ice shatter effect in the ice attack, is that the ice attack will eventually do damage to Biter, and if it were to stay around for an extra second while it plays this animation, it would be difficult to know when not to subtract damage. Creating another object for the ice shatter effect negates that and makes things easier overall.

The End of Biter

Speaking of the little bugger, it's time to give some health to Biter just so we can take it away. Open Biter's create event and add some variables for health, like currentHealth and maxHealth. I'm giving Biter 2 health, enough to test that our attack works, but not enough to be a real pain.

Open Biter's Step event and do a check to see if Biter is colliding with an ice attack object. If so, change its state to damaged, set its sprite to damaged, set its image_index to 0, destroy the ice attack, and subtract its health by 1 **(Figure 23.3)**. And then in the damaged state, check to see if Biter has any health left. If so, revert Biter back to idle after finishing the animation, but if not, set its state to dead and play the explode animation **(Figure 23.4)**.

```
//Getting Hurt
if (place_meeting(x, y, objIceAttack)) {
    myState = EnemyState.damaged;
    sprite_index = sprBiterHurt;
    image_index = 0;
    instance_destroy(objIceAttack);
    --currentHealth;
}
```

Figure 23.3 Biter Getting Hurt

We've done all this before, which is why I'm just giving you instructions and not much else. This stuff needs to get done, but it's nothing new and exciting. Plus, we're almost totally done with Biter so I'm getting excited for what's coming next! Let's wrap this up.

```
#region Damaged State
case EnemyState.damaged:
    if (currentHealth > 0) {
        if (image_index >= image_number - 1) {
            image_index = 0;
            sprite_index = sprBiterIdle;
            myState = EnemyState.idle;
        }
    }
    else {
        sprite_index = sprBiterExplode;
        image_index = 0;
        myState = EnemyState.dead;
    }
break;
#endregion
```

Figure 23.4 Biter Damaged State

The explode animation needs to be altered a bit, so open it up. Change its FPS to 10, add a new empty frame at the end, and trim the entire sprite so it doesn't have a bunch of excess space **(Figure 23.5)**. The extra space makes the explosion be created above Biter which looks weird. In the transition to dead state, set the x and y scale to half, as the explosion is still too large. Also bring Biter down by 5 pixels so the explosion looks more centered. You don't have to, but I think it helps.

There's also a sound to accompany Biter exploding, so let's not forget that. It's in Assets, Sounds, and called Monster Death. Bring it in and name it sndBiterDeath. Play the sound when Biter is transitioning into the dead state.

And the last thing to do is check when the animation has finished, then destroy Biter. Since the FPS is at 10, you don't need to subtract 1 from image_number. And after that, we're all done with Biter! You may find a weird quirk or two, such as attacking Biter in the charge state turns him around and back to walking. Personally, I don't mind this, but if you wanted Biter to continue charging, you might hold the previous state of Biter in a variable and return him to that state instead of defaulting to idle.

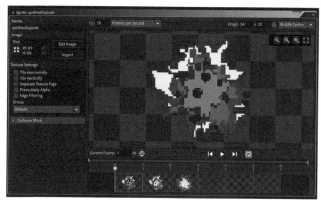

Figure 23.5 Explosion

The only real issue you may discover is that because we're just changing the sprite of Biter, we can still collide with it and take damage while it's exploding. This is a problem, but not a big one since the attack is ranged, and the animation is so short. A few ways to fix it would be destroying Biter and replacing it with an explosion object, just like the ice shatter object. Or you can make the collision mask on the explosion tiny, so the player would have an awfully hard time running into it. As for me, I'm not going to worry about it, since it forces the player to think a little more when fighting, which is the kind of game I enjoy.

Let's Talk

The time has finally come. Are you ready for it? We're going to add a dialogue box into the game! Exciting, I know. With this power comes great responsibility, as it will allow you to send the player messages, instructions, jokes, and so much more. Our dialogue box will be fairly simple, but I have several tutorials on my channel where I go much more in depth, so after you're done with this book, you should check them out.

What we need first is the sprite we'll be using for the dialogue, which is in the Assets folder, Sprites, and it's called Message Box. Bring that into the Sprites folder in your game and rename it to sprMessageBox. It's a simple sprite

175

but works great for what we need. Now create an object called objMessageBox and give it this sprite.

And there's also a sound to play when the message box appears, so let's bring that in, too. It's called New Message, in the Sounds folder, so bring that into your game. Rename it to sndMessageBox. We don't need to do anything else with it.

Before we begin coding, let me lay out what we'll be doing. The main idea is to create a message box, or dialogue box, and be able to pass in any text we want. That text will then be displayed onto the box, one letter at a time, like a typewriter. The player will be able to make the entire message appear instantly or wait until the end and then destroy it. This message box will only be able to fit one message, it won't have multiple screens. It's possible to make a system that can break up long messages and have them displayed one after the other. If you want to see that check out my advanced course where we create an entire dialogue system like that, plus so much more.

For this game though, we'll be sticking to a simple dialogue box. I'll drop some hints along the way of how to upgrade in the future, though. And now, with all that out of the way, let's dive into creating our message box.

Add 4 events to objMessageBox; Create, Step, Draw, User Event 0. User Events are something we haven't looked at yet, but you can image them as a custom event that we can trigger with a specific function. It's almost like a function, but only for that one object. I find them useful and want to show you how to use them, as the more tools you have, the better off you'll be.

User Events

Every object can have 16 User Events, like functions defined specifically for the object they're created in. They are a onetime event but can be triggered as often as you want. They're great for writing a bit of code that you want to decide when it runs.

In the Create event, we're going to add a good number of variables, but we'll start small. Create a variable called myMessage and set it to undefined. This variable will hold the entirety of the message to be shown to the player. Next add a currentText variable and set it to an empty string. This variable will hold the text that is actively on screen, which will grow over time. And finally, add textIndex and set it to 0. This variable will be the spot within myMessage we're currently at **(Figure 23.6)**. And then play the sound we brought in here.

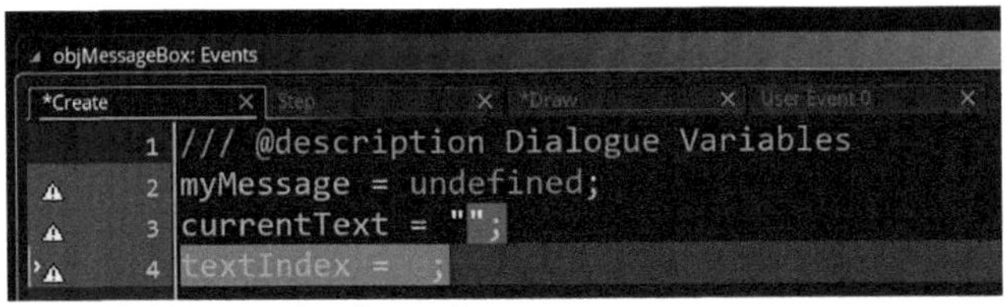

Figure 23.6 Message Box Create Event

Now open the Draw event and add draw_self at the top. Then we're going to align the horizontal and vertical axis for drawing. The two functions we'll use to do this are:

```
draw_set_halign();

draw_set_valign();
```

These functions determine where text is drawn at, when drawing it on screen. The first one is for horizontal and you have 3 options: left, center, right. The second function is for vertical alignment, and again you have 3 options: top, middle, and bottom. **Figure 23.7** show the differences. There are times you want each one, but for our message box we want the text to draw in the top left corner, and go until it reaches the edge of the sprite, then continue on a new line below.

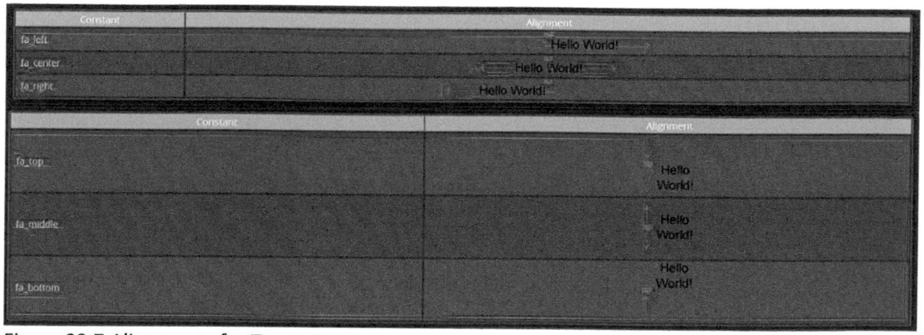

Figure 23.7 Alignments for Text

So, set halign to fa_left, and valign to fa_top. And then below that, draw text using the function draw_text_ext. This function allows us to draw multiple lines of text on the screen, as opposed to a single line. With that power comes more options though, such as the distance between the lines, called line separation, and the total width of any line. Add it in like this:

```
draw_text_ext(bbox_left + 8, bbox_top + 2, currentText, 12, 190);
```

We'll replace those last two numbers with variables down the road, but for now they'll be fine. I want to show you how to get the text on the screen before we worry about how it looks. And now jump over to the Step event where we'll set the text to be displayed.

There are many dedicated functions to manipulating text in GameMaker, but the one we want is called string_copy. It copies over text from one to another, but not at all once. We get to specify how much we want, which is where our textIndex comes into play. We want to copy over 1 character at a time and add it to currentText. This will create that typewriter effect which is so often used. Add these lines in the step event:

177

```
currentText = string_copy(myMessage,
0, textIndex);

textIndex += 0.5;
```

The first line copies over the text, and second increases the amount to be copied for the next frame.

And that's all we need to display some text, so let's give it a go! Jump into the Create event of the player and create our message box object at our players location. Then set the variable myMessage to a message, a string, and run the game. You should see a message box appear with your message **(Figure 23.8)**!

Figure 23.8 Message Box

Error Help

- If you get the error "string_copy argument 1 incorrect type (undefined) expecting a String (YYGS)", you've not set myMessage to a string as required. Or you haven't done it soon enough before the function tries to copy an undefined string. Be sure to set myMessage immediately after creating the object.

Conclusion + Challenge

Making a dialogue box is a huge step in your game dev journey. Every game needs a way to communicate with the player, even if it's just to give instructions on how to play. I imagine that whatever you game want to create, whether it be story driven, or action-focused, you'll be using dialogue in one form or another.

There are a thousand different ways of presenting dialogue in games, and your challenge today is to find a few of those. Maybe play some old and new games or watch some random gameplay videos and check out their message boxes. What features do they seem to have? Which features do you think you'll want in your game project?

Dwell on these things and hit me up on Twitter when you know!

Day 24

Ooooh, Pretty Text

Yesterday's Challenge

I'm sure you discovered that there's extraordinarily little rhyme or reason to dialogue boxes. Sure, there are some universal features that all need, but that commonality is quite small to how diverse they can be. And that's a big reason why I'm not going into too much depth on them. That, and the fact it can get overly complex very quickly and could easily become its own book.

But for now, just keep in mind the features you want and think on how you might create them in your next game. Anything you want to do is possible, you'll just need the patience and ability to create it.

Fine-Tuning the Message Box

Our job today is to get the message box looking great! We're going to accomplish this by adjusting the font and ensuring our text stays inside the message box. The first things we'll tackle is the font, so let's make one of those now.

Create a font and name it fntMessageBox. You can choose a unique font, but I'm going to stick with Arial. Set the font size to 10, or whatever 10 Airal looks like in the font you select. Then return to the Create event in the message box and set the font to what we just created by using the function draw_set_font. This draw function doesn't need to be in the Draw event, it can be set anywhere. It's a good idea to always set it right before what you'll be drawing, as it is system wide. That means if we had a UI in our game and changed the font to message box, all the UI font would also change.

As a rule of thumb when it comes to using draw functions, like setting fonts, colors, and alignment, always call them before you draw something on screen to ensure what you're drawing there is the way you want. If you're only ever drawing things that use the same font, color, and alignment, it won't matter. But once you begin using multiple fonts and adding a UI, it's essential to repeat these functions often, sometimes even in the draw or step event. Overkill is better in this scenario.

Two things we need to set are the width and line separation. Right now, they're hard coded in, so let's make those variables and give them more dynamic values. First let's set the width to be sprite_width – 16. This allows you to use other message boxes that have a similar border size. The amount of border you want on the text is up to you, but I find this to be a good amount.

Next create lineSeperation and set it to this function:

```
lineSeperation = string_height("Aby");
```

String height is a function that returns, in pixels, the height of whatever string you pass in. In this case, we're passing in a capital, lowercase, and hanging letter so get what the height of any given line could be. If you set the font before this, and then call this function, your message box will now always be separated correctly, which is pretty neat.

Now, pop on over to the Draw event and replace the last two values in the draw_text_ext function with the variables we just created. Next, return to the Create event and make another variable called messageSpeed and set it to 0.5. Then go to the Step event and replace the 0.5 there with our new variable. This part isn't necessary, but it does make it easier to adjust the text speed in the future, which is always nice.

Now let's set up the User Event 0. The goal with this event is to call it when the user clicks a button. If all the text is displayed, we'll destroy the message box, otherwise we'll skip to the end of the message.

So, let's create a check if currentText is equal to myMessage. If it is, then destroy the message box, otherwise increase textIndex by 1000, which will be plenty to skip it to the end. I'll show how to call this event shortly. But for now, that's everything we need to do with the message box. I'll post images of all the code, so you can ensure you got it all correct.

Figures 24.0 – Figures 24.3 are the events of message box.

The last thing we need to do is create a function where we can pass a message in and it creates the message box. So, create a new Script and call it Messages. Inside, make a function called ShowMessage that accepts one argument called message. The argument message may show green for a second, as it's a built-in variable. I don't quite know what it does, as the manual pulls up blank and I've never used it before, but it will turn into a local variable after a second.

We'll only create this one function, but you could easily make more. You could create one to display the message box in a certain area, or at a certain speed, etc... For now, this function will make a message box in the middle of the screen and display the message we pass inside. Simple but effective. However, that raises a question. How do we create the message box in the middle of the screen, when we're using views and can move all over the room? I'm so glad you asked.

```
objMessageBox: Events
Create                    Step              Draw              User Event 0
1  /// @description Dialogue Variables
2  myMessage = undefined;
3  currentText = "";
4  textIndex = 0;
5  audio_play_sound(sndMessageBox, 1, false);
6  draw_set_font(fntMessageBox);
7  width = sprite_width - 16;
8  lineSeperation = string_height("Aby");
9  messageSpeed = 0.5;
```

Figure 24.0 Message Box Create Event

Views, Cameras, and More Functions

Recall back to when we set up the room we're in and the camera we're using. We did it all through the room GUI, not code. We set the up viewports and enabled the first viewport with some specific numbers. Although we didn't create it in code, we are using a camera to see our room, it's just the default camera GameMaker created for us. We'll create our own camera later on, when we do room transitions, but for now we can just get the data from the default camera.

```
objMessageBox: Events
Create          Step            Draw            User Event 0
1  /// @description Add Text Over Time
2  currentText = string_copy(myMessage, 0, textIndex);
3  textIndex += messageSpeed;
```

Figure 24.1 Message Box Step Event

What we see on the screen is what the camera sees, and it stores a lot of useful information. We can use that information to get the coordinates of where we're at and where we should place the message box, so it appears in the middle of the screen/camera. This is something you will use all the time in future games, so we're going to create functions to get at this information. They're simple, and yet will save you so much time and frustration later down the road.

```
objMessageBox: Events
                Draw
1  /// @description Draw The Text
2  draw_self();
3
4  draw_set_halign(fa_left);
5  draw_set_valign(fa_top);
6
7  draw_text_ext(bbox_left + 8, bbox_top + 2, currentText, lineSeperation, width);
```

Figure 24.2 Message Box Draw Event

So, create a new script and call it CameraHelpers. In this, we'll put all the functions for getting at different locations on screen. Do note that we will be accessing the camera in the first viewport specifically, which means if you create another camera and assign it elsewhere, these functions won't work. Of course, you can modify them to accept an argument of which camera you want, which wouldn't

```
objMessageBox: Events
Create          Step            Draw            User Event 0
1  /// @description Go to end / Destroy
2  if (currentText == myMessage) {
3      instance_destroy();
4  }
5  else {
6      textIndex += 1000;
7  }
```

Figure 24.3 Message Box User Event

be very difficult at all. But let me show you what I mean, instead of just rambling on.

For the first function to create, call it CameraX. And inside all we need is this code:

```
return camera_get_view_x(view_cam-
era[0]);
```

This function simply gets the x coordinate of the camera assigned to view_camera[0], which is an array of all the cameras, and returns it. The x coordinate for the camera will be on the left edge, as the camera's origin is essentially 0,0. But we can work with this information to find the rest.

Next, create a function called CameraY and, as you can probably guess, call the same function except this time use y instead of x. This returns the top edge of the camera's position in the room. With these two functions, we can easily get everywhere else within the camera's view by also getting the height and width. **Figure 24.4** is an example of all the camera coordinates we'll be accessing.

Create another function called CameraMiddleX, and this time we're returning CameraX() + half the width of the camera. It looks like this:

```
return CameraX() + camera_get_view_
```

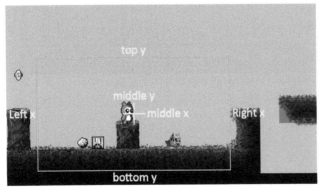

Figure 24.4 Camera Coordinates

```
width(view_camera[0]) / 2;
```

By knowing where the left side of the camera is at in the room, and how wide it is, we can get the middle of the camera, too. This same principal is what we'll apply to get the right side, middle for the y, and bottom for y. Here are the rest of the functions we'll use:

- CameraMiddleY
- CameraRightX
- CameraBottomY

They're all terribly similar, just changing either the x and y, or width and height. We're using smaller functions, like CameraX, to create more complex functions. That's what advanced programming is really all about. You build small pieces and ensure they work, then put them together to create something complex. You test that complex piece thoroughly, then put it together with another piece to create your game. It goes on and on, but this is how it starts. Pretty cool huh?

Figure 24.5 is all the functions you need to create. I have descriptions on them because we can use what's called JSDoc Script Comments to write our own comments for our functions, including the arguments. You can check out all the details by opening the manual and typing JSDoc and clicking on the first thing that pops up. I use these all the time, and I'd encourage you to do the same.

Now that we have all of those in place, let's use them with the script ShowMessage to create the message box in the middle of the screen. The code for the function is this:

```
var messageBox = instance_create_
depth(CameraMiddleX(), CameraMid-
dleY(), depth - 100, objMessageBox);

messageBox.myMessage = message;
```

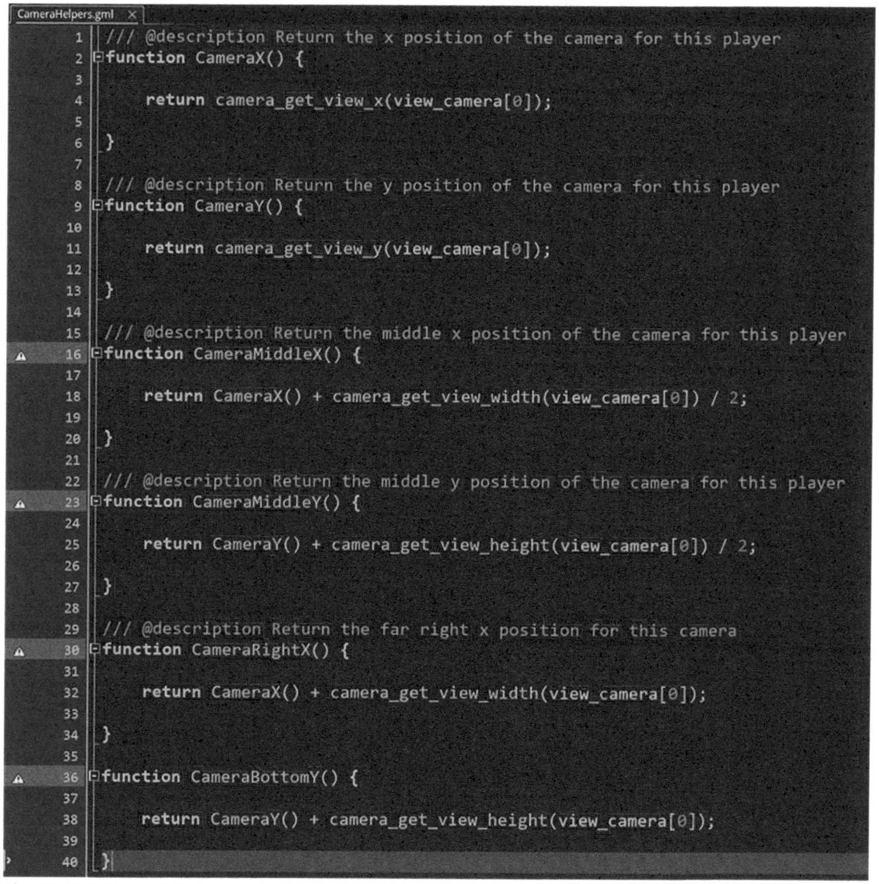

```gml
/// @description Return the x position of the camera for this player
function CameraX() {

    return camera_get_view_x(view_camera[0]);

}

/// @description Return the y position of the camera for this player
function CameraY() {

    return camera_get_view_y(view_camera[0]);

}

/// @description Return the middle x position of the camera for this player
function CameraMiddleX() {

    return CameraX() + camera_get_view_width(view_camera[0]) / 2;

}

/// @description Return the middle y position of the camera for this player
function CameraMiddleY() {

    return CameraY() + camera_get_view_height(view_camera[0]) / 2;

}

/// @description Return the far right x position for this camera
function CameraRightX() {

    return CameraX() + camera_get_view_width(view_camera[0]);

}

function CameraBottomY() {

    return CameraY() + camera_get_view_height(view_camera[0]);

}
```

Figure 24.5 Camera Helper Functions

It's a long first line, I know. But just image if we didn't have those scripts to call and had to use the full functions to get the middle x and y of the camera. This way is shorter. Let's do a quick test to see that all our new scripts are working correctly. In objPowerJump, use the script in the Collision event. Then run your game and collect the coin to see if a message box appears.

It worked for me! What about you? The reason we can't use it just anywhere is because the camera needs a frame to set up and move from where it is initially in the top left corner. After a frame, you can call it anywhere, but I thought that would be easiest thing to do.

Conclusion + Challenge

We got off on a little bit of a tangent, but that's alright. We'll be needing all those functions soon, and they're ones you can take with you into every game you make. Reusable code is a great thing!

Today's challenge is a big one, are you ready for it? I want you to tackle the dialogue state. All of it. What I'll be doing with the message box specifically is telling the players what the power-up coin does when they collect it. I'll freeze the player in place while the message box is on screen. They can skip to the end of the message, and then destroy it by pressing any key or mouse click. When it's destroyed, they continue falling since they were in mid-air.

You don't have to try and do all that but see if you can set it up so the player can enter and exit the dialogue state. The one function you'll need is called event_perform, and you must use with in conjunction with the with statement. There is another function called event_perform_object, but it does work the way you expect it to, so I'd ignore it.

Well, get to it!

PRO TIP

Ideas Don't Matter

John Watson
Developer of Gravity Ace

GravityAce.com

Ideas don't matter as much as you think.

Lots of developers and designers hoard ideas and keep them secret. Their thinking is that they have something so unique and wonderful that it's worth a goldmine all by itself. But that's almost never true. Players only care about your idea to the extent that they'll be able to play it one day. And other developers don't care about your idea either. Every developer I know has a hundred ideas of their own that they care about way more than yours. And even if several developers all make a game based on the same idea, those games will all turn out differently. On top of that, your idea probably isn't even unique. And a strong indicator that an idea is good in the first place is that other people are already doing it.

Players only really care about the actual game that you made and how well it was executed. That's the only thing they can download or pay money for. If fun was a math equation it might look something like: fun = idea × execution. A great idea executed poorly won't be any fun (imagine a really great game idea but it crashes every 2 minutes). And great execution on a terrible idea won't be any fun either (imagine the most amazing version of a game where you watch grass grow). My personal belief is that ideas aren't nearly as important as execution. That is, it's good to choose an idea that delights people vs. ideas that no one likes. But that doesn't mean the idea has to be super unique or weird or novel. Lots of games do just fine rehashing old ideas — just think of how many sequels come out every year. It's more important to execute that idea to a very high level. Because even the most novel and interesting idea in the world won't matter at all if you can't execute it well.

Day 25

Let's Learn About Sequences

Yesterday's Challenge

Well, I left you with a doozy of a challenge yesterday. How'd it go? I hope you were able to figure it out and get the dialogue state up and running. It should have been one of the shorter states to code, although getting the User Event to trigger can be difficult and annoying. Let's walk through it together now.

The first thing is to display the message when the user collects the power up coin. Open objPowerJump and in the collision with the player event, call ShowMessage with a message like:

"Your jumping power has increased! Use it wisely."

Then jump over to the Player's Step event beneath where we're moving into the attack state and add a check if a message box exists. If so, we'll transition into the dialogue state. Change our state to dialogue and our image_speed to 0 **(Figure 25.0)**.

```
//Dialogue
if (instance_exists(objMessageBox)) {
    myState = PlayerState.dialogue;
    image_speed = 0;
}
```
Figure 25.0 Into the Dialogue State

In the dialogue state, the way to get out is when the message box no longer exists. So add a check to see if it doesn't exist, and if that's true, revert our image_speed back to 1, and change back into the moving state. If the user presses any key, activate User Event 0 with the message box **(Figure 25.1)**.

```
#region Dialogue State
case PlayerState.dialogue:
    //Return to walking when message box is no more
    if (instance_exists(objMessageBox) == false) {
        myState = PlayerState.moving;
        image_speed = 1;
    }
    //Speed up or destroy message box
    if (keyboard_check_pressed(vk_anykey) || mouse_check_button_pressed(mb_any)) {
        with(objMessageBox) {
            event_perform(ev_other, ev_user0);
        }
    }
break;
#endregion
```
Figure 25.1 Dialogue State

If you tried using event_perform_object you would have come across some issues. I don't know why they designed it the way they did, but as far as I can tell, that function takes all the code in that User Event and then runs it on the object that is calling the code. So essentially it would be making our player run the code, instead of the message box running it. It makes zero sense.

The other new thing here is the event_perform function, which if you looked up in the manual, you would have found the necessary arguments for. This function can manually trigger any event, given you know the correct constants, which are all listed out in the manual. It's a pretty cool function, with far-reaching possibilities. Today though, we're just using it to trigger one event in another object.

And that's all there was to it. With that code in place, our message box appears, pauses our player in the air, and allows them to read it at their pace. When they're done, they dismiss it and resume playing, all powered up. Pretty neat stuff, right?

Sequences

Sequences are an extremely powerful tool to create many different things, such as cut scenes, complete animations, and more. Sequences can have sequences nested inside them for even more complexity. All parts of a sequence can also be controlled through code, giving you fine-grain control over how a sequence plays out.

Sequences!

With the core gameplay wrapped up, we're going to move onto some more technical and difficult subjects. But don't worry, you're ready for them. Today we start creating the main menu for our game. That's going to involve data structures, sequences, saving and loading, and more! This is when we truly transition from the beginner to the intermediate. I'll do my best to make it a natural transition, not even noticeable, except for what I'm telling you now. Ready? Let's go!

The first thing new subject we're going to tackle are sequences. I'm only going to touch on their power and awesomeness, but it should be enough to get you started. So, what are sequences? Sequences are the newest feature in GameMaker, having been added in the middle of 2019. They are a powerful set of tools that allow for easy design of cut scenes, animations, object interactions, and more. They share a lot in common with other programs like Adobe After Effects, Hitfilm, and Blender. So, if you've used any of those, you'll be right at home with the interface. But if you haven't, don't fret, we're going to walk through it together.

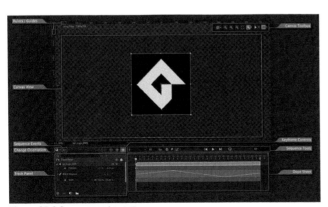

Figure 25.2 Sequences Layout

Figure 25.2 lays out all the different parts of a sequence. In fact, go ahead and create a sequence now to see it for yourself. It's going to look completely different from everything else in GameMaker, but that's because it's like another program built in.

The three big parts to pay attention to are the Canvas View, which is the big area in the middle with the checkered background. This area is where you place all of your assets, including sprites, objects, sounds, and more. It's where you can easily move and manipulate them, and where you can preview the sequence when you press play.

Then there's the Track Panel on the bottom left, which begins empty. Let's go ahead and drag objPlayer onto the Canvas and see what shows up in the Track Panel. Now the Track Panel has objPlayer as an object there. Click the little arrow to the left of its name to see which properties you can manipulate. By default, only Position is shown, but you can add 7 properties all together: Position, Rotation, Colour Multiply, Image Index, Image Speed, Origin, and Scale. By clicking on the small plus icon, next to the eye, you can add more properties **(Figure 25.3)**.

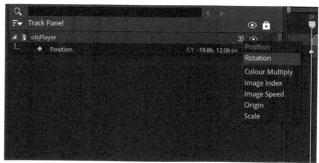

Figure 25.3 Adding Track Proporties

And finally, for now at least, is the Dope Sheet. You can see that it has an orange rectangle since we added in objPlayer to the canvas. The Dope Sheet controls the length and when changes occur to your assets in a sequence. Click on the orange bar and drag it to 20f, which stands for frames. Then move Pinky to the right. A white dot with an arrow appears at that orange bar, which indicates the end of a change **(Figure 25.4)**. Move the orange bar back to the beginning and you'll notice Pinky now moves, too. The Dope Sheet has recorded Pinky's initial position, and then by moving along in the sequence and making a position change, it has created a linear interpolation. Pinky moves from point A to point B in a smooth line, increasing evenly the whole time.

Figure 25.4 Dope Sheet Changes

There are many, many different kinds of interpolations, or more commonly known as curves, that you can create to have more interesting movement. Think about any YouTube video intro, or just text on an ad. Remember how some if it comes flying in, hits some invisible point, then snaps back a little bit into place? That's a special kind of curve of motion. You can make it quick, slow, quick and slow at different parts, and so on. There's really no end to what you can do, especially in GameMaker because you can create your animation curves.

Figure 25.5 Position Curve

To see that for yourself, right click on the white dot/arrow, and click on convert to curve **(Figure 25.5)**. Let's focus on my curve for now, since I can't see yours and it is probably different. Every property you can manipulate has different curves in it, specific parts of the property. For Position, it's x and y. Blue is x and red is y, and on mine I've only moved Pinky to the right, so the blue line as changed while the red remains static. How do I know that? Well, I expanded the curves view and it labels the curves.

To expand it for yourself, click on the little curves button,

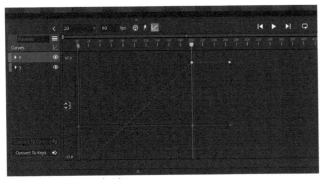

Figure 25.6 Curve Mode View

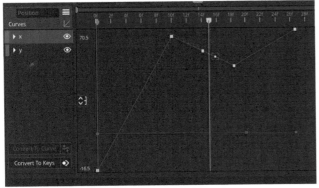

Figure 25.7 Adding More Points to a Curve

Figure 25.8 Changing Curve Type

the one to the right of the lightning bolt. It expands what you've selected, so be sure to click on Position first, then click on the button, it's called Toggle Curve Mode. And now we have a totally new view, with labels for each line on the graph **(Figure 25.6)**!

I know this is a lot to take in, especially if something like this is new. If you're getting confused or overwhelmed, take a small break, and come back. We're not going to do anything else today, just learn a bit more about Sequences. One of the most valuable lessons I've learned as a programmer is to let new ideas marinate for a while. That means learning one day, then sleeping on it before you really give it a go. This works in all areas of life, but I've found it most helpful in the technical areas, where new ideas can seem daunting at first, but eventually become commonplace with enough repetition and endurance.

Take a look at your curve and look for the squares along the lines. These indicate changes you've made, or changes elsewhere in this property that are being stored. That's all the Dope Sheet is, in reality. It simply remembers a properties position at a certain time within the sequence, so by changing where those are, you change the sequence itself. Grab the box on frame 20 of whichever axis you moved Pinky and drag it back 10 frames. You probably won't get it exactly lined up, so now Pinky mostly snaps to its new position, but then slides the rest of the 10 frames.

You've changed the curve, making it your own. You can also click anywhere on the curve to add more spots **(Figure 25.7)**. By adding more points, you can make the curve go quicker, slower, or go totally crazy. But it's all still linear, not really curve like. It's more like a mountain. To change the curve type, click on the graph icon next to the word Curves and select Smooth **(Figure 25.8)**. Now it looks curvier! There are 3 kinds of curve types you can use, Linear, Smooth, Bezier. I'm not an expert in this area, but you should experiment around with each when using Sequences to get the effect you're looking for.

And lastly, I want to show you how to create a shared curve, one that multiple assets can use. It can save a lot of time creating a shared curve. Click on the little hamburger menu above where the Curves button is **(Figure 25.9)** and select Export To Shared Curve. This creates a new asset in your Asset Browser, called an Animation Curve. Double click on it to open a new window. You'll find the same curve here that was in the sequence's editor, only now you can name it and then use this curve on other assets **(Figure 25.10)**.

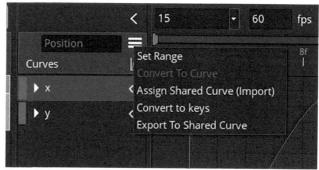

Figure 25.9 Creating a Shared Curve

And that's all I wanted to show you for today. It's a lot. We'll be using sequences to make a really cool animation for our menu. Sequences are only going to grow and become more powerful and more people understand what they can do and how to best use them, which is why it's important to start learning now.

Conclusion + Challenge

Sequences are a huge section of GameMaker, nearly a program unto itself. It's a little daunting, but they're also really cool. My challenge for you today is to play around with sequences more and see what you can discover. Browse the manual and see what functions are available and what you might be able to do with them.

Tomorrow we'll start creating our menu with sequences!

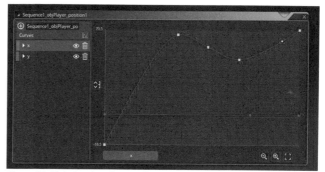

Figure 25.10 Animation Curve Editor

Day 26

Crafting the Perfect Scene

Yesterday's Challenge

I hope you took some time relax, think about Sequences, and even play around with them a bit. There's a lot there, and we're only going to scratch the surface today, so keep your eyes open and your mind ready to learn!

Your First Sequence

Go ahead and delete the sequence and animation curve we created yesterday. When I first deleted a shared animation curve that was still attached to a sequence, GameMaker did become unstable, so if that happens to you, don't worry. Just save and restart. Now let's create a new sequence called seqMenuAnimation.

In our menu, we're going to use several sprites and a couple sounds. Let's bring those all in now to save time later. Navigate to Assets, Sprites, Menu and bring in all 4 of those sprites. I'm bringing them into a new group called Menu and making a Sprites folder inside of it. Rename them each and put a spr in front of them. Then navigate to Assets, Sounds, and bring in Menu Move, and Menu Selection. Create a folder named Sounds inside of Menu and toss them in there. Rename them appropriately.

Lastly, we'll need 2 objects. Create one called objMenuCircle, and one called objMenuBox. Assign the play sprite to objMenuCircle, and box sprite to objMenuBox. ObjMenuCircle will be one object that will change sprites, based on the menu box attached to it.

Now jump over to our sequence. The goal here is to create snappy animation that plays when we open the menu, and when scrolling through the options. We're going to use both of our menu objects, so grab them and put them into the sequence. The canvas size and where we put these objects does matter, so let's get those settings correct right now.

Click on the top right arrow, the one next to the highlighted box. Set the width to 640 and the height 480, leaving everything else the same. Then expand objMenuCircle in the Track Panel and set its x and y position to -1. You can click on the numbers and write in your own, although double clicking to select all of it doesn't seem to work well. Once you've got that, add in tracks on objMenuCircle for rotation and scale **(Figure 26.0)**.

Figure 26.0 Adding Tracks

For objMenuBox, add a track for Colour Multiply. Colour Multiply can also control transparency, which is good to note. Next, line up the two objects in the canvas, so they connect **(Figure 26.1)**. Now we're going to create a small animation that, in my opinion, looks pretty cool. The circle will start rotated bottom, spin to the right, grow and shrink, then the box will appear and snap into place. All of this will happen in 22 frames.

Figure 26.1 Menu Option

We can set the length for our sequences, so let's do that now. There are two places you should see the number 60, we want to change the one on the far right, which determines how long this sequence is. Change it from 60 to 22. You'll now see the frames go from 0 to 22. Grab the tracks of objMenuBox, all 3 of them, and drag them to begin at 10 frames, instead of 0. The box won't show up until part way through the sequence.

We're going to stick to keyframed parameters, instead of using the curves. It's easier when starting out and when copying another, like from a book. This way I can tell you the values and the frame to set them for, so we come out with the same result. However, I highly suggest you experiment throughout this process, as you can probably create some much cooler than I can. I'm not an artist, just trying to work with what I have.

All that aside, let's get to creating this animation. The position of objMenuCircle won't change for the entire animation, so don't worry about keyframing that track, in fact, go ahead and delete it. I didn't know you could delete Position, but then I tried and learned something new.

The first track we're going to alter is Rotation for objMenuCircle. I'm going to layout it in a series of frames and degrees, just add them in until you're all done.

0f, -90

8f, 0

And that's all for rotation. If you press play now, you'll find that the circle disappears after the second frame. This is because the asset, in the Dope Sheet, has a track that controls when it's in the sequence. It's the brighter, more solid color track. Drag from the right of it all the way over to the end of the sequence, so it's in it for the entire sequence. Drag the objMenuBox all the way over as well **(Figure 26.2)**.

Figure 26.2 Full Length Assets

Error Help

- If you're entering values and find that they're not being saved on the Dope Sheet, it's because the setting to automatically record changes has been turned off. It's a toggle you can set by pressing F10 or selecting it. It's the button to the left of the number box showing your current frame.

Next let's do the scale for objMenuCircle. I'm just going to put out the frames and values, as before. This time, however, there are two values. Do them in the order I set out here:

0f, 100, 100

10f, 125, 125

19f, 100, 100

On the first keyframe, right click and select the option Stretch Parameter Key, at the bottom. This will take this value and stretch it until it finds the next change. This can work to change the kind of curve, without adding curves. What I want it to do is stay its normal size until suddenly growing. This way it will.

Next is the Colour Multiply on objMenuBox. This one takes hex values, so it's a little bit of a pain to copy, but I'm sure you can manage. Here we go:

10f, 00FFFFFF (Alpha set to 0)

21f, FFFFFFFF (Alpha set to 255)

Almost there! But you may have run into a slight issue on this track. For whatever reason, changing just the Alpha doesn't create a new keyframe on this track. The workaround for this is to create your own keyframe using the plus icon on the Track Panel. You can add and remove keyframes with these buttons, instead of relying on the automatic keeper to notice changes. Add a keyframe at frame 21 and set it to fully white and you're good to do.

Now onto the last section, Position for objMenuBox:

10f, 47, -0.82,

17f, 57, -0.82,

21f, 48, -0.82

And there we have it **(Figure 26.3)**! Nothing too fancy, but cool looking enough to catch the eye of the player. How was that experience of crafting a sequence? Hopefully, it wasn't too bad. There's so much that can be done with sequences, especially for those that are patient. As for me, that was pretty hard to do originally. But it does save a lot of time as compared to doing it through code, or hand drawing it.

Figure 26.3 Finished Sequence

- If you're pressing play and it seems like it's chopping off parts of your sequence, check that the two red lines are at the beginning and end, and there's no red highlighted section. These are the beginning and ends of the sequence, which you can drag around. Move each one to their respective ends to get the sequence playing fully.

```
//In-Game Menu
if (isIdle && keyboard_check(vk_escape)) {
    myState = PlayerState.gameMenu;
    image_speed = 0;
    layer_sequence_create("Instances", x, y, seqMenuAnimation);
}
```

Figure 26.4 In-Game Menu Code

Using That Sequence

So, we've created a cool little sequence, but what do we do now? How do you actually use it in any meaningful way? Let me show you.

We only want the player to do this when they're idle, standing on the ground. You could allow them to access it anytime, there's nothing wrong with that idea, but it would take a bit more work to ensure the player returns to the right state, animation, motion, etc.... Forcing them to be idle is a lot easier, and generally accepted in video games. So let's jump to the top of the player's Step event and create a local variable called isIdle. This variable will check if the player is on the ground and their speeds are both 0.

```
var isIdle = onSolid && (xSpeed == 0
&& ySpeed == 0);
```

With that variable in place, go down to the end of the moving event, right after the dialogue check, and only enter the menu if they're both idle and press escape. Inside the if

statement change the state to gameMenu and set image_speed to 0. Then call this code (**Figure 26.4**):

```
layer_sequence_create("Instances", x,
y, seqMenuAnimation);
```

And now run your game. You'll see the sequence appear on top of the player and play. It looks cool, but we do freeze up since we haven't figured out yet how to get out of the menu state. Our sequence also doesn't really do anything since we can't interact with it.

For today, this is where we're going to end. The next few days will be jam packed full of new stuff and combining old knowledge into some pretty advanced code.

Conclusion + Challenge

Sequences are a super powerful tool that the community is still learning how to harness. Play around with them and experiment, maybe you'll come up with the next great idea that will be in everyone's game!

The challenge for today is to read up on the functions GameMaker has for sequences. We'll be using a good chunk of them tomorrow, so getting a head start now would help you out a lot. Keep thinking about sequences and letting them marinate.

Day 27

Embracing Sequences

Get Ready for Some Awesome!

Today's the day we build a menu and harness the power of sequences! It's going to get a little complex, and I'll be introducing some new programming concepts and terminology but stay with me and we'll make it through. If you struggle, just keep going and do your best. At the end if you're still confused, delete everything you did, take a small break, and then read this chapter again and follow along. Doing something twice, thrice, or more, is a great way to ensure you're really learning. You can also download the finished project and compare your code it mine if you're having some issues.

As you saw yesterday, it's not too hard to create a sequence and then have it play by default. However, for our menu that's not what we want to happen. We want to create multiple sequences, as we'll have multiple choices in our menu, and only have the one play that we select. When we move off of that menu option, it should play in reverse and then stop at the beginning. There will be 4 options in the game menu: Resume, Save, Load, and Quit. Each of the menu options should have that text inside of the box, and when we click on it, run the appropriate code. That's our goal for today.

Starting Easy

All of that explained, it seems like a lot. But we're going to break it down. The first we'll do is get the menu drawing text inside of itself. Open the objMenuBox and add a Create and Draw event. In Create, add one variable called myText, which will hold the text to display when the box portion of the menu object is visible.

Then go into the Draw event and add draw_self at the top. Now recall what I was saying about drawing text, and ensuring you've always got the right settings. We're going to draw some text, and the settings here are different from the dialogue box drawing settings. That means we need to reset the drawing in this event to this event, with all those functions we used in the message box. Those functions were all draw_set functions, including: halign, valign, font, and color. Go ahead and set them now, like this:

```
draw_set_halign(fa_center);

draw_set_valign(fa_middle);

draw_set_font(fntMenu);

draw_set_color(c_white);
```

We don't yet have a fntMenu, so let's quickly create that.

```
objMenuBox: Events

Create          ×   *Draw          ×
1   /// @description Draw the Text
2   draw_self();
3
4   draw_set_halign(fa_center);
5   draw_set_valign(fa_middle);
6   draw_set_font(fntMenu);
7   draw_set_color(c_white);
8
9   draw_text(x, y, myText);
```

Figure 27.0 Menu Draw Box Event

This time around get creative with the font you use, as menu font can be a little more different, since it's not as long and complex as dialogue. I'm going to use the font labelled Oswald and set its size to 10. Depending on your font, you may need to increase or decrease the size so it fits in the menu box.

Lastly, return to objMenuBox and draw the text in the myText variable at x and y **(Figure 27.0)**. Because we set the halign to center, the text will center itself on the object's sprite, which is what we want. Let's test it out and see how it looks. Set myText to a word, like Resume, and press play **(Figure 27.1)**.

What do you think? Personally, I find it looks pretty awful. The text is too small and blurry, barely legible. Changing the font might make it look better, but at this size the font isn't ever going to look great. Fortunately, there's a neat trick we can employ to make it look much better, which we could also apply to the message box. Find the function draw_text and add this to it: _transformed. It will become a new function that allows you to draw text at different scales and angles. Using it, we can choose a larger font size, then scale it down programmatically, keeping its sharpness but not its original size.

Figure 27.1 Resume Button

Figure 27.2 Resume Button Larger Font

This new function also takes 3 more arguments, x and y scale, and angle. Put .5 for each of the scales and 0 for the angle, which will keep it facing the right, as it normally does. Then open the font you're using for the menu and double its size. Run your game and try it out, you'll find it's much nicer looking now **(Figure 27.2)**.

If you're motivated enough, return to the message box, and do the same thing. That font doesn't look near as bad, but it could look better. Transforming the size of the font through code is the key to small font looking good. I'm also going to add 1 to the y component when drawing the text, as I think it needs to be moved down ever so slightly.

Also, set myText to undefined again.

Menu Options

Now that we're done with the menu object, open objPlayer and navigate to the Create event. In here we need to add some data to make the menu work. In a menu, we need to know which option the player is currently on, which we can store in a variable called menuChoice, setting it to 0. Zero will be the top of the menu, and we'll increase that number as we go down. This way of thinking about a menu can be confusing at first, as we might think the bottom of the menu should be 0 instead. However, we'll be creating the menu from an array, and since arrays start and 0 and we'll be navigating through one with our menu, we begin counting at 0 as well. Once you do it enough, it will become natural, but I know for more that increasing a number is associated with going up, while decreasing one is associated with going down. Just reverse that association for the menu.

Next, we need an array that will hold all the values for our game menu, such as the text we want to display, the function to call when we click on it, and the sequence id associated with that menu object. Create a 2D array and name it gameMenu. Set the first entry, 0,0, to the string Resume. Then continue on, increasing the first dimension by 1, and adding in the rest of the strings. The code looks like this:

```
gameMenu[0,0] = "Resume";

gameMenu[1,0] = "Save";

gameMenu[2,0] = "Load";

gameMenu[3,0] = "Quit";
```

This is also the order the menu will appear in, so make sure it's the order you prefer. This system will also make it quite easy to add more menu items down the line, which is nice. As your game grows, your menu will, too.

Now expand the array and make the second dimension for index 1 equal to undefined (**Figure 27.3**). This will hold the sequence id, but it's undefined until we create the sequence and save it there.

Figure 27.3 Game Menu with 2 Dimensions

And the next part of this array is the function we'll run when the user selects the menu item. Let's quickly create a script called Menu and inside create 4 functions called Resume-Game, SaveGame, LoadGame, and QuitGame. Don't put any code inside, we'll do that later. Once those functions are made, set the correlating function to index 2 of the second dimension in our array. (If that sentence is confusing for you, don't worry, it's confusing to me, just check out **figure 27.4** to see what I mean). Describing how to fill out 2D arrays is

199

```
55  //The string to be displayed
56  gameMenu[0,0] = "Resume";
57  gameMenu[1,0] = "Save";
58  gameMenu[2,0] = "Load";
59  gameMenu[3,0] = "Quit";
60  //Sequence ID, starts out undefined
61  gameMenu[0,1] = undefined;
62  gameMenu[1,1] = undefined;
63  gameMenu[2,1] = undefined;
64  gameMenu[3,1] = undefined;
65  //The script to execute
66  gameMenu[0,2] = ResumeGame;
67  gameMenu[1,2] = SaveGame;
68  gameMenu[2,2] = LoadGame;
69  gameMenu[3,2] = QuitGame;
```

Figure 27.4 Game Menu Almost Complete

very confusing, for both the listener and speaker.

Do note that I don't have braces at the end of my functions here. By including the (), the function will actually get called on these lines, which isn't what we want. Instead, but just putting the name of the function, we can store it for later use, like when the user presses enter on one of the menu items.

And finally let's store the sprite we'll assign to each of these menu options as the last index of the array. The first index, 0, will hold sprPlay. The next two will hold sprOptions, and the last will hold sprCancel. The finished array can be seen in **figure 27.5**.

Sequence Time!

We now have all the data and code filled out that we need to get started on creating and interacting with the menu. So, let's get to it!

Find where the player transitions into the game menu state and delete the line creating the sequence. We will be creating the sequences, but we need to do so inside of a for

```
55  //The string to be displayed
56  gameMenu[0,0] = "Resume";
57  gameMenu[1,0] = "Save";
58  gameMenu[2,0] = "Load";
59  gameMenu[3,0] = "Quit";
60  //Sequence ID, starts out undefined
61  gameMenu[0,1] = undefined;
62  gameMenu[1,1] = undefined;
63  gameMenu[2,1] = undefined;
64  gameMenu[3,1] = undefined;
65  //The script to execute
66  gameMenu[0,2] = ResumeGame;
67  gameMenu[1,2] = SaveGame;
68  gameMenu[2,2] = LoadGame;
69  gameMenu[3,2] = QuitGame;
70  //The sprite to display
71  gameMenu[0,3] = sprPlay;
72  gameMenu[1,3] = sprOptions;
73  gameMenu[2,3] = sprOptions;
74  gameMenu[3,3] = sprCancel;
```

Figure 27.5 Game Menu Array Finished

loop. Now the time has come to combine the power of for loops and arrays. So, add this code in:

```
for(var i = 0; i < array_length(game-
Menu); ++i) {



}
```

We've used for loops, so that part should be familiar to you, but the function in the middle will be new. This function, array_length can get the number of indices in any array, for any given dimension. It's extremely useful and almost always used when combining arrays and for loops. It gives your code that dynamic ability to stretch and shrink, simply by changing the size of the array. This is how you can add or remove menu items with ease. Our for loop will only create the number of items we've set in the array, and you never have to change the for loop for it to work correctly.

Now, array_length returns the count of the dimension you specify, which by default is the first dimension. To get the length of other dimensions, simply add a 0 surrounded by brackets, like so:

```
array_length(gameMenu[0]);
```

And then to get the third dimension, add another 0 surrounded by brackets after the first. Because the first dimension holds the number of menu items, it's the length we need.

IMPORTANT SIDE NOTE

- You must remember this, or you'll end up very frustrated and confused. The function array_length returns the number of entries, starting at 1. It counts in a normal, human way, which makes sense. However, because we're dealing with arrays, which always start at 0, it's extremely easy to mix them up, or try to use that function to set the value of an array, only to have it be set in the wrong spot, or even crash your game.

- In our for loop, we use the < symbol, which is less than. So, our loop will run while it's less than 4, the number array_length returns. This works as expected, since our array begins at 0 and goes until 3. But anywhere else you use this function you'll probably need to subtract 1 from its response, otherwise your game won't work as expected. I'll expand on this when we get to it on our code, which we will soon.

Now, inside our for loop, we first create the sequence and assign it to our gameMenu array, using i as the first index and 1 as the second to save it to. This time create the sequence using CameraMiddleX and CameraY. On the y coordinate, however, add 18 to it, and then add i * 35 as well **(Figure 27.6)**. This will create the first menu item near the top, but then move the next ones down by 35 pixels each time. Finally, add the last argument of the sequence itself.

At this point we can run our game and see the sequences be created and fill up our screen. It looks fairly good, and they're all evenly spaced.

```
for(var i = 0; i < array_length(gameMenu); ++i) {
    gameMenu[i,1] = layer_sequence_create("Instances", CameraMiddleX(), CameraY() + 20 + i * 35, seqMenuAnimation);
}
```

Figure 27.6 Creating the Sequence

The next step is to pause each one of them at the beginning of their animation, as we only want the one currently selected to play. So, underneath where we create them, use the function layer_sequence_pause to pause each one. Use i for the first index in the array, and 1 for the second index, once again. If you run your game now, you'll find each sequence created and paused, as expected.

What comes next is a little confusing, so I'll try to explain it a bit first. When we created each sequence, what was returned from the function, and subsequently stored in our array, was an integer ID of that sequence. It doesn't hold any information about the sequence, such as where in the room it is, if it's at the beginning or end of its sequence, etc.... But we can use that integer ID along with another sequence function to get all of that information. The function we need is layer_sequence_get_instance, and it returns that sequences struct. Now, a Struct is a variable that can hold other variables, functions, and data types. It's kind of like its own object that we get to create.

Struct

A struct is a variable that can hold data. Structs can hold variables, functions, arrays, even other structs. It's super-efficient and quick but uses up memory when you create one. Structs are a very special kind of variable with a lot of power and possibility.

When we use that function to get the struct associated with our sequence, it gives us access to all of the data about that struct, such as its name, loop mode, playback speed, and so much more. Our goal is to get that struct, save it as a local variable, and then use it. So, let's go ahead and do that.

On the line below where we're pausing the sequence, use the function layer_sequence_get_instance, and store it to a local variable called seqStruct. The function takes one argument, the id, which we've got stored in our array. The code looks like this:

```
var seqStruct = layer_sequence_get_
instance(gameMenu[i,1]);
```

Inserting Objects into the Sequence

With that stored away, we'll be able to do some pretty cool stuff in just a little bit. But first, let's create an objMenuCircle at the same location as the sequences, and save it is a local variable. This is the object we'll assign the correct sprite to, as Resume will use the green, saving and loading the blue, and quitting the red. The sequence itself only uses the green, but we can take these objects we create and insert them into the sequence with the proper values, and then the sequence will continue to operate as normal.

This is where the power of sequences starts to shine. Being able to take objects in your game, with custom data, and then insert them into a sequence and have them play out the sequence. It makes custom characters in cut scenes a breeze, or custom menu buttons easier than eating pie (well not really, it actually takes a fair bit of code, but I'm really hungry right now).

So, create and store objMenuCircle in a local variable called circle, creating it outside of room at -100, -100, and a depth − 1. By creating these objects outside of the room, we won't see them appear until they're injected into the scene. If you create them in your camera view, you'll see them for just 1 frame until they take over for the objects in the sequence, but for that 1 frame it looks terrible.

Next, let's assign the correct sprite to our object. We've got the sprite we want already in our array, so assign that sprite to circle with this code:

```
circle.sprite_index = gameMenu[i,3]
```

And finally, we inject this object, circle, into the sequence with the newly changed sprite. The function to do that is sequence_instance_override_object, and it takes 3 arguments, the sequence struct, the object id you're inserting (the name of the object from the Asset Browser), and the specific instance. **Figure 27.7** shows the entire process of creating the circle, altering its sprite, and inserting it into the sequence.

```
//Create the circle part of the menu and assign its specific data
var circle = instance_create_depth(-100, -100, depth - 1, objMenuCircle);
circle.sprite_index = gameMenu[i,3]
sequence_instance_override_object(seqStruct, objMenuCircle, circle);
```
Figure 27.7 The Circle Object

I know this chapter is getting really long, by far the longest yet, I just don't want to stop. This is exciting stuff, and it's all so closely related that I think it's easier if we do it all at once. We're really close to being done though, so let's push through!

We're now going to do the same thing with objMenuBox that we just did with objMenuCircle. We'll create it, assign its text, and insert it into the sequence. Nothing new here, so try doing it yourself first. Here's how I did it:

```
var box = instance_create_depth(-100, -100, depth - 1, objMenuBox);

box.myText = gameMenu[i,0];

sequence_instance_override_object(seqStruct, objMenuBox, box);
```

And that's everything in the for loop. The only thing left to do is play the first sequence, as that's the option the player starts on when the menu opens. So, outside of the for loop, call layer_sequence_play and pass in gameMenu[0,1]. Check out the complete code in **figure 27.8**.

```
//In-Game Menu
if (isIdle && keyboard_check(vk_escape)) {
    myState = PlayerState.gameMenu;
    image_speed = 0;
    //Create the sequences, assign their image, text, and script
    for(var i = 0; i < array_length(gameMenu); ++i) {

        //Create the sequence, pause it, and save the sequence struct in a local variable
        gameMenu[i,1] = layer_sequence_create("Instances", CameraMiddleX(), CameraY() + 20 + i * 35, seqMenuAnimation);
        layer_sequence_pause(gameMenu[i,1]);
        var seqStruct = layer_sequence_get_instance(gameMenu[i,1]);

        //Create the circle part of the menu and assign its specific data
        var circle = instance_create_depth(-100, -100, depth - 1, objMenuCircle);
        circle.sprite_index = gameMenu[i,3]
        sequence_instance_override_object(seqStruct, objMenuCircle, circle);

        //Create the box and assign its text
        var box = instance_create_depth(-100, -100, depth - 1, objMenuBox);
        box.myText = gameMenu[i,0];
        sequence_instance_override_object(seqStruct, objMenuBox, box);
    }
    //Play the first menu option
    layer_sequence_play(gameMenu[0,1]);
}
```
Figure 27.8 Transitioning into Game Menu

Now run your game and watch it in action! Boom! The sprites are changed, the first sequence plays beautifully, and the text we want is in that menu box. Everything's working as it should. It was a long day, the longest in this book, but you did it!

Conclusion

As you've seen, sequences are pretty awesome and powerful, although they can be confusing, too. There's a lot to them, including the power to insert your own objects into the sequence. I find that to be the coolest part of it all, at least until I learn something new tomorrow.

There's no challenge today. Go rest and enjoy what you've done. You've earned it!

PRO TIP

Is Being a Programmer just Memorizing the Language?

Avea Krause | Game Developer, Technical Artist, Content Creator

spheroustwitch@gmail.com

While knowing your language is important, learning how to identify when to use an applicable programming pattern is far more valuable. Rote memorization of syntax doesn't help with that at all, as the same patterns can be used in many different languages. You will learn the ins and outs of a language simply through repeated use, not to mention the fact that most modern languages have extensive online documentation to make your life easier. Furthermore, compilers are extremely advanced now and some, like Rust's, will make it incredibly difficult to write bad code. Learning to read and interpret the messages your compiler throws at you will go a long way. Beyond this, critical thinking, organization, and patience will be key to your success as a programmer.

Day 28

Pretty Things Ahead!

Navigating a Menu

Yesterday was a long day, but we accomplished an incredible amount. Today we're going to finish that project, by getting navigation for our menu set up and functional. Let's go ahead and dive right in by opening up objPlayer and scrolling down to the gameMenu state.

In this state the player can move between the options, making the sequences play each time they move into and out of one, and then select an option and trigger the function associated with it. We'll be using the up and down arrow keys, which we don't already have assigned to local variables. So, create an if check for when they press down, up, and enter. Use keyboard_check_pressed this time around, as we only want them to move one at a time, not cycle through the entire menu in one click.

Let's start in the down if check. The goal here is to reverse the sequence of the menu option the player is currently on, then begin player the sequence of the menu option they're moving onto. We can use menuChoice to know where we're at and where we're going. The new function we'll be using today is layer_sequence_headdir, which controls which way the sequence plays when you tell it to play. When the sequence is at the end and stopped, if we reverse the head direction and then tell it play again, it will play in reverse. Cool, right?

So, in the down check, use layer_sequence_headdir, passing in the sequence id we have stored in our array, and then the constant seqdir_left. The code looks like:

```
layer_sequence_headdir(gameMenu[menuChoice,1], seqdir_left);
```

At this point, menuChoice is still 0 as we haven't changed it. And we know all the sequence id's are stored in the second dimension of the array, at the second index (which is 1, since we start at 0). Then the constant comes from the menu **(Figure 28.0)** which you can open by selecting this function and pressing F1. Once we've set the direction for this sequence, tell it to play and then increase menuChoice by 1 **(Figure 28.1)**.

Constant	Description	Value
seq_dir_right	The sequence will play frames in an incremental order from left to right	1
seq_dir_left	The sequence will play frames in a decremental order from right to left	-1

Figure 28.0 Head Direction Constants

```
//Move down the menu
if (keyboard_check_pressed(vk_down)) {
    //Play the sequence in reverse of our current menu item
    layer_sequence_headdir(gameMenu[menuChoice,1], seqdir_left);
    layer_sequence_play(gameMenu[menuChoice,1]);

    ++menuChoice;
}
```

Figure 28.1 Playing a Sequence in Reverse

Run your game and test it out. The new selected item won't play yet, but the first item plays in reverse and looks great. Keep clicking down and you'll find your game crashes, however. That's because we're increasing menuChoice by 1 every time we click down, and eventually it exceeds the length of our array, and when that happens, the next time you press down, the layer functions activate and try get data that's outside of the array, crashing the game. We can remedy this by adding a check after increasing our array to see if it's outside of its boundary.

The code to do that looks like this:

```
if (menuChoice >= array_length(gameMenu)) {

    menuChoice = 0;

}
```

When menuChoice grows too large we reset it to 0. This will allow the player to cycle through the menu, which may not be want you desire. If you want them to reach the bottom and stay there, then set menuChoice to the length of the array, instead. Do note here that I use >=, greater than or equal to, because array_length returns a number that begins counting at 1, instead of 0. You could also say array_length(gameMenu) − 1.

If you run your game now it will not longer crash. You'll see the sequences play as you press down, although they only play in reverse. The reason is that's how they're all set. We need to add a little more code, after increasing menu-Choice, to play the menu option we're on in the correct direction, from left to right. Go ahead and add that now **(Figure 28.2)**.

```
//Move down the menu
if (keyboard_check_pressed(vk_down)) {
    //Play the sequence in reverse of our current menu item
    layer_sequence_headdir(gameMenu[menuChoice,1], seqdir_left);
    layer_sequence_play(gameMenu[menuChoice,1]);

    ++menuChoice;
    if (menuChoice >= array_length(gameMenu)) {
        menuChoice = 0;
    }

    //Set the direction of the new item to normal and play
    layer_sequence_headdir(gameMenu[menuChoice,1], seqdir_right);
    layer_sequence_play(gameMenu[menuChoice,1]);
}
```

Figure 28.2 Moving Down the Menu

And that's all that we need for the down key. The menu now looks great when going down. Now it's time to tackle going up, which is almost identical except we subtract from menuChoice and set it to the max length of gameMenu when going below zero. Give this a try on your own and refer to **figure 28.3** when you're done.

```
//Move up the menu
if (keyboard_check_pressed(vk_space)) { //This must be space because we've mapped vk_up to space
    //Play the sequence in reverse of our current menu item
    layer_sequence_headdir(gameMenu[menuChoice,1], seqdir_left);
    layer_sequence_play(gameMenu[menuChoice,1]);

    --menuChoice;
    if (menuChoice < 0) {
        menuChoice = array_length(gameMenu) - 1;
    }

    //Set the direction of the new item to normal and play
    layer_sequence_headdir(gameMenu[menuChoice,1], seqdir_right);
    layer_sequence_play(gameMenu[menuChoice,1]);
}
```

Figure 28.3 Moving Up the Menu

Error Help

- If you're pressing up and nothing's happening, it's only kind of your fault. Recall what buttons we press to jump in our game. We can press w, space-bar, and the up key. We've mapped all of them to the spacebar, so trying to map vk_up specifically here will not work. Instead, map it to vk_space and you'll be good to go.

- If you're moving up the menu and your game crashes with an out of bounds array message, it's because you set menuChoice to array_length directly, without subtracting 1 from the function's result. Remember that array_length begins counting at 1, so if you set menuChoice to array_length, it will always be outside of the bounds of your array. Subtract 1 from array_length and you're all set.

If you're having trouble, be sure to read the common error issues. I ran into the first one myself, as I forget we'd mapped vk_up to space. Once you get it working, it should look and feel good and no longer crash.

Executing functions

Now comes the time to execute the functions when the user selects one of the menu options. And to execute the function itself is amazingly simple, just one line of code:

```
gameMenu[menuChoice,2]();
```

That's it. The function stored in our array will run because the brackets we put there. To test that out and see it for yourself, add a show_message call in one of the functions and run your game. You'll find it works as expected. That means our attention can now turn to coding in these functions.

Let's start with at the top and work our way down. The first function we'll fill in is ResumeGame. This just needs to destroy the sequences and return the player to the moving state. So, first change the players state and set their image speed to 1. Then use a for loop and destroy each of the sequences we created. The function to destroy a sequence is layer_sequence_destroy **(Figure 28.4)**.

```
//Destroy the sequences
for(var i = 0; i < array_length(gameMenu); ++i) {
    layer_sequence_destroy(gameMenu[i,1]);
}
```

Figure 28.4 Destroying Sequences

Run your game and test it out. You'll quickly notice that the objects are created are still there, though the sequences are destroyed. We'll get to destroying the menu objects in a second, but first I want to explain why we destroy the sequences if we can't even see them anyway. The reason is memory. Whatever computer is playing your game has a finite source of memory, and every time you create something in your game, especially things like data structures and sequences, it takes up that memory. Over time, if you don't delete the things you've created and are no longer using, it can eat into all the available memory and crash the game unexpectedly. To prevent this, always clean up after yourself, just like I'm always telling my kids to do.

To destroy the menu objects, we don't need to find each one and get rid of it, instead the instance_destroy function can take an argument of an object and then it will destroy all instances of that object. Super powerful stuff! Go ahead and destroy both objects we created, objMenuCircle and objMenuBox.

Voilà! It's done. We can now get into and out of our menu and destroy all the things we created. Next on the hit list is SaveGame, although that one won't be as simple or quick as ResumeGame was. But I have every confidence in you!

Map

DS (Data Structure) Maps are a great tool for saving data to a file to read at a future time. Maps are made up of unique keys and values. No key can be a duplicate, although the values can. Maps can hold a nearly infinite amount of data, as much memory as the game can allocate, and the data stored can be of any type. Maps, like every other data structure in GameMaker, should be destroyed when you're done using it to avoid memory leaks.

Saving Your Game

The idea behind game saves is fairly simple. You take a snapshot of everything in the game and that the player has done, such as their coordinates, health, experience, room, quests completed, etc... and save it in a file. Then when they want to load you read it all back and fill in those values instead of the default ones the player would have started with. How you do this saving and loading can get pretty complex, especially for larger games, but that complexity can be broken down into manageable chunks. The code itself isn't that complex, it's more about how much you want to save, and taking the time to save it all, since every piece of data is another line of code.

We'll be saving the important information for our player, but we won't be saving everything in the game. Once you know the basics, adding more usually just takes more time, although sometimes it can be more complex. I cover saving much more in depth in my advanced course, where I show how to save and load information from multiple rooms. For now, we'll only be handling the data of the player.

To save our game, we'll be using a data structure called a map, also known as a hash table and dictionary. In GameMaker a Map is a data structure that has keys and values associated with those keys. It is a data structure, something you create and takes up memory, which means it should be deleted after you're done with it. This is our first time using a data structure, but fortunately maps are one of the easiest to use and are a wonderful starting point.

In SaveGame, create a local variable called data and set it equal to the function ds_map_ create. It doesn't take any arguments. With that one line of code, you've created your first data structure! Data Structures are ways to store data with specific rules attached to each one. For DS Maps, the rules are that no key can have a duplicate, and you don't know where in the map the data is being stored. That's about it. I won't go into the rest of the data structures, but each one has its use, so definitely do some reading on them.

The primary function we'll be using with our map data structure is ds_map_replace. You pass in the map you're using, the key name, and the piece of data you want to store. The data to store can be anything, including another map (although there is a specific function you should use when inserting a map data structure into another map). The reason we're using replace instead of add, which is a function, is that add can fail if there's already a key in there. Replace, on the hand, will always work, assuming you pass in a valid map, because it will replace an existing value, or create a new key and value pair if it didn't already exist.

So, let's give it a go then! Use the function ds_map_replace to store the x and y coordinates of your player. Use any string for the key, I'm using a lowercase x, and then pass in the players x position. Do the same for their y position. Our map now has this data inside of it, but what we need to do is save the map to a file, because all this information is lost when the game is turned off or reset.

To save our map to a file, we need to use some file functions. GameMaker has a lot to stay about its sandboxed nature and what that means for reading and writing files. What we're going to do is more on the simple side, saving a file to our own directory, then reading that same file later. We don't need to worry about trying to read outside files or wandering into areas our game isn't allowed. If you're interested in the sandboxed nature of GameMaker, check out the manual, it's got a lot in there.

Here's the code we need to save our file to the computer:

```
var dataToSave = ds_map_write(data);

var file = file_text_open_write("GameData.sav");

file_text_write_string(file, dataToSave);

file_text_close(file);
```

The first function is a map function that writes it out in a way we can save. There's a corresponding one for reading, which we'll use when loading. Next, we open a file called GameData.sav, and if it doesn't exist it gets created. The file name is completely arbitrary, as is the extension on it. You can name your file whatever you want, and give it any extension, or none at all. Then we do the actual writing of our data to the file, passing in the file we've opened and the data. Finally, we close the file, as GameMaker suggests only having one file

Data Structures

Data Structures are a way of storing data in a precise and structured way. Each DS has its own rules about how it can be used and accessed. In GameMaker the data structures you can create are Grids, Lists, Maps, Priority Queues, Queues, and Stacks. Each one is useful for different things, but they are all dynamically created. That means they must be destroyed when you're done with them or you may cause a memory leak which will eventually crash your game.

```
function SaveGame() {
    var data = ds_map_create();
    ds_map_replace(data, "x", objPlayer.x);
    ds_map_replace(data, "y", objPlayer.y);

    var dataToSave = ds_map_write(data);
    var file = file_text_open_write("GameData.sav");
    file_text_write_string(file, dataToSave);
    file_text_close(file);

    ds_map_destroy(data);
}
```

Figure 28.5 SaveGame Funktion

ever open at a time. So, when you open one, you close it as soon as you're done.

The last thing to do is destroy our data structure since we're done with it. Use the function ds_map_destroy and pass in data. If we want to save again, we'll create a new one and fill it up with the current data, no need to keep one around and risk a memory leak. The entire SaveGame function should look like **figure 28.5**.

Run your game and try saving. It looks like nothing happened, but your game just created a file and filled it with your map.

To see this information, you have to find your game in the directory of your computer. For Windows you also have to enable the ability to see hidden files (Open Windows Explorer (Windows+E), and click View -> Options. Then change to the View tab, and in the Advanced Settings, about 6 checkboxes down select 'Show hidden files, folders, and drives). Once you can see hidden files go to This PC, then click on your primary hard drive (probably C) -> Users -> Your user name -> AppData -> Local -> Your GameMaker Project Name. Then you'll find your save file. You can open it up in notepad, although all you'll see is numbers.

On a Mac you'll find it in some hidden files in Users -> Your Name -> Library -> Application Support -> com.yoyogames. To view the hidden files, press CMD+Shift+. If you have any issues, follow this support article, as it has solutions for many problems you may run into.

Conclusion + Challenge

Well, we got the menu up and running, looking awesome I might add, and created our first save file. We did a lot today, and we're nearing the end of this book. I do hope it's been good for you and you've enjoyed it thoroughly.

Today's challenge is to tackle loading. We'll do it tomorrow together, but it would be good for to try on your own. It's the last big thing we're doing. It is a little different from saving, but if you comb through the manual and begin trying things, I bet you can figure it out. The most difficult part is loading which room you were in and then moving to that room, but we haven't even saved that data yet, so only try it if you're feeling super confident.

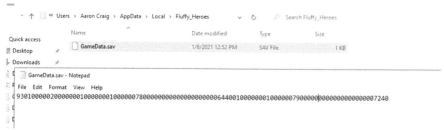

Figure 28.6 Viewing Save Data on Windows

Figure 28.7 Viewing Save Data on Mac

Day 29

Reading What You Wrote

Now Where Were We?

Alright, let's just jump straight into loading! If you got it up and running, great work! If not, follow along and let's do it together. I'll be giving you some tips to make the saving/loading process easier and smoother, and pointing out several of the bugs and common pitfalls that you'll probably run into, if you haven't already.

Find your LoadGame function and inside let's open up the file we saved to yesterday. It's gotta be the same file name, otherwise it won't find it, so be sure to type the same thing. This time use the function file_text_open_read instead of write, to be able to get the contents of that file. Save the result to a local variable called file. When opening a file, the function will either return the file ready to read, or -1 if no file could be found. Using that information, we can perform an if check and only load the information if the file was found.

The best way to handle the lack of a file is to let the player know there was no file found and then exit the function with the return keyword. We can use our ShowMessage function to display that information to them **(Figure 29.0)**. And while we're at it, we should have also let the player know when we saved the game with a message. Let's add that to the end of the SaveGame function.

```
var file = file_text_open_read("GameData.sav");
//No file found
if (file == -1) {
    ShowMessage("No saved game file found.");
    return;
}
```

Figure 29.0 No File Found

Let's test those two things out really quick. Put in a file name, in the LoadGame function, that doesn't exist so we can see the message. Run your game and try loading. The message appears as expected, but we encounter an issue. The message box stays over top, and we can only get rid of it after we leave the menu and then click a key. That's no good!

Navigate to the gameMenu player state. Inside here, let's add an if check at the top for a message box, and when there is one, any key press will destroy it. Remember to use the message box's User Event 0 to actually destroy it, as it will also trigger the message to jump to the end first if it's not completed. It's the same code we have in our dialogue state, so that's easy enough to implement.

Now run your game again. Is it all fixed? Well, no, not totally. When the message appears, we can click down or up to make it vanish, but the menu also changes. That's not super intuitive, as I think if a message box is covering up the menu, we shouldn't be moving the menu around. The nice quick fix for this is to wrap all the rest of the gameMenu code in an else statement. Then the message box takes priority, and only after if it's gone can the player continue navigating the menu **(Figure 29.1)**.

```
//Destroy the confirm boxes that appear when saving and loading
if (instance_exists(objMessageBox)) {
    if (keyboard_check_pressed(vk_anykey)) {
        with(objMessageBox) {
            event_perform(ev_other, ev_user0);
        }
    }
}
else {
    //Move down the menu
    if (keyboard_check_pressed(vk_down)) {
    //Move up the menu
    if (keyboard_check_pressed(vk_space)) { //This must be space
    //Run a function
    if (keyboard_check_pressed(vk_enter)) {
}
```

Figure 29.1 Taking Care of Message Box

Boom! Now that's done, let's return to loading. Put in the correct file name into the reading of the file. As a quick side

note, I always use Macros for file names. They can store strings and that way I never worry about a typo, because the Macro can't change. I also do this for the key names of my DS Maps, as even one typo can throw a wrench into the entire saving/loading process. I would encourage you to do the same. My Macros look like **figure 29.2**. In a small project like this it isn't essential, but it's a good practice to have, nonetheless.

```
//Saving and Loading Data
#macro FileName "GameData.sav"
#macro PlayerX "XPosition"
#macro PlayerY "YPosition"
```

Figure 29.2 Macros for Names

After we've checked that the file we want exists, it's time to read the data out of the file and into our game. To do that, use the function file_text_read_string and pass in the file we've opened. Then, since we have everything we need from it, close the file.

And from here, the bulk it just takes time. Create a new DS map called data. Then use the function ds_map_read, passing in the map we just created and the contents of the file:

```
var data = ds_map_create();

ds_map_read(data, fileData);
```

Once done, your loaded ds map works just like you would expect it to. It's got all the data it had when you saved the game and can be accessed by all the same key names. All that's left to do is apply that data to the player. Go ahead and give it a shot. The function to get data from a map via key is ds_map_find_value, passing in your map and the key **(Figure 29.3)**.

Once you're done, try running your game. Save the game,

```
//Load a DS map with that data
var data = ds_map_create();
ds_map_read(data, fileData);

//Apply values from save file
objPlayer.x = ds_map_find_value(data, PlayerX);
objPlayer.y = ds_map_find_value(data, PlayerY);
```

Figure 29.3 Applying Loaded Data

then move around a bit and load. Did it work? Did you get warped back to where you saved? It should all be working as expected. So far, we've only done the simple saving and loading.

Error Help

- If your game isn't loading, the most likely reason is there's a typo in the file name between your SaveGame and LoadGame function. Create a Macro and use that instead of a string.

- If your player isn't loading back to where they were saved, the most likely case is a typo in the key names. Create a macro and use that for both saving and loading the values.

Restart your game and save it. Then go and move the boulder, pick up the coin and then load. What happens? My guess is several things. First, you'll notice the menu has either moved or disappeared completely, depending on how far away you went. Second, the coin is gone but you still have your powers. And third, the boulder has remained moved.

All we've done in our loading is move the player. Everything else in the game has remained the same, even though it should also get changed. Can you start to see why it can become tedious to save and load? To do so well, you need to store a lot of information, data you probably hadn't even considered. Do you want to remember exactly where the boulder was and the rotation it was at? That's gotta be saved as 3 different data points. Coin collected and powerup given? You need 2 data points to ensure it stays that way when loading. Then you've got health and Biter to consider, since it has health, state data, and a position to restore. And what about your state and health?

It can get overwhelming, which is why it's best to begin your saving and loading process early in your game. Adding two or three things here and there isn't too bad but going in near the end of a project and saving hundreds of data points would be cumbersome, and you would most likely miss a few key ones.

And what's up with the menu moving or disappearing when we load? Well, since we created the sequences in a specific spot in the room, that's where they stay unless they're told to move. We could move them, but we could also just delete them and put the player back in the moving state, since normally when you load a file it puts you right back into the game, not the menu. Let's do that option, since it's easier and, in my opinion, makes more sense.

What's really cool is we can call our ResumeGame function at the end and it will take care of everything for us, including destroying the sequences. Reusing code is pretty awesome!

And that's all we're going to cover for loading data. Like I said, most of it is tedious work, just taking time to do.

Get Me Out of Here!

The last function on our menu is the QuitGame function. This one is pretty easy. Call game_end and the game quits. If you want to be generous, you could save the game before quitting, which is what I'm going to do.

Well, that was easy.

Figure 29.4 Check Persistent

Changing Rooms

Let's add another room to our game by duplicated our current room. You can name it whatever you want, just remember it since we'll need that name to move into the room. Take out something from this new room, so we can easily tell it's a different room, like Biter or the boulder. You could even grab a different background from the assets and throw it in there, which is what I'll do for visual clarity. Delete the player object from the new room since we only want to have 1 player. And open objPlayer and click the checkbox marked persistent, because without it Pinky won't move into the new room as we change rooms **(Figure 29.4)**.

For quick testing purposes, add a key check event for the letter R to the player. In that event, use this code:

```
room_goto(Room2);
```

Use your rooms name. Then run your game and change rooms. What happens? You should have changed rooms that's about it **(Figure 29.5)**. Everything still seems to work as expected. However, a large part of that is because we duplicated our original room which had all the right settings. But if we created a room from scratch, that wouldn't be the case.

Figure 29.5 New Room

To show you what I mean, open the new room, and disable ViewPorts entirely. Reset all those settings. Now run the game and change rooms and you'll see that things look different **(Figure 29.6)**. Since we disabled viewports, the camera is no longer the way we had it in the first room. Since our camera was designed in the GUI, it must be set that way in every room, otherwise it reverts to the default GameMaker camera, which isn't what most games need or want.

You can see that changing rooms in and of itself is quite simple, it's only one line of code. But there's a lot more that goes into changing rooms well than you may have thought. That's especially true when you want to add a nice transition between rooms, such as fading to black, swiping to the side, or anything else you've seen. Some of that can be done with a sequence now, which would make your job easier, but the camera system still needs to be taken of. And that's what we're going to tackle tomorrow: creating our own camera in code.

There are many benefits to creating your own camera, such as the ability to set each new room to use it, smooth following, local multiplayer, and more. It's one of the last major things we'll cover in this book because I think it's essential to have a good grasp on them before you begin your dream game.

Figure 29.6 Default Camera Settings

Conclusion + Challenge

Today we tackled loading and you figured out why it can take so long to do right and to do it well. There's almost always more to a subject than you might think, remember that.

Your challenge for today is begin researching GameMaker's cameras. The manual does an ok job at explaining them, though it's always confused me. But sometimes confusion isn't a bad thing. Read up, maybe try creating one for yourself, and then we'll do it together and I'll make known everything there is to know about cameras.

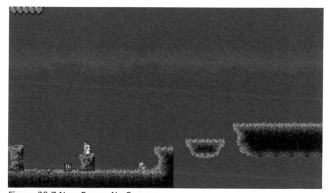

Figure 29.7 New Room, No Camera

Day 30

Lights, Camera, Action!

Let's create a new object called objCamera and put it in System, Objects. Add 3 events to it, Create, Begin Step, Room Start. We'll begin in the Create event.

The first thing we'll do is enable full screen. We haven't done so yet because we had no way of quitting the game, but now that our menu is up and running, let's do it. The function to use is window_set_fullscreen and set it to true.

After that create four macros called CameraWidth, CameraHeight, and CameraSpeed. We're using Macros here because we'll need to access them in other objects. We could use global variables, but they require more typing, and these values won't ever change so Macros work great. Set their values in order: 256, 144, 0.1.

The width and height are the same values we are already using, whereas the scale and speed are settings we'll get to shortly. To test out this camera we're creating, we need to turn off the views from our room. Open the main room and uncheck Enable Viewports and Viewport 0. We'll be enabling them through code from here on out.

To enable the views in code, return to objCamera and type this out:

```
view_visible[0] = true;

view_enabled[0] = true;
```

This checks both of those boxes. It does so for the first viewport, as you can have up to 8 on screen at once. Next up let's create the camera itself and store it in a local variable called myCamera. There are two ways to create the camera, with the function's camera_create, and camera_create_view. We'll be using the view function, as it allows us to set a lot of the properties right there. Every camera property can be adjusted and set with a camera function, but that would just take more code when it isn't necessary, since we know what the values of our camera will be.

The first two arguments are for where the camera is at in the room, which won't matter since we're going to assign it to follow the player. For static cameras you'd want to position them where they should be when created. For ours, go ahead and set those two arguments as 0. Then for the next 2 use our macros for width and height. The rest of the arguments are an optional array, meaning you can pass them in if you want, but you don't have. I'm not going to here, since I don't want to set all of them, and you have to do all or none.

To show you that you can adjust all the camera settings through other functions, let's now set the border by using the function camera_set_view_border, passing in our camera and the width and height macros. Remember the border is how close the player can get before the camera begins moving if the camera is set to follow an object. And then to make the camera follow our player, use the function camera_set_view_target, passing in the camera and player object **(Figure 30.0)**.

```
14 var myCamera = camera_create_view(0, 0, CameraWidth, CameraHeight);
15 camera_set_view_border(myCamera, CameraWidth, CameraHeight);
16 camera_set_view_target(myCamera, objPlayer);
```
Figure 30.0 Creating Camera and Applying Settings

Lastly, we need to set the camera to the first viewport, which we've already enabled. Use the function view_set_camera, choosing 0 as the viewport to assign the camera to and passing the camera. Now place the camera object in the first level and run your game. You'll notice that the game starts super small but than expands to full screen, which is natural, and that the camera looks and functions just as it did before. Awesome!

If you didn't want your game to start full screen, there are ways to adjust the size of the window itself. Look through the manual and you'll find window functions that deal with it. I'm not going to touch on it anymore, as it's outside the scope of this book, but just remember that you have that power.

So Smooth

The last thing I want to touch on with the camera is the following. The default follow target that the camera does is fine for starting out. We've been using it this entire book and you probably haven't noticed anything. However, once you see it compared to some smooth movement, you'll instantly notice how terrible it is. Let me open your eyes!

Move over to the Begin Step event. This is where we'll manually move the camera around, instead of relying on it following the player. The idea here is to check every step if the player is in the middle of the cameras view, and if not, move to make that happen. But instead of instantly moving to fit the player in the middle, like it does now, we're going to smoothly, linearly, move from where we are to where we want to be, eliminating all the jerkiness.

So, first create two local variables called cameraX and cameraY and set them equal to our CameraX and CameraY functions. Then we need to get the x and y coordinates of the player, but in relation to where the camera is at in the room.

```
var targetX = objPlayer.x - (CameraWidth / 2);

var targetY = objPlayer.y - (CameraHeight / 2);
```

Those variables are where we're headed to. But to ensure that the camera never leaves the room or goes outside of where it should be (which can happen if you're moving fast), we're going to clamp those values. Clamp is both a function and something you can do in real life. To clamp values means to keep them from going outside of a certain range, which we can set.

To clamp values in GameMaker, use the function clamp, and then pass in the variable you're checking, and the minimum and maximum values allowed. Like so:

```
targetX = clamp(targetX, 0, room_width - CameraWidth);

targetY = clamp(targetY, 0, room_height - CameraHeight);
```

The clamp function only returns a value within the range we specify. The function doesn't change the value of the variable, so we have to set our variables equal to whatever clamp sends back. That ensures our camera never goes somewhere it shouldn't.

Then comes the smooth movement part. It's using a new function called lerp, which stands for linear interpolation. Remember the linear curves from sequences? This function produces a linear result based on two points and how quickly you want to get there. It looks like this:

```
cameraX = lerp(cameraX, targetX, CameraSpeed);

cameraY = lerp(cameraY, targetY, CameraSpeed);
```

Finally, we tell the camera to move the amount we got back from that lerp function using the camera function camera_set_view_pos. For this function, specifically, you need to tell it which view camera to use, which is 0, not the camera id you had stored in the create event. That's why we could create the camera and store it in a local variable, we wouldn't need it here. **Figure 30.1** contains the entirety of this step event.

```
1  /// @description Smooth Follow
2
3  //Get at where the camera is
4  var cameraX = CameraX();
5  var cameraY = CameraY();
6
7  //Get at where the camera needs to go
8  var targetX = objPlayer.x - (CameraWidth / 2);
9  var targetY = objPlayer.y - (CameraHeight / 2);
10
11 //Clamp the possible values, keep camera in room
12 targetX = clamp(targetX, 0, room_width - CameraWidth);
13 targetY = clamp(targetY, 0, room_height - CameraHeight);
14
15 //Get how much to move
16 cameraX = lerp(cameraX, targetX, CameraSpeed);
17 cameraY = lerp(cameraY, targetY, CameraSpeed);
18
19 //Move the camera
20 camera_set_view_pos(view_camera[0], cameraX, cameraY);
```

Figure 30.1 Begin Step Event

Before testing it all out, return to the Create event and comment out the setting of the border and following of the player. We don't need that anymore since we're taking manual control. Now run the game and check out the follow. If you can, jump from a high place, or get moving quickly. If you run or fall fast enough, the camera sort of snaps to you when it catches up, and it all looks really good.

Now that we have a custom camera, we can use it in every room. We could create a global camera and use that everywhere, but we can also just re-create the camera we want and set that whenever we enter a new room, which works just as well. To do that, copy the code where we create the camera, including enabling the views, and set it in the Room Start event. Then set the camera to be persistent, either by clicking the checkbox or through code with the built-in variable persistent.

Run your game and try changing rooms! We now have a working camera with smooth follow, and it works even when you go into a new room! Fabulous stuff. There is a snapping effect when entering a new room, including some strangeness where if you click on the change room button you can see the leftover room in the background as the camera moves. This isn't something you'll ever see in a finished game, since you wouldn't be having the player just activate room_goto over and over again. But as for the snapping, let's take care of that by putting in a nice transition.

Sweet Transitions

Our goal here is to create a system that can easily and beautifully transition from 1 room to the next with just a function call. Let's start by designing that function.

This function doesn't really fit with any of the others we already have, so let's create a script called Rooms and a function inside called ChangeRooms. This function will take 1 argument called newRoom. The code for this will be creating a new object at a very a low depth and then setting that objects properties. We don't have said object yet, so go ahead and create one under System called objTransition.

Then let's finish the function before doing anything with our new object. In ChangeRooms, create a local variable to hold the transition object. We'll eventually add a variable called newRoom to the transition object, so set that future variable now to the argument passed in **(Figure 30.2)**. And that's all we need to do here.

```
function ChangeRooms(newRoom){
    var transition = instance_create_depth(x, y, depth - 100, objTransition);
    transition.newRoom = newRoom;
}
```

Figure 30.2 Change Rooms Function

Let's return to objTransition and add a Create and Draw event. We'll be crafting our transition in code instead of using a sequence. It's good practice to know how to do it if you ever need to. The transition will be color swipe to the right, followed by another color swipe to the left when we're in the new room. We'll be creating these colors dynamically in code, which is pretty cool.

To do all of this, we'll need several variables. Here's all the ones we need for our transition to work:

```
rightFade = 0;

leftFade = 0;

fadeSpeed = 6;

newRoom = undefined;

oldRoom = room;
```

We'll be drawing the color swipes, and to do so we need to know where the swipes are at, in relation to the room. We'll be using the rightFade to know when we've reached the right edge of the screen, and leftFade for the left side. The fadeSpeed controls how quickly it goes. newRoom is obviously which room we're going to, and oldRoom holds the current room (at least until we switch to the new one, then it's the previous room).

In GameMaker you can create colors from RGB (red, green, blue) values and from HSV (hue, saturation, value). We'll be using RGB since it's what I'm more familiar with, but either one could work here. Create three local variables called r, g, and b. Then assign them a random number between 0 and 255, you can just using random(255) for this, as it begins at 0. These will be the RGB values.

Then we want to call draw_set_color, which we can do in the create event, passing in another function called make_color_rgb, with our local variables. Check out **figure 30.3** to see exactly how it works. Calling draw_set_color in the Create event is a little odd, but fine here, because when we do this the only thing going to be shown on screen is the transition.

```
8  //Pick a random color
9  var r = random(255);
10 var g = random(255);
11 var b = random(255);
12
13 draw_set_color(make_color_rgb(r, g, b));
```

Figure 30.3 Creating a Random Color

225

Next comes the changing of the rooms and drawing of the color swipes across the screen. The first thing we check for is what room we're in. If we're in the old room (room we want to leave), then we draw a rectangle and increase the rightFade variable. When that covers the entire screen, we'll change rooms, position the player, and draw the swipe disappearing. When it's all done, it will destroy itself.

So, add an if check to see if we're still in oldRoom. Add an else at the bottom. Draw a rectangle, using draw_rectangle, starting at the top left of the camera and going to the bottom. The second x coordinate is what we'll change here over time, so make it CameraX() + rightFade. Do not make it just an outline, we want to cover the entire screen.

Then increase rightFade by fadeSpeed. And finally when rightFade is greater than the width of the camera, which you can get the value of through camera_get_view_width, change rooms **(Figure 30.4)**.

```
if (room == oldRoom) {
    draw_rectangle(CameraX(), CameraY(), CameraX() + rightFade, CameraBottomY(), false);
    rightFade += fadeSpeed;
    if (rightFade > camera_get_view_width(view_camera[0])) {
        room_goto(newRoom);
    }
}
```
Figure 30.4 First Swipe + Room Change

And now inside of the else we need to do almost the same thing, except we're drawing the rectangle finish its swipe from left to right. That means the first x coordinate is changed by leftFade. And when the leftFade gets to the end, destroy itself **(Figure 30.5)**.

```
9  else {
10     draw_rectangle(CameraX() + leftFade, CameraY(), CameraRightX(), CameraBottomY(), false);
11     leftFade += fadeSpeed;
12     if (leftFade > camera_get_view_width(view_camera[0])) {
13         instance_destroy();
14     }
15  }
```
Figure 30.5 Second Swipe

Let's test this out by changing the code in the R key press to our function. Run your game and give it a shot. It should produce a colored swipe from left to right, move rooms, then the swipe vanishes to the left. If you try it again, however, your game will freeze. Our transition object requires the room not be the same, which makes sense as you'd never need to go to the room you're already in. This transition looks nice and mostly covers up the camera jumping to catch up to the player.

The only issue is the player. How do we position them in a new room? We also have a state for the player to be in when changing rooms that we need to fill out. Fortunately, the state is just a few lines of code, so we can take of that. The more difficult part is knowing where to put the player. There are many ways to solve this problem, some elegant, others gross. When I say elegant, I mean simple and effective, not overly complex and involving dozens of objects.

Elegant Room Placements

This method works great for pretty much any game. It will allow an infinite amount of entrances to every room, and those entrances can be easily changed at any time.

Figure 30.6 Level Warp

Create a new object called objWarp in System and either create a new sprite or assign one you already have. It just needs a collision mask so we can collide with it, we won't see the sprite. Uncheck Visible. I'm going to create a new sprite and just fill it with a nice blue. I'll place that created sprite in System, Sprites. Then add three variable definitions to objWarp called newRoom, newX, and newY. Set the type of newRoom to Asset, and select Rooms (by clicking the little gear and choosing Rooms).

Place this warp in your level somewhere it makes sense. I tend to place my warps slightly outside the room, that way the player walks out of the level before the warp begins (**Figure 30.6**). Now, double click on that warp object and its properties will be revealed. Click on Variables, and then click on the little pencil icon to allow changes. Put in here the information for your next level. This method allows you to place the player anywhere and to any room. You can have as many warps as you want, each instance with different data.

We need to add in these two pieces of data as arguments to our ChangeRooms function and as variables in objTransition, so do that now. Then, in the Draw event, move the player to these new coordinates once inside the new room (**Figure 30.7**). Once finished, jump over to objPlayer's moving state and scroll to the bottom.

```
else {
    //Move the player
    objPlayer.x = newX;
    objPlayer.y = newY;
    draw_rectangle(CameraX() + leftFade, CameraY(), CameraRightX(), CameraBottomY(), false);
    leftFade += fadeSpeed;
    if (leftFade > camera_get_view_width(view_camera[0])) {
        instance_destroy();
    }
}
```

Figure 30.7 Move the Player

In here, add a check if we're colliding with a warp object, and if so capture that warp object as a local variable. Also set the new state, set both speeds to 0, and change the sprite to idle. Finally, call ChangeRooms, passing in the values from our warp object (**Figure 30.8**).

```
//Changing Rooms
if (place_meeting(x, y, objWarp)) {
    myState = PlayerState.changingRooms;
    sprite_index = sprites[hero][Idle];
    image_speed = 1;
    xSpeed = 0;
    ySpeed = 0;

    var warp = instance_place(x, y, objWarp);
    ChangeRooms(warp.newRoom, warp.newX, warp.newY);
}
```

Figure 30.8 Changing States

And then, to get out of the changingRooms state, check to see if objTransition still exists. When it doesn't, change to moving. Now you can test your finished game! Don't forget to delete the R key event in objPlayer.

And that's it. That is the end of the game and the end of this book, sort of. I'll have some more to say after today, but let me wrap up today, first.

Conclusion

Wooh! We did a lot today. You should be proud you made it this far, it's a great accomplishment. You're now ready to tackle whatever game idea you want to make. You may now know how to do everything, but you know how to learn to do everything. I knight thee a Game Developer! Go out there and keep up the practice of coding and game development, and you'll be finishing your game in no time!

PRO TIP

Hiring A Game Artist

Maura Miller | Sentient Perspectives

Maurstomi@gmail.com

What many game developers forget is that artwork is a form of communication. Oftentimes, what you present artistically will be one of the first things that catches a player's attention. Art style will often be what your game is remembered for along with gameplay. For this reason, it's so important to choose an artist that really captures the theme of your game design. It is very common for artists to have a "resume" of some sort, whether that be a website or social media page. This is where you can discover whether or not an artist's style will work for you. If you have a specific artist in mind, I suggest reaching out to them through their contact information. Another way to go about finding an artist is to post on a work website, like Fiverr or Reddit, and take applications. Keep in mind, there is a chance you will have multiple offers to look through, so be sure you are prepared to take on this task! It's also great to reach out to local artists; those who are your classmates, friends, or family.

When communicating with an artist about cost, many tend to "undersell" themselves. As a rule of thumb, I suggest paying an artist at least minimum wage per hour worked, in addition to the cost of supplies, if an artist does not already have a price point in mind. Many can give you an estimate of how long they estimate a piece will take. Keep in mind that art takes a long time to make, so be sure to speak to an artist far before you expect the game to be "finished". It may be cliche to say, but communication is important, especially when it comes to talking over private messages or email. Specify what you need and when you need it, and allow feedback and suggestions from the artist. It's always important to write up a contract of some sort, so that both parties are able to refer back to the goal.

One of my favorite aspects of the relationship between a game designer and an artist is that they can bounce ideas off of one another. Don't be afraid to listen to aesthetic or design suggestions, as artists often have the most experience in this matter. The relationship between artist and game designer should be a collaborative one as you move towards creating a finished product: the game!

Conclusion

Congratulations, Game Developer

Maybe you thought you'd never get here, or perhaps you knew it all along. Whatever the case was, you've finished this book, absorbed all the knowledge I had for you, and come out the other side of this book a verifiable game developer, ready to begin working on your dream game.

Be sure to take some time to celebrate. Go out to eat, buy yourself something nice, take a day off to relax and just revel in your accomplishment. Not everyone who starts this book is going to finish it, but you did. I am proud of you.

So, what now? Well, that all depends on your goals. After completing this book, you should have a great handle on GameMaker, programming, and game design. You're also in the rhythm of coding every day, which is something you shouldn't stop. That was one of the big benefits of completing this book, building a habit of making games. So many people want to make a game but don't create the habits necessary to complete a big project like that. You now have that, so leverage it to your advantage.

From here, the path is wide open. You can continue down the line with GameMaker and build the game of your dreams, as you have all the knowledge to either make it yourself, or at least know how to learn everything you'll need to make it. Any game you can imagine, 2D game at least, you can create with GameMaker. We didn't touch on it, but it has network capabilities for online play.

Or you can pick up a new engine, like Unity, Godot, or Unreal. There are dozens of game engines out there, and after learning 1 the rest will come much easier to you. Each engine will use different languages, but again, after learning GML, new languages won't be as difficult. Don't feat the unknown, embrace it!

There's also the option of joining a team. My guess is there are thousands of indie game devs out there who would love to work with you if you can find them. Reach out through social networks like Reddit, game forums, and more. In the games industry, networking plays a huge role in landing gigs, so don't be afraid to send messages to strangers, attend conferences, and join in on forums. You're an indie game dev, too, remember?

If you're dream is to work in more a corporate setting, then the best thing you can do is start building games for your portfolio and networking. Many companies want to see what you've done, not what you've learned. So many people go to college and create a resume with their classes on it and think that's enough, but they're wrong. You don't need a college degree to get jobs these days, you just have to show you're qualified with an awesome portfolio of how you've applied your knowledge. The best way to do that in the games industry is to create games.

And that's the last thing I want to leave you with. DON'T STOP MAKING GAMES. If you want to be the best game developer and designer you can be, keep making and keep learning. Game development is a skill, just like running, playing basketball, and singing. The more you practice it the better you'll become. Natural talent can give you an edge, just like in real life, but without the practice you'll be left behind.

And of course, I would be remiss to not invite you to check out my YouTube channel and website, Let's Learn This Together, for more content from me. I've got tutorials, discussions, and courses you can check out to upgrade your skills even more.

But whatever you decide to do, I wish you the best of luck. You're ready for the world, and I know you're going to take it by storm!

Glossary